Guide to America's Outdoors

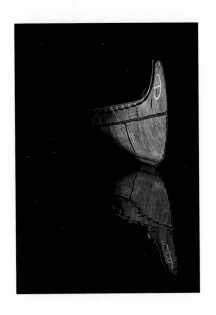

Great Lakes

Guide to America's Outdoors
Great Lakes

By Tina Lassen
Photography by Mark R. Godfrey

NATIONAL
GEOGRAPHIC
WASHINGTON, D.C.

Contents

Cover: Split Rock Lighthouse, Minnesota's North Shore *Page 1:* Simulated birchbark canoe, Voyageurs National Park *Pages 2-3:* Lake of the Woods *Opposite:* Isle Royale National Park

Treading Lightly in the Wild

A fritillary resting upon a wood lily

NATIONAL GEOGRAPHIC GUIDE TO AMERICA'S OUTDOORS: GREAT LAKES takes you to some of the wildest and most beautiful natural areas of a region famed for its tangle of boreal North Woods, crystal-clear lakes, limestone bluffs, and rolling hills. In addition, the Mississippi and Ohio Rivers play host to a wealth of birdlife.

Visitors who care about this spectacular region know they must tread lightly on the land. Ecosystems can be damaged, even destroyed, by thoughtless misuse. Many have already suffered from the impact of tourism. The marks are clear: litter-strewn acres, polluted waters, trampled vegetation, and disturbed wildlife. You can do your part to preserve these places for yourself, your children, and all other nature travelers. Before embarking on a backcountry visit or a camping adventure, learn some basic conservation dos and don'ts. Leave No Trace, a national educational program, recommends the following:

Plan ahead and prepare for your trip. If you know what to expect in terms of climate, conditions, and hazards, you can pack for general needs, extreme weather, and emergencies. Do yourself and the land a favor by visiting if possible during off-peak months and limiting your group to no more than four to six people. To keep trash or litter to a minimum, repackage food into reusable containers or bags. And rather than using cairns, flags, or paint cues that mar the environment to mark your way, bring a map and compass.

Travel and camp on solid surfaces. In popular areas, stay within established trails and campsites. Be sure to choose the right path, whether you are hiking, biking, skiing, or riding. Travel single file in the middle of the trail, even when it's wet or muddy, to avoid trampling vegetation. If you explore off a trail in pristine, lightly traveled areas, have your group spread out to lessen impact. Good campsites are found, not made. Travel and camp on sand, gravel, or rock, or on dry grasses, pine needles, or snow. Remember to stay at least 200 feet from waterways. After you've broken camp, leave the site as you found it.

Pack out what you pack in—and that means *everything* except human waste, which should be deposited in a hole dug away from water, camp, or trail, then covered and concealed. When washing dishes, clothes, or yourself, use small amounts of biodegradable soap and scatter the water away from lakes and streams.

Be sure to leave all items—plants, rocks, artifacts—as you find them. Avoid potential disaster by neither introducing nor transporting non-native species. Also, don't build or carve out structures that will alter the environment. A don't-touch policy not only preserves resources for future generations; it also gives the next guy a crack at the discovery experience.

Keep fires to a minimum. It may be unthinkable to camp without a campfire, but depletion of firewood harms the backcountry. When you can, try a gas-fueled camp stove and a candle lantern. If you choose to build a fire, first consider regulations, weather, skill, and firewood availability. Where possible, employ existing fire rings; elsewhere, use fire pans or mound fires. Keep your fire small, use only sticks from the ground, burn the fire down to ash, and don't leave the site until it's cold.

Respect wildlife. Though they may appear tame, animals in the wild are just that. Watch wildlife from a distance (bring binoculars or a tele-photo lens for close-ups), but never approach, feed, or follow them. Feeding weakens an animal's ability to fend for itself in the wild. If you can't keep your pets under control, leave them at home.

Finally, be mindful of other visitors. Yield to fellow travelers on the trail, and keep voices and noise levels low so that all the sounds of nature can be heard.

With these points in mind, you have only to chart your course. Enjoy your explorations. Let natural places quiet your mind, refresh your spirit, and remain as you found them. Just remember, leave behind no trace.

MAP KEY and ABBREVIATIONS

National Park	N.P.
National Lakeshore	N.L.
National Monument	N.M.
National Recreation Area	N.R.A.
National Scenic Riverway	N.S.R.
National Forest	N.F.
State Forest	S.F.
State Forest Recreation Area	S.F.R.A.
National Wildlife Refuge	N.W.R.
Preserve	PRES.
State Natural Area	S.N.A.
State Natural Preserve	S.N.P.
Wildlife Area	W.A.
State Park	S.P.
Historic State Park	H.S.P.
Provincial Park	P.P.
Recreation Area	R.A.
State Recreation Area	S.R.A.
Scenic Waters Area	
Indian Reservation	I.R.
National Wild & Scenic River	N.W. & S.R.

U.S. Interstate, Trans-Canada Highway   (80) (17)

U.S. Federal, state, and Canadian Provincial Highway   (2) (93) (21)

Other Road   [164] [C]

Trail

Ferry

Canal

BOUNDARIES
STATE, PROVINCIAL, or NATIONAL

FOREST

UNDERWATER PRESERVE

WILD.

POPULATION
● **CHICAGO**	above 500,000
● **Duluth**	50,000 to 500,000
● Athens	10,000 to 50,000
· Munising	under 10,000

ADDITIONAL ABBREVIATIONS
B.	Bay
Br.	Branch
B.W.C.A.	Boundary Waters Canoe Area
Cr.	Creek
D.N.R.	Department of Natural Resources
E.	East
Fk.	Fork
I.-s.	Island-s
L.	Lake
Mt.-s.	Mount-ain-s
N.	North
Pen.	Peninsula
PKWY.	Parkway
Pt.	Point
R.	River
Ra.	Range
S.	South
RD.	Road
Rec.	Recreation
TR.	Trail
WILD.	Wilderness

□ Point of Interest

◉ State or provincial capital

+ Elevation

╫ Falls

⤬ Swamp or Marsh

⟊ Dam

△ Campground

⊞ Picnic Area

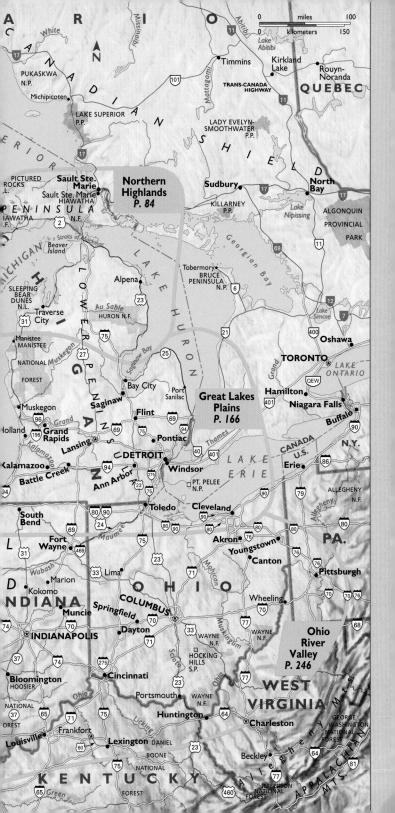

The Secret of the Great Lakes

"FLYOVER LAND," some people call the middle of America, implying that nothing between the coasts—at least nothing between the Rockies and the Appalachians—merits a stop. Good-natured by temperament, we Midwesterners just shrug it off. Their loss, we collectively agree.

So it's out of curiosity, not frustration, that I wonder: What exactly do those people picture when they look at a map and see the enormous blue mass of the Great Lakes—oversize farm ponds? An industrial wasteland? Swampy backwaters?

Raised along these shores, I can only speculate. But I doubt they conjure the Sleeping Bear Dunes rising like great pyramids out of the water, hammered gold and copper at sunset. I doubt they think of kayaking among the wooded Apostle Islands in water so clear it sometimes makes your boat feel suspended in midair. I doubt they contemplate walking for miles on a Lake Huron beach littered only with black bear paw prints and accompanied only by the haunting bellow of a loon. And I doubt they can even imagine the cliffs and coves of Isle Royale or the North Shore, where a timber wolf stands on an outcrop of ancient rock, throws back its head, and lets out a call so timeless it makes your hair stand on end.

Maybe that's a good thing. With more awareness comes more people—and, inevitably, change. But the writer in me wants to share this place. The proud Midwesterner does, too.

As a travel writer, I've been fortunate to explore at least a modest chunk of the world, especially some of the most spectacular natural areas in North America. When people ask me to name my favorite spot, my mind swims with images.

But in the end, the answer is easy: It's Lake Superior. It always has been. Nothing on the planet can yet match the sensation it gives me when I come over that last rise, and there it is, spilling across the horizon: the most magnificent body of water in the world, cobalt blue, crystal clear, almost primal in its beauty and its power.

This guidebook shares some of the most special spots along Lake Superior and throughout the Great Lakes region. They are places that can easily trigger inspiration and awe, from classic fly-fishing streams to glacial lakes and roiling waterfalls hidden deep in the pines to somnolent river valleys evocative of the Old South.

Though hardly encyclopedic, this collection of natural treasures found throughout the Great Lakes region may help define, describe, and offer a little direction to this oft-misunderstood place. And if I shatter a few stereotypes along the way, well, that's probably okay, too.

So the secret's out. With the help of this book, may you lose any misconceptions and find your own memories along these magical shores.

Tina Lassen

Lake Michigan, Sleeping Bear Dunes National Lakeshore

Trail to Lake Superior's shore, Little Presque Isle SFRA

The North Coast

THE FIVE GREAT LAKES—Superior, Michigan, Huron, Erie, and Ontario—
hardly seem to be lakes at all. To anyone who has stood along their shores,
they look and feel like inland seas, each powerful enough to heave into
earth-pounding waves, each vast enough to curve far over the horizon.
The 8,000-mile Great Lakes shoreline represents the nation's fifth seacoast.
The North Coast, they sometimes call it here.

Interconnected by rivers and canals, the Great Lakes form the largest
freshwater system in the world. They spill across nearly eight degrees of
latitude and sixteen degrees of longitude, lap the shores of eight states and
one Canadian province, and contain nearly one-fifth of the world's surface fresh water. They are one of the most prominent geographic features
on the face of the Earth, instantly recognizable even from the moon.

A combination of soupy tropical seas and cataclysmic volcanic erup-
tions initially formed the Great Lakes region. Billions of years ago, in the
northern tier around Lake Superior and northern Lake Huron, erupting
volcanoes laid down thick layers of basalt, which later tilted and faulted to
form the area's rugged, rocky topography of ancient mountain ranges and
steep, saw-toothed shorelines.

Farther south, a shallow sea covered the vast Michigan Basin, an area
that now encompasses the lower four Great Lakes. Over millions of years,
sand, shells, and other detritus compacted into thick layers of sedimentary
rock—the limestone, dolomite, sandstone, and shale now found from the
shores of northern Lake Michigan south to the Ohio River Valley.

But glaciers left the most indelible marks on the Great Lakes landscape.

Four different ice ages scrubbed and scoured their way across the region, the last one as recently as 10,000 years ago. As they advanced and retreated, the massive sheets of ice rearranged the Earth's surface. They bulldozed the land flat in some places and left high ridges of glacial debris in others. They carved out valleys and created rivers; they dammed up rivers and formed lakes; they dug depressions that filled with meltwater and became thousands upon thousands of additional lakes.

This is the watery landscape that defines the Great Lakes region today.

The idea that the Midwest is all farm and field is probably one of the greatest misconceptions out there. Along with the Great Lakes themselves, the region encompasses two of the nation's grandest rivers—the Mississippi and the Ohio—and countless other lakes, rivers, and streams. Minnesota, after all, is the "land of 10,000 lakes." Wisconsin claims even more. Two areas in the Great Lakes region—along the Minnesota-Ontario border, and the border between Wisconsin and the Upper Peninsula of Michigan—comprise the world's largest concentrations of lakes. Michigan is virtually surrounded by water, with more shoreline (3,288 miles) than any other state except Alaska.

All of this glorious water makes things a little cumbersome when you try to categorize the region for a guidebook. Areas of similar topography, such as northern Minnesota and the Upper Peninsula of Michigan, are separated by a hundred miles of open lake; in other cases, vastly disparate regions—steep river bluffs and flat outwash plains—end up side by side. Man-made distinctions are even crazier: The state of Michigan is severed in two, linked only by a bridge that spans the strait between Lakes Michigan and Huron.

Still, if you're willing to ignore political boundaries and accept those whims of nature, you can divide the northern Great Lakes into five basic biogeographic regions. The Superior Uplands and Canadian Shield region encompasses those areas of volcanic activity, stretching from the Ontario/Minnesota border and along the western and southwestern shore of Lake Superior. The northernmost area covered in this book, it is characterized by a thick boreal forest of fir, spruce, and birch—and the dramatic Superior shoreline.

South of the Superior Uplands lie the Northern Highlands, stretching across most of northern Wisconsin, the eastern Upper Peninsula of Michigan, and the northern half of Michigan's Lower Peninsula. Here basalt bedrock gives way to sandstone and limestone, and boreal forests segue into pine and hardwoods. Once heavily logged for its vast, valuable stands of white and red pine, today the area is prized largely for the recreation provided by its woods, water, and wildlife.

The Great Lakes Plains received the full brunt of the Ice Age and its powerful glaciers. Thick ice sheets marched across southern Wisconsin, southern Michigan, and northern Ohio, leaving behind a flattened tableau of sandy glacial lake beds, grasslands, prairie remnants, sedge meadows, cedar swamps, peat bogs, and immense marshlands.

Glacial debris and torrents of meltwater also chiseled out the Mississippi and Ohio River Valleys. The Upper Mississippi River Valley traces North America's mightiest river and some of its key tributaries from its northern reaches in Minnesota to the southern tip of Illinois. Nearly grazing the 37th parallel, it marks the southernmost reaches of this book. The Ohio River Valley also strays far to the south, covering the folded hills of southern Ohio, Indiana, and Illinois, a natural boundary distinguishing the Great Lakes region from the Appalachian Plateau.

All that water. For centuries it has given us fish for our tables, water for our crops, power for our mills, and an extraordinarily convenient transportation system. The Mississippi River carries grain from the Great Plains to the sea, where it ends up in ports around the world. Massive lake carriers annually haul nearly 200 million tons of heavy commodities, such as iron ore and limestone, from the northern Great Lakes to industrial centers along southern Lakes Michigan and Erie. Without these waterways, farmers could not compete, mines would shut down, and factories would grind to a halt.

Dawn along Minnesota's North Shore

And as our world population grows and our resources shrink, the water itself will likely prove to be the most valuable commodity of all. We must realize what an invaluable resource we have in our midst, and continue efforts to curb industrial pollution, agricultural runoff, and other abuses. But as conservationist Aldo Leopold taught us, writing from his farmstead in central Wisconsin, we should appreciate and protect our waters not just for our own consumptive needs, but because the Great Lakes region is a rich, wonderful, diverse ecosystem that should be treasured for its own intrinsic value.

The treasures here are large and small. It's a moose trundling out of the balsams and slipping into a wild Lake Superior bay. It's a centuries-old white pine scraping at the sky. It's also a tiny orchid. A rare horsefly. A tenacious blade of marram grass, building a monumental dune.

So pick a lake, pick a stretch of river, pick one tiny little patch of forest or one solitary bay. Get up close. Explore. Discover the watery wonders of the North Coast. ∎

Lake Superior and the Canadian Shield

Lighthouse, Raspberry Island, Apostle Islands National Lakeshore

GREATEST OF THE GREAT LAKES, Superior sprawls across the U.S.-Canadian border in a grand arc, stretching 383 miles between the port of Duluth, Minnesota, on its western end and the St. Marys River that links it to Lake Huron in the east. It seems a paradox to call Superior a lake at all; its size better qualifies it as an inland sea, a body of water so large it overflows with superlatives.

At 31,700 square miles—larger than the state of South Carolina—Lake Superior tops the list as the largest freshwater surface in the world. Plunging to depths of 1,333 feet, it also ranks as the world's third largest freshwater lake (after Baykal and Tanganyika) in volume. To put it in perspective, Superior holds enough water to cover all of North America, Central America, and South America to a depth of one foot.

What's more, Lake Superior's rather remote location has largely protected the quality of this vast waterway. Though mining, paper manufac-

turing, and a few other industries have presented some environmental challenges, Lake Superior remains far enough from major population centers that it has dodged many of the water-quality, water-rights, and shoreline-development problems faced by lakes elsewhere. Its water remains largely unpolluted and gin clear; its shore—characterized by rugged escarpments, rocky coves, and turbulent white-water rivers—is still wonderfully uncivilized.

This wild beauty is all part of the Precambrian Canadian Shield, an immense region of ancient rock that dips down in a giant horseshoe from the Canadian Arctic at Baffin Island, across portions of the northern Great Lakes region, and back up the west side of Hudson Bay. (Only Lake Superior's southeastern corner lies outside the Canadian Shield.) It encompasses a wealth of cherished natural areas, including perhaps the last expanse of true wilderness between the Adirondack Mountains in the east and the Rockies in the west.

The Canadian Shield formed about 2.7 billion years ago as the Earth's crust cooled. This cataclysmic era was marked by spewing volcanoes, colliding continents, and mountain ranges rising up and breaking apart. Much later, about 1.2 billion years ago, the Earth's hardened crust broke apart, forming a rift. Molten rock poured out at least a hundred different times, hardening like pancake batter in a griddle. Wind and rain then carried sand and other sediments onto these lava flows (or flood basalts, as they are known), creating slabs of soft rock sandwiched between layers of basalt. Groundwater percolated into the rock, too, filling the bubbles, cracks, and any other air spaces with minerals. Eventually the rift sank, creating a basin surrounded by tilted, uplifted rock. Today these high spots form much of the lakeshore's headlands and large islands such as Isle Royale.

The result is a rockhound's delight. The basalt visible in uplifted areas such as Minnesota's Sawtooth Mountains and Michigan's Keweenaw Peninsula is believed to be some of Earth's oldest exposed volcanic rock. Superior's beaches are also excellent places to hunt for agates, zeolite, rhyolite, granite, quartz, flint, jasper, and other specimens. And that mineral-rich groundwater that seeped into the bedrock a billion years ago? It became silver, copper, iron ore, and lead, prompting the development of huge mining industries across much of central Canada, Minnesota's Arrowhead region, and portions of Michigan's Upper Peninsula. The Keweenaw Peninsula still contains some of the largest and most pure deposits of copper found anywhere in the world.

Glaciers added a finishing touch to the region as recently as 10,000 years ago. Massive ice sheets scoured away many of the softer rock layers, leaving behind cliffs, coves, corrugated ridges, rivers, valleys, and thousands upon thousands of lakes. The Ontario-Minnesota border is pockmarked with the most intense concentration of glacial lakes on the globe, much of it protected as Quetico Provincial Park and the Boundary Waters Canoe Area Wilderness. When the last ice sheet began melting, rock debris carried by the glaciers blocked the natural drainage outlets of the basin and formed Lake Superior.

The retreating glaciers also carried away much of the region's topsoil. That's why pitching a tent in the Canadian Shield often entails a lot of bent tent stakes—you frequently hit solid rock just a few inches below the surface. Yet the landscape is surprisingly thick and verdant. Several species manage to cling and survive in the shallow, infertile soil, a northern coniferous forest of white pine, spruce, balsam, jack pine, birch, aspen,

Stones at water's edge, North Shore

berries, and numerous other shrubby plants. The southern end of the region merges into northern hardwood forest, marked by specimens that include hemlock and sugar maple.

The woods teem with wildlife—a fact quickly capitalized on by the French fur traders, or voyageurs, who traveled the lakes and rivers in enormous canoes to trap beaver and mink. Today those two species continue to thrive, along with healthy populations of black bear, white-tailed deer, moose, red fox, bobcat, and several smaller mammals. Loons, mergansers, and other waterfowl bob in quiet bays, while eagles, hawks, and ospreys soar overhead, searching the water for fish. Their quarry: the lake trout, lake herring, whitefish, and lake sturgeon that ply the frigid, almost sterile waters of Superior.

The Lake Superior region also happens to be the only area in the continental United States where the eastern timber wolf (also called the gray wolf) has managed to survive without being reintroduced by humans, the wolf's arch predator. Though extirpated from much of the Great Lakes region in the 1930s, the wolf was able to hang on in the large swaths of wilderness in the Superior uplands. Today its numbers are a far cry from the time when tens of thousands of wolves freely roamed the area, but some 2,200 animals still survive in northern Minnesota; another 350 to 400 live in Wisconsin and the Upper Peninsula of Michigan.

Perhaps some tranquil evening as you stare into your campfire deep in the heart of a white pine forest or along a rocky Lake Superior beach, you will hear it: an eerie, almost primeval whine that starts low and slowly warbles into a hollow wail. It is a sound at once so beautiful and so sad that you will be transfixed, never to forget the long, hollow call that connected you to the sublime. In that moment, like the wolves of Superior, you will have found your own piece of wilderness. ■

Lake of the Woods

■ 31,900 acres ■ 27 miles north of Rainy River, Ontario, near borders of Ontario, Manitoba, and Minnesota ■ Year-round ■ Camping, hiking, boating, swimming, fishing ■ Contact the park, R.R. 1, Sleeman, ON P0W 1M0; phone 807-488-5531. www.assabaskapark.com

WITH ITS WANDERING BAYS, leggy channels, and endless islands, it's difficult to tell if Lake of the Woods is land punctuated with lakes, or a lake punctuated with land. The confusion is understandable: Lake of the Woods is a giant among freshwater lakes, with 65,000 miles of shoreline, 80 miles of which stretch from its northernmost harbor in Kenora, Ontario, to its U.S. gateway in Baudette, Minnesota. In between, more than 14,000 islands—some of scoured granite, others covered in thick forest—stipple nearly 1,500 square miles of cool, clear water.

A major waterway in the immense Rainy River system, Lake of the Woods absorbs three-quarters of the river's flow, then spills north into Lake Winnipeg and eventually into Hudson Bay. The lake is a remnant of glacial Lake Agassiz, which once covered the ancient bedrock of the Canadian Shield. Erratics—huge boulders left behind by the ice fields—dot the landscape, providing further evidence of the area's glacial past.

The lake's warming influence supports a jumble of species, ranging from southern hardwoods such as elm, ash, and basswood to northern

Early morning on Lake of the Woods, near Nestor Falls, ON

spruce, balsam, and pine. Wild blueberries and raspberries are common, as is a wide variety of wildflowers such as pasture roses and spotted touch-me-nots. The mix of species also shows up in the park's birdlife. Most surprising are white pelicans: They have colonized several remote islands and waterways, turning them into permanent nesting grounds. Only a few of the islands provide undisturbed habitat for black bears, moose, deer, wolves, coyotes, foxes, beavers, and other woodland animals.

Assabaska Ojibway Heritage Park, made up of several islands in the lake's east, provides a convenient gateway to this watery wonderland.

What to See and Do

Visitors head for the lake for some of the finest sportfishing in the United States and Canada. Species include northern pike, muskie, large- and smallmouth bass, and yellow perch. Walleye fishing reigns supreme, especially in spring. Boat launches, charters, and guide services are easy to find, particularly in the Ontario gateway communities of Sioux Narrows and Rainy River. If you have your own boat, you can explore islands that have changed little over the centuries.

You won't find trails, but the islands' barren rock makes for easy walking. Along the shore, you may spot arrowheads and pottery sherds half buried in sand—signs that people have enjoyed the lake's bounty for generations. ■

Voyageurs National Park

■ 218,054 acres ■ North-central Minnesota, 15 miles east of International Falls via Minn. 11 ■ Year-round; access limited during fall freeze and spring thaw ■ Camping, hiking, boating, fishing, cross-country skiing, snowshoeing, wildlife viewing ■ Contact the park, 3131 Hwy. 53, International Falls, MN 56649; phone 218-283-9821. www.nps.gov/voya

FLOATING THROUGH THE CRAZY QUILT of waterways that make up Voyageurs National Park, you gain a new appreciation for the French-Canadian traders and explorers for whom the park is named. Loaded with furs and other trade goods, the voyageurs paddled this labyrinth of island-studded lakes, part of an elaborate water highway stretching from Montréal deep into northwest Canada. Situated flush against the Ontario border, at the western edge of the Canadian Shield, the park lies just a few miles east of a vast expanse of prairies. Rainy River, flowing between Rainy Lake and Lake of the Woods, eased the voyageurs' journey by allowing them to continue west by water.

Forming the backbone of the park is the 75,000-acre Kabetogama Peninsula, a largely untouched landmass nearly surrounded by the park's three largest lakes—Rainy, Kabetogama, and Namakan. This trio is linked by smaller lakes and waterways, all perfect for paddling. Water accounts for nearly 40 percent of the park, which encompasses 30 lakes, 900 islands, and thousands of miles of shoreline.

What to See and Do

Boating

The road ends where the national park begins, so you'll need access to a boat if you want to explore the park properly. You can bring your own, or rent a boat (the park has a list of outfitters) from one of the many resorts that hug the park's southern and western borders near the gateway towns of Ash River, Crane Lake, Rainy Lake, and Kabetogama Lake. The noise and speed of motorboats churning the larger waters may be offputting to canoeists, but there are more than enough smaller waterways to make the park a prime paddling destination.

Houseboating is also exceptionally popular here; several char-ter companies operate in the area. Voyageurs has 78 special house-boat campsites with mooring aids and fire rings. The Park Service provides canoes and rowboats at some of the hike-in campsites located on inland lakes. You can reserve one at the **Rainy Lake Visitor Center** (218-286-5258) or **Kabetogama Lake Visitor Center** (218-875-2111). Otherwise, they're available on a first come, first served basis.

Because Voyageurs' vast waterways disperse boaters—and because the lion's share of them overnight outside the park's perimeter—it's easy to surround yourself with solitude virtually anywhere in the park. You can explore

Black Bay Narrows, Voyageurs National Park

hidden harbors, set up camp at one of more than 200 water-accessible campsites, make a few casts into a placid bay for your dinner, or marvel at the precision of ospreys and bald eagles as they dive for fish.

Beyond sheer recreation, you may wish to learn about the park's wildlife and history by taking advantage of some of the boat adventures offered by the park *(218-286-5258; fee)*. Cruise with a naturalist aboard a 63-foot passenger boat to view wildlife at sunset, or visit the renovated 1910 **Kettle Falls Hotel** *(reservations 888-534-6835; accessible only by boat or floatplane)*, where you can also lodge. The hotel once housed lumberjacks and served as a rollicking center for gambling, bootlegging, and "fancy ladies." Relive the past aboard the park's 26-foot replica of a voyageur canoe *(free)*.

Fishing

Voyageurs has long been renowned for its fishing—these are considered some of the finest walleye and bass waters in the coun-try—and many resorts have skiffs available for guests' use.

Hiking

Few people take advantage of the park's 35 miles of hiking trails, especially those on isolated Kabetogama Peninsula. At the peninsula's west end, the **Locator Lake Trail** proceeds 2 miles to a chain of inland lakes, where the park service maintains canoes and campsites. Arrange for a water taxi at one of the park's four entry points to and from the trailheads *(for information call International Falls Convention and Visitor's Bureau 800-325-5766)*.

The 9-mile **Cruiser Lake Trail** bisects the peninsula as it makes its way through boreal forest of pine and aspen, scaling knobs of pink granite, skirting several inland lakes, and passing bogs and beaver ponds. Beaver pelts fueled the early fur trade, and about 3,000 of the rodents still thrive here—the largest concentration in the lower 48 states. Beavers share the park with wildlife such as moose, black bear, river otter, and the elusive timber wolf. ■

Fur trading, 1777 engraving

The Voyageurs:
Canoemen of the North

BEGINNING IN THE mid-1600s—generations before Europeans would explore North America in earnest—French-Canadian voyageurs, or travelers, ventured deep into the wooded wilderness of present-day Canada. Working for fur-trading companies, the voyageurs had a straightforward but arduous job: Transport beaver and other pelts from the far northwest to Montréal, capital of the fur trade. From there, the furs were shipped to Europe, where they were crafted into fashionable felt top hats and other upper-crust accessories. With Europe's appetite for furs nearly insatiable, the pelts were considered "soft gold."

Paddling immense birchbark canoes, the voyageurs followed a network of lakes, rivers, and streams that formed a nearly continuous waterway across North America. One of their most difficult overland hauls was at well-named Grand Portage on Superior's North Shore—an 8.5-mile trek involving a 700-foot climb. Because they usually carried three loads, that walking distance was actually 42.5 miles.

There were two types of voyageurs, a distinction that evolved based on geography. The "Montréal Men" transported trade goods from the east to Grand Portage, and returned to Montréal with furs destined for Europe. They paddled 36-foot lake canoes, propelled by as many as 14 men and carrying three tons of cargo, up the St. Lawrence Seaway and across Lakes Huron and Superior to Grand Portage.

At that busy post, the Montréal Men met up with a second group, the "Winterers," who transported the goods to Rainy Lake and farther west into the interior; here the men spent the long, cold winter, trading for furs with the Indians. When the waters thawed in spring, the Winterers, now loaded with furs, retraced their route of the year before. They paddled 24-foot canoes—large enough to carry four to six men and nearly two tons of cargo, yet small enough to navigate narrow, rapid waters and the inevitable woodland portages. From as far north as the Great Slave Lake in the present-day Northwest Territories, they journeyed along a web of rivers to immense Lake Winnipeg and Lake of the Woods, up the Rainy River, across the lakes of what is now Voyageurs National Park, through the maze of smaller lakes and portages in the Boundary Waters, and finally down the Pigeon River to Grand Portage.

The stamina and good cheer of the voyageurs became legendary. Singing folk songs as they paddled and sleeping in the wilderness with little more than upturned canoes for shelter, they labored from sunrise to sunset.

The July meeting, or rendezvous, in Grand Portage was the highlight of the year for the voyageurs. They camped for the better part of a month at the North West Company fur trade supply depot, taking full advantage of this rare chance to trade, rest, and socialize. Liquor flowed freely as Europeans and Indians alike shared in raucous entertainment.

The voyageurs relied heavily on the native Ojibwa and Cree (and other tribes farther west) to teach them survival skills and navigable routes. They learned to craft strong, lightweight canoes; they used birchbark for the skin, cedar roots to tie the bark together, and spruce resin to make the hull watertight. The Indians, in turn, were forever changed by the trade goods brought by the voyageurs. Wool blankets and woven cloth replaced animal skins; iron traps and firearms changed age-old hunting practices; and kettles and tools modernized everyday life. By the 19th century, European culture had left an indelible mark on even the most remote tribes.

The fur trade went on for more than a century. By the 1820s, however, trapping had diminished the beaver population and Europeans had moved on to new fashions. The Grand Portage post ceased operation, and the vocation of the voyageur soon became obsolete. Thanks to land donated by the Grand Portage band of Ojibwa, the fur-trading site is now a national monument, with a palisade enclosing reconstructed buildings and exhibits (see p. 41). ■

Voyageurs working their way upstream

The Boundary Waters

■ 2.2 million acres ■ Minnesota-Ontario border, between International Falls, MN, and Lake Superior ■ Best months May-Oct. ■ Camping, hiking, canoeing, fishing, skiing, snowshoeing, dogsledding, wildlife viewing ■ Permits required; call 877-550-6777 ■ Contact BWCAW, Superior National Forest, 8901 Grand Avenue Pl., Duluth, MN 55808, phone 218-626-4300, www.snf.superiorbroadband.com; or Quetico Provincial Park, Atikokan, ON P0T 1C0, phone 807-597-2735, www.ontarioparks.com/quet.html

AMONG PADDLERS, MINNESOTA'S Boundary Waters Canoe Area Wilderness (BWCAW) enjoys legendary status as one of the premier canoeing destinations on the planet. Comprising the northern tier of Superior National Forest, the wilderness area stretches 150 miles along the Canadian border, its one million acres a jumble of more than 1,000 lakes and 1,500 miles of interconnected water routes. Across the border, Quetico Provincial Park protects nearly one million acres of additional pristine wetlands. Quetico and the Boundary Waters Canoe Area Wilderness together make up an area referred to as the Boundary Waters—the largest swath of wilderness east of the Rocky Mountains.

Like the Yellowstone ecosystem, BWCAW serves merely as the center-

Camping beside Nym Lake, just north of Quetico Provincial Park

piece of a vast preserve, this one characterized by lakes. It is virtually surrounded by other protected lands: two million non-wilderness acres of Superior National Forest to the south and east, Voyageurs National Park to the west, and, of course, 1.2 million acres of Ontario's Quetico Provincial Park to the north. BWCAW and Quetico combined equal the size of Yellowstone National Park.

For the avid canoeist, these statistics engender an almost irresistible pull: to paddle and portage your way hundreds of miles deep into the wild North Woods. Traveling the paths of the Indians and the French-Canadian voyageurs, you'll find that the landscape has remained essentially unchanged. The Boundary Waters is still devoid of roads, cars, and power lines; it is largely free of motorboats and airplanes. This primordial setting invites you to revel in timeless delights: wind sighing in the pines, fish rising to feed at dusk, a startled moose crashing through the underbrush.

Formed by ancient volcanoes and scoured by glaciers, the landscape is dominated by northern forest of spruce, pine, and birch, rock-rimmed lakes, and exposed bedrock rising up in the form of rounded knobs or shattered cliffs. Though almost all of the red and white pines that once blanketed the region were logged in the late 1800s, you can still find isolated stands of these magnificent trees. In 1999, one of the most punishing

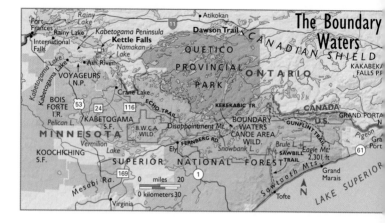

windstorms in North American history ravaged the forest (see sidebar, p. 32); recovery from that disaster is just beginning.

Your chances of spotting wildlife in the Boundary Waters are excellent, especially from the vantage point of a quietly floating canoe. You may see black bears browsing near the shore, beaver and muskrat gliding along the water's surface, eagles and ospreys soaring overhead, and loons, mergansers, and other birds gliding on mirror-smooth waters. In summer, nearly 100 species of birds nest in the region.

Paddlers can usually count on fresh fish dinners, avoiding the low romance of freeze-dried meals. Though best in spring and fall, fishing for northern pike, walleye, and smallmouth bass is generally good all summer long. But be forewarned: Mosquitoes and black flies plague the backcountry, especially in June and July. (Be sure to pack plenty of repellent, and perhaps a head net.)

Then again, as you rest your weary shoulders at a campsite miles from the modern world, listening to a fresh walleye sizzle in the pan over the campfire and watching the northern lights dance across the limitless sky, a few annoying insects may turn out to be a small price to pay for the sensation.

What to See and Do

Both the BWCAW (nicknamed "the bee-dub" by locals) and Quetico are primarily canoeing preserves. Depending on your experience or expectations, plan a canoe trip that lasts a couple of days or several weeks. In most areas, you can map out a circular route that covers several lakes, portages, and campsites. Or paddle to a specific campsite and enjoy day trips from there, forgoing the toil of having to pack up and portage your camping gear every day.

Even if your stay is limited to one day, you can enjoy a taste of the Boundary Waters region by trying a short day paddle on one of the outermost lakes that serves as an entry point to the wilderness. These lakes don't necessarily promise the solitude you can expect from the interior, but crystal-clear waters and undeveloped shorelines make for a magical outdoor experience.

Though renowned for its canoe routes, BWCAW contains fine hiking trails as well, from short day hikes to week-long backpacking treks. Some options are listed below under the appropriate entrance points. For maps and other suggestions, stop by the Quetico office or a Forest Service office in one of the gateway towns.

From Ely, Minn.

Ely (EE-lee), self-proclaimed "canoe capital of the world," is the best-known entryway to Boundary Waters from the southwest. Its downtown overflows with canoe outfitters happy to help you provision your trip or orchestrate the whole adventure. In winter, Ely transforms itself into a premier dogsledding and Nordic-skiing community; polar explorers Paul Schurke and Will Steger both have

businesses in town. Ely is also home to the International Wolf Center *(800-359-9653)*, which offers excellent exhibits and educational programs—not to mention the chance of viewing the center's resident wolf pack. More than 400 wolves—the largest population in the lower 48 states—roam freely in the surrounding national forest.

Two of the main access roads into the region depart from Ely. The **Echo Trail,** or County Road 116, heads north and west toward Voyageurs National Park. Fernberg Road wanders east out of Ely, leading to some of the most popular BWCAW access points, including Fall Lake, Moose Lake, and the aptly named Lake One. For an inaugural day paddle or short trip, Lake One offers a lot of interesting inlets and islands to explore. You may see other paddlers—likely heading for Lakes Two, Three, and points beyond—but you'll probably have few other distractions.

The backbone of the trail network is the **Kekekabic Trail** (the "Kek"), a 38-mile route that stretches eastward from the end of

Boundary Waters marsh

Fernberg Trail near Snowbank Lake to the Gunflint Trail north of Grand Marais. Built in the 1930s as an access trail for firefighters, this rugged route ascends high hills, crosses beaver dams, and arcs past hundreds of lakes.

Snowbank Lake Trail shares the Kekekabic's western trailhead. The 24-mile route circles Snowbank Lake, climbing rocky ridges for several fine overlooks. Also near the west end of the Kek, you can pick up the **Old Pines Trail,** which loops through a stand of old-growth pines to the south, and **Disappointment Trail,** which crosses Disappointment Mountain north of Kekekabic Trail. You can easily create lengthy treks of 20 to 30 miles by combining various loop trails.

From Echo Trail, access the **Herriman Trail network,** where moderately steep loops of 3 to 14 miles follow lakeshores and the Echo River. For an all-day outing, try the rolling **Angleworm Trail,** a

Storm of the Century

On July 4, 1999, a windstorm unlike any other blasted through the Boundary Waters. Winds reached speeds of 100 miles per hour, toppling an estimated 40 million trees and rendering 700,000 acres of forest almost unrecognizable. Within minutes, century-old pines were strewn across the forest floor like matchsticks. Remarkably, even though the storm occurred on a holiday weekend, no one was killed.

The National Weather Service categorized the storm as a derecho—a straight-line wind that can wreak far more destruction than circular or spiraling winds. It rocketed across Superior National Forest in a 40-mile-long, 10-mile-wide path from Ely, across the Gunflint Trail and into Ontario. It inflicted its heaviest damage in the Boundary Waters Canoe Area Wilderness.

Cleanup—a grueling task that entailed clearing portages and hiking paths where downed trees sometimes formed walls 20 feet high—continued for more than a year. Trail crews had to locate once-familiar portages and methodically cut through tangles of trunks, sometimes progressing just 25 feet per hour.

By spring 2000 a new problem loomed: the risk of fire. The litter of downed trees had turned the region into a tinderbox, with the potential for an inferno that could have rivaled the 1988 Yellowstone fire. Fortunately, that scenario never materialized, thanks to favorable weather, prescribed burns outside the BWCAW, and legions of firefighters snuffing out blazes as quickly as they began. (Special fire precautions may remain in effect; check with a ranger station.)

Within the wilderness area, the forest will be left to regenerate naturally. Outside the wilderness, the forest service plans to reseed 5,000 acres of pine and spruce. Like Yellowstone, the devastated portions of the Boundary Waters will rebound. In the meantime, the blowdown and its aftermath serve as an outdoor laboratory for scientists—and as a sobering reminder of the wild inherent in wilderness.

View of Bass Lake, Superior National Forest

scenic 14-mile hike around the perimeter of Angleworm Lake, 18 miles north of Ely.

From Tofte/Grand Marais, Minn.

These two towns, both with forest service offices, provide access to the BWCAW from Lake Superior's North Shore. The **Sawbill Trail,** or County Road 2, leads north from Tofte to well-known access points on Sawbill and Brule Lakes. Located between the two but less trafficked than either one, **Baker Lake** (a narrow, pretty body of water easy to reach from the Sawbill Trail) is ideal for day paddles. Popular, 8-mile-long **Brule Lake,** with its maze of bays, rocky outcrops, and islands and inlets, promises great day or overnight paddles, especially during the off-season.

The famous **Gunflint Trail** punches northward into the forest from Grand Marais for nearly 75 miles to the trail's terminus at Sea Gull Lake. Sea Gull and immense **Saganaga Lake**—which straddles the international border—are portals to Quetico Provincial Park and the eastern end of BWCAW. Outfitters and lake resorts are strewn at intervals along the Gunflint Trail, as are plenty of lake access points. About two-thirds of the way up the trail, you'll cross the Laurentian Divide; waters north of here drain into Hudson Bay, while those south drain into the Gulf of Mexico.

Twenty miles from Grand Marais, the 7-mile out-and-back **Eagle Mountain Trail** climbs through jack pine and birch forest to a rocky knob: 2,301-foot Eagle Mountain—Minnesota's highest point. From here you get a sense of the Boundary Waters' staggering scale: The seemingly endless rise and fall of forested terrain is interrupted only by dark patches of wilderness lake, and on clear days Superior is visible along the southern horizon.

As its name implies, the **Border Route Trail** follows the United States-Canada frontier for 75 miles through some of the Boundary Waters' most scenic sections, ascending high ridges that yield panoramic overlooks and passing waterfalls and old-growth pines. The trail extends from Gunflint Trail to Pigeon River, with a half-dozen access points that allow you to hike just a portion of the route, if the idea of the full 75 miles strikes you as a bit daunting.

From Atikokan, Ontario

The only way to access the Quetico wilderness by car is at the modern **Dawson Trail Campground** on French Lake, 30 miles east of Atikokan, Ontario. The rest of Quetico can be reached only by canoe from six access points, four of them in Superior National Forest's wilderness area.

Rimmed with granite cliffs and sparkling with waterfalls, Quetico's lakes seem even wilder than those in the BWCAW. Only veteran paddlers should travel independently in this country, where many find it easy to confuse the unmarked portages and lakes.

The Dawson Trail Campground provides informative displays about the area's geology, biology, and history. Park rangers host nature talks throughout the summer here, and three interpretive hikes wind through the woods from the campground. ■

Sigurd F. Olson: Voice of the Wilderness

Sigurd F. Olson (1899-1982) once described himself as "a freelance canoeman, trying to get the rest of the world excited about saving the finest recreational resource on the continent." He was speaking of the Boundary Waters canoe country that straddles the Minnesota-Ontario border. Olson's appreciation of that lakeland wilderness established him as one of the most influential (and beloved) conservation writers of the 20th century.

Sigurd F. Olson

Born in Chicago, Olson grew up in the pine forests of northern Wisconsin, where he discovered the wonder of woods and water. At 24, he migrated north to Ely, Minnesota, and began a lifelong love affair with the Boundary Waters.

Olson's writing style was simple and eloquent. His eight books—most notably The Singing Wilderness—espouse a "wilderness theology," describing the gift of the natural world and the deep peace it can bring to the human spirit.

As an activist, Olson lobbied tirelessly to protect the wilds of the Boundary Waters. In the 1920s, he fought to keep out roads, then power company dams. In the 1940s, Olson was at the forefront of a precedent-setting fight to restrict airplanes from flying into the Boundary Waters area; in the 1970s he was at it again, lobbying to ban boat motors from its lakes and grant it wilderness status. For that, he was booed, ostracized, and hanged in effigy in Ely.

But by then, Olson's legacy was assured. Over the years he had served as president of the National Parks Association, president of The Wilderness Society, adviser to the National Park Service, and adviser to the U.S. Secretary of the Interior. Olson helped draft the 1964 Wilderness Act, the pivotal law that established our nation's wilderness preservation system. He played a key role in setting aside the Arctic National Wildlife Refuge in Alaska and Point Reyes National Seashore in California.

In the end, that freelance canoeman did indeed get the world excited about northern Minnesota's lakeland wilderness. Olson's dream was realized in 1978, when President Jimmy Carter signed the bill granting full wilderness status to the Boundary Waters Canoe Area Wilderness.

"Some places should be preserved from development or exploitation," said Olson, "for they satisfy human need for solace, belonging and perspective. This is the most beautiful lake country on the continent. We can afford to cherish and protect it."

Minnesota's North Shore

■ 150 miles along Lake Superior ■ Northwest Lake Superior, between Duluth and Grand Portage via Minn. 61 ■ Year-round ■ Camping, hiking, boating, fishing, skiing, snowshoeing, wildlife viewing ■ Day-use permits for state parks ■ Contact Superior National Forest, 8901 Grand Avenue Pl., Duluth, MN 55808, phone 218-626-4300, www.snf.superiorbroadband.com; or Superior Hiking Trail Association, Minn. 61 & 8th St., Two Harbors, MN 55616, phone 218-834-2700, www.shta.org

AH, THE NORTH SHORE. To Minnesotans, the term refers to the state's precious patch of real estate along the northwest shore of Lake Superior. Though a popular vacation area peppered with resorts, cabins, and lakefront homes, this rocky coast somehow manages to remain untamed.

It's a prime example of the Canadian Shield, part of a broad band of igneous rock blanketed with boreal forest. Along the North Shore, the rock forms a high escarpment at the lake's edge, interrupted only by white-water rivers—fed by springs or snowmelt—that thrash their way toward Lake Superior.

Beginning at Lake Superior's western tip, near the busy shipping port of Duluth, the North Shore extends northeastward to the Ontario border at Grand Portage. Along this 150-mile stretch lie several of Minnesota's finest state parks, offering ample access to the big lake. Just inland, Superior National Forest spans a staggering 3 million acres; the forest climbs into the ancient Sawtooth Mountains, encompassing hundreds of glacial lakes and a wilderness that remains a stronghold of wolves, moose, deer, and other wildlife.

No wonder the North Shore ranks as such a legendary destination: Its broad appeal offers something for everyone. Sightseers, beachcombers, and hikers can remain near Minn. 61, the paved road that hugs the shoreline for almost all its length, linking state parks and charming villages. Anglers, boaters, and those seeking backcountry adventure can follow the Gunflint Trail (Forest Road 12) or one of the other roads that leads into the interior. Attracting distance hikers, the Superior Hiking Trail traces the high ridgelines above Lake Superior for more than 200 miles.

What to See and Do

Heading northeast from Duluth along Minn. 61, you'll pass several lakefront towns (notably Knife River) that serve as sportfishing hubs. Lake trout is the area's most popular native game fish. Weighing 5 to 20 pounds, these swift predators are the only species of trout or salmon that spawn in lakes. Lake trout reigned as Lake Superior's most valuable commercial fish during the period that lasted from the early 1900s until the 1950s, when they were nearly wiped out by the sea lamprey, an eel-like parasite.

Other popular game fish—

Cascade River State Park, Minnesota's North Shore

among them chinook salmon and brown, brook, and rainbow trout —were introduced to these waters for sport or to control unwanted predators. Rainbow trout have fared best, thanks to the North Shore's fine spawning streams.

Knife River is one of the few North Shore communities that still harbors a commercial fishery. Hundreds of fishermen worked along the North Shore around 1900, pulling lake trout, whitefish, and herring from the area's waters. By the mid-1900s, North Shore fishermen were netting more than 5 million pounds of lake herring each year. Today, only a handful of commercial fisheries remain.

Gooseberry Falls State Park

About 12 miles north of Two Harbors, Gooseberry Falls State Park

Lake Superior's Tides

The Great Lakes do not experience true tides—those caused by the moon's gravitational pull—but weather on the giant bodies of water still produces a tidelike rise and fall called a seiche (SAYSH). A seiche occurs when wind and barometric pressure push water against the lake's shore. Behaving rather like a glass of water that's been jostled, the lake's water rebounds, sloshing back to the other side. Seiches rarely rise and fall more than one foot on Lake Superior, and are usually less pronounced on the other Great Lakes. Yet to anyone who spends time along these shores, the periodic rise and fall appears to mimic a tide.

(*3206 Minn. 61 East, Two Harbors, MN; 218-834-3855; fee*) is known for its waterfalls. On both sides of the highway bridge, the Gooseberry River tumbles over dark lava flows, now splintered into hard-edged ledges. **Middle** and **Lower Falls,** the most impressive, lie just downstream from the bridge, where the river plunges 60 feet. Footpaths wind around the pools for several fine vantage points.

To see the fifth and most secluded cataract, follow the aptly named **Fifth Falls Trail** upstream. The 3-mile route winds up one bank and down the other, crossing a bridge just past the falls. Several mountain bike trails depart from the visitor center, bound for more remote sections of the park. You'll likely spot some immense tree stumps—arboreal headstones marking the site of a large stand of old-growth white pines logged off in the 1890s. On the other side of the highway, a 1.5-mile out-and-back walk on **Gitchi Gummi Trail** (the Ojibwa name for Lake Superior) leads to a ridgetop view of the big lake. **Lower Rim Trail** (1.5 miles round-trip) follows Gooseberry River to its mouth at **Agate Beach,** where you can hunt for the lovely mineral-banded quartz stones.

Split Rock Lighthouse State Park

This nearby state park (*218-226-6377; fee. www.dnr.state.mn.us*) preserves one of the North Shore's most famous landmarks. The 1910 lighthouse sits atop a dramatic bluff that rises 120 feet out of Lake Superior. Sailors are said to have given Split Rock its name because the cliff appears split in two at

Minnesota's North Shore

0 miles 20
0 kilometers 30

certain angles from the water. The cliff and much of the surrounding shoreline is composed of gabbro—a rock similar to basalt, flecked with black and white crystals.

The region's most valuable mineral is iron ore. From about 1870 to 1950, hundreds of mines across northern Minnesota's "iron ranges" produced the ore, then sent it by railcar to Lake Superior ports for shipment to steel mills. A huge upsurge in commercial shipping resulted, prompting the construction of more and more lighthouses. They were especially vital along the Lake Superior shore, where vicious storms can form quickly and the ships' highly magnetic cargoes played havoc with compass readings.

Tettegouche State Park

Just north of Silver Bay, Tette-gouche's **Palisade Head** marks the highest lookout along the North Shore. Formed by ancient lava flows that reached thicknesses of more than 200 feet, Palisade Head was a well-advertised stop for motorists who cruised the scenic highway after it was completed in 1924. The sheer face now attracts accomplished rock climbers.

The **Baptism River** meets Lake Superior at the main entrance to **Tettegouche State Park** *(218-226-6365)*. A small bridge here provides a good view of the river's gorge, while **Baptism High Falls Trail** leads 1.5 miles upstream to 65-foot **High Falls,** the state's second tallest cascade. Several other trails wind farther inland, through a mature forest of sugar maple, eastern white cedar, white spruce, and yellow birch, to four lakes accessible only by foot.

At the park's east end, **Shovel Point** extends 1,000 feet into Lake Superior. Follow the **Shovel Point Interpretive Trail** for less than a mile through three distinct ecosystems: Spruce, balsam, and other northern species grow on the cool eastern shore; a "dwarf forest" of scrub pines clings to areas of shallow soil; and little more than

Fishing, Cascade River State Park, Minnesota's North Shore

lichens survive on the exposed rock outcroppings. The highest point affords terrific views of Palisade Head and, on a clear day, the Apostle Islands of Wisconsin 30 miles southeast.

George Crosby-Manitou State Park

A trip to this park *(218-226-6365)* promises easy access to a backcountry free of most man-made intrusions. It lies 15 miles off Minn. 61 on County Road 7, remote enough that its few visitors do not scare off wildlife. Black bears, moose, and wolves have been sighted here, the wolves often feeding on the large deer population.

Twenty-three miles of trails begin at the entrance and lace the 3,320-acre park, circling **Benson Lake** and rolling through river valleys. Rocky and narrow, the 4-mile **Manitou River Trail** parallels spring-fed Manitou River, home to a population of native brook trout. The park also contains fine old-growth northern hardwood and eastern white cedar forests.

Temperance River State Park

Of all the North Shore rivers rushing toward Lake Superior, none is more dramatic than the **Temperance** as it bounds through its namesake state park *(218-663-7476)*. It drops 160 feet in its last half mile, crashing through chasms and carving out potholes in the lava riverbed. **Cauldron Trail** (1.5 miles) traces the river up one bank and back down the other *(keep a firm grip on children here)*. On the banks you will be able to spot several dry potholes, formed when

the river ran higher or followed a different course.

Like many other rivers in the area, the waters of the Temperance have a reddish-brown hue. This is caused by tannin released into the water by hemlocks, cedars, tamaracks, and other trees and plants, as well as by minerals leaching from soil. Local tanneries relied on the bark of hemlocks and cedars to tan leather in the 19th century.

Grand Portage State Park

The **Pigeon River** forms part of the United States-Canada border—and thus the end of Minnesota's North Shore. Largely undeveloped Grand Portage State Park *(218-475-2360)* was established to protect 120-foot **Pigeon Falls** (known locally as High Falls), the state's largest. Several vantage points, including one from **Middle Falls Provincial Park** in Ontario, provide views of this grand cascade.

The Pigeon River's falls and rapids required Native Americans (and, later on, French-Canadian voyageurs) to bypass this section of river as they traveled a well-established water route across North America. **Grand Portage National Monument** *(218-387-2788; fee)* commemorates the place where paddlers beached their birchbark canoes and hauled them overland, uphill, to a navigable point more than 8 miles upstream. (You can hike the trail, but it tends to be muddy and buggy.) A reconstructed stockade, artifacts, and displays at the monument set forth the fascinating life of the voyageur and the raucous rendezvous that took place here each summer.

Following pages: Split Rock Lighthouse at dusk, Minnesota's North Shore

Superior National Forest

Stretching along the North Shore from about Temperance River State Park to beyond Grand Marais, and inland for some 150 miles, Superior National Forest encompasses classic North Woods beauty in a water-rich forest of glacial lakes, rivers, and bogs. Nearly one-sixth of the forest's 3 million acres is surface water.

From the North Shore, four well-marked and well-maintained dirt roads cleave the forest: the **Sawbill, Caribou, Gunflint,** and **Arrowhead Trails.** From these, other forest and logging roads and single- and double-track trails spin into the woods. Buy a topographic map at a Forest Service office in Duluth, Tofte, or Grand Marais.

One of the nation's great footpaths, the 235-mile **Superior Hiking Trail,** largely parallels Lake Superior on a high ridgeline that rises more than 1,000 feet above the lake and overlooks the water at many points. The trail clambers up rock outcroppings and cliffs, drops into valleys, and often follows rivers for a mile or more, showcasing waterfalls, rapids, and deep gorges where thousands of years of rushing water have cut into layers of ancient volcanic rock. Rustic campsites are located every 6 miles or so along the trail.

Though a few hikers tackle the entire trail each summer, numerous access points make it a great day-hiking destination as well. The trail links seven state parks and other trail networks, so you can easily create a loop route. Local businesses offer shuttle services *(Superior Shuttle 218-834-5511)* and lodge-to-lodge hikes *(Lutsen-Tofte Tourism Association 218-663-7804 or 888-616-6784).* In winter, the trail is open to snowshoers but not cross-country skiers.

One of the most scenic segments lies east of Grand Marais. Just beyond the **Devil Track River,** take County Road 58 north to a well-marked parking area. Follow Superior Hiking Trail west. Within a mile, you'll reach Minnesota's deepest canyon, where the **Devil Track River** careers through a narrow slot far below. The trail weaves along the canyon rim before descending to the river at the 2.4-mile marker. Cross the footbridge and continue 0.8 miles to **Pincush-**

Caribou Resurgent?

Woodland caribou were spotted north of Grand Marais as recently as 1981, probably wandering down from Ontario. The sighting surprised everyone because the migratory mammals had disappeared from Minnesota in the 1930s. Caribou once freely roamed the upper Great Lakes region, but logging obliterated the mature pine forests they favored, pushing them farther and farther north. They also fell victim to ringworm, a parasite carried by the white-tailed deer who moved into the browsing areas created by the newly logged land. (Deer can carry ringworm with no ill effects; caribou and moose succumb to the parasite.)

No additional caribou have been seen in recent years. As the pine forests mature once again, many people hope that the caribou will return with the conifers.

High Falls, Tettegouche State Park

ion Mountain, or 2.5 miles to the Gunflint Trailhead, enjoying panoramic views of Lake Superior and Grand Marais en route.

North of Tofte, the trail climbs to several high points offering magnificent Lake Superior vistas. From the Sawbill Trailhead take the 4-mile round-trip to the summit of **Carlton Peak,** a bald dome of granite. Alternatively, head east to link up with the **Oberg** and **Leveaux Mountain National Recreation Trails,** 1,000 feet above Superior. For a special treat, visit in fall when the hardwoods glow fiery bronze and crimson.

The **North Shore State Trail**—a 153-mile route from Duluth to Grand Marais—lies farther inland. The trail winds through forests behind the bluffs of Lake Superior where you're sure to find plenty of solitude. Anglers favor this trail because it crosses dozens of creeks and rivers, most abounding with brook, rainbow, and brown trout.

This multiuse trail is also open to horses, but not to mountain bikes. Camping is permitted on adjacent public lands and at 14 rustic shelters along the way *(contact North Shore Trail Headquarters, 218-834-5238, for maps and information).*

Boaters can choose from more than 2,000 lakes within the national forest. Most of those outside the Boundary Waters Canoe Area Wilderness allow motorboats, assuming a boat launch is available *(see Forest Service topographic map for launches).* A good choice for paddlers is the **Timber Frear Canoe Route.** About 15 miles northwest of Tofte, **Whitefish Lake** offers a launch restricted to kayaks and canoes. From there, short portages lead to five other wilderness lakes, none with motorboat launches. As you glide over the water, the only sound you're likely to hear is the call of a loon or the slap of a beaver tail. Rustic campsites dot the shores of five of the six lakes. ∎

Apostle Islands National Lakeshore

■ 69,372 acres ■ Northwestern Wisconsin, along tip of Bayfield Peninsula and 21 islands in Lake Superior ■ Best months for island access via commercial boats May–Oct. ■ Camping, hiking, boating, fishing, diving ■ Adm. fee ■ Contact the lakeshore, Route 1, Box 4, Bayfield, WI 54814; phone 715-779-3397. www.nps.gov/apis

WISCONSIN CLAIMS BUT A SMALL CORNER of Lake Superior's vast shoreline, yet what it lacks in quantity it makes up for in quality. Like emeralds in a sapphire sea, 22 forested islands lie scattered off the tip of Bayfield Peninsula. All but the largest, Madeline Island, are undeveloped and uninhabited, and feature sculpted sandstone sea caves, pristine stretches of sandy beach, and remnant old-growth hemlocks and hardwoods.

Jesuit missionaries and French fur traders named the islands after the 12 followers of Jesus. The honor, though reverential, is not particularly appropriate: Historians believe the missionaries did indeed realize there were more than 12 islands. The national lakeshore now protects 12 miles of mainland shore and the entire archipelago, with the exception of Madeline Island (it already had year-round residents when Congress created the national lakeshore in 1970). The protected islands range in size from 3-acre Gull to 10,000-acre Stockton.

The Apostles serve as visible remnants of the last ice age. As the glaciers advanced, they deposited high hills of sand and gravel, and carved a deep, broad basin; when they retreated about 10,000 years ago, meltwater filled the basin, and the high spots became islands.

The relatively hard red sandstone of the Apostles became a popular building material in the late 1800s. "Brownstone" quarried from Stockton, Basswood, and Hermit Islands was used to construct many buildings throughout the East and Midwest, including those rebuilt in Chicago after the great fire of 1871. The old county courthouse in Bayfield, now the National Lakeshore Visitor Center, consists of brownstone from the Apostle Islands.

People have exploited the Apostles for generations. Well-protected, the islands became an important fur-trading post in the 1600s. The Ojibwa tribe lived on Madeline Island, and the Huron came here to trade with French-Canadian voyageurs. The fur trade lasted nearly two centuries. As it declined, commercial fishing began to develop in the 1830s. Two decades later the fishing industry was harvesting enormous stocks of whitefish, herring, and lake trout. Today, you can visit restored fish camps at Little Sand Bay on the mainland and on Manitou Island. All those fishing boats on the water prompted the construction of lighthouses, and the Apostles now lay claim to one of the nation's highest concentrations of beacons. Six lighthouses—the largest collection in the national park system—are located within the national lakeshore.

Little Sand Bay, Apostle Islands National Lakeshore

Logging followed fishing, and clear-cutting the islands was almost too easy: Large tracts of white pine, red pine, fir, spruce, and hemlock could be felled, stacked on the nearby ice, then floated to mainland mills come spring. By the 1930s, the islands were so denuded that the National Park Service resisted the idea of making them into a national park when Herbert Hoover's Administration suggested it. Indeed, the only areas that had escaped the logger's saw were those purposely left as a firewood supply for lighthouse keepers or those growing on steep shorelines. Today these areas are protected as the Apostle Islands Maritime Forest State Natural Area, and they include Devils Island, Raspberry Island, and portions of Outer and Sand Islands.

Fortunately, wilderness has slowly reclaimed the Apostle Islands, and native species thrive once again in this transition zone between the boreal forest of fir and spruce and the northern highland forest of maple, hemlock, birch, and pine. Devils Island showcases blufftop boreal forest, with balsam fir and spruce clinging to its exposed rock, while arctic plants such as butterwort and sedges grow from raw, north-facing cliffs. Bear Island protects northern mesic—requiring a moderate amount of moisture—and wet-mesic forest, with acres of hemlocks and perched bog.

A sizable community of birds inhabits the islands, including bald eagles and loons, both of which seem almost commonplace here. To protect their nesting colonies of double-crested cormorants, herring gulls, great blue herons, and others, Eagle, Gull, and North Twin Islands have been placed off-limits. Some visitors are surprised at the number of large mammals—including deer, black bears, and coyotes—that inhabit the Apostles. Stockton Island, in fact, harbors one of the greatest concentrations of black bears in North America—as many as 2.1 per square mile.

What to See and Do

Magnificent natural bounty sets the stage for a wonderful escape, especially for hikers and boaters. After exploring a few mainland areas, hikers will want to arrange transportation to the islands for the park's best trails. The proximity of the islands to one another and to the mainland enables experienced sea kayakers to paddle throughout the area, exploring sea caves and sandstone cliffs. Sailors enjoy plying the deep island waters and dropping anchor in protected, crystalline bays.

The Mainland

Head for the mainland's **Little Sand Bay**, 13 miles north of Bayfield, where the national lakeshore begins. Here the National Lakeshore Visitor Center offers a variety of fishing and shipping displays, as well as the restored **Hokenson Brothers Fishery** (*free tours*)—a living museum with a fishing tug, herring shed, ice house, and other buildings filled with fascinating relics and interpretive displays.

Farther west, the 13 miles of shoreline at **Mawikwe Bay** include a dramatic stretch of sandstone sea caves. Exposed to the furious weather of the open lake, the brilliant red sandstone has been shaped into gaping chasms and flying buttresses that rise as high as 65 feet. In winter, ice and snow sculptures build up along the cliff faces and ooze off the top like icing on a cake. The best view of the sea caves is from a kayak on the lake, or from the lake's frozen surface in winter (*call first for ice conditions, 715-779-3398, ext. 499*).

Accessing the Islands

Allow at least half a day to see the islands. The Apostle Islands Cruise Service (*715-779-3925*) offers three-hour or all-day tours from mid-May through mid-October. The tours wind past lighthouses

Kayaks, Apostle Islands National Lakeshore

and dramatic rock formations as narrators share information on the area's history and natural resources. This is a good way to enjoy the beauty of the water—some tours even stop at several of the islands. Through the same company, you can arrange for a shuttle to drop you at an island for a few hours or a few days.

Another excellent means of visiting the islands is via charter boat *(for information, contact the Bayfield Area Chamber of Commerce, 715-779-3335 or 800-447-4094)*. Several sailing charters operate in the area, offering captained or bareboat arrangements, depending on your experience. Sportfishing charters allow you to pit your skills against salmon, lake trout, and whitefish.

The Apostles are a sea kayaker's dream. Even rank beginners can take to the waters on guided trips through local outfitter Trek & Trail *(800-354-8735)*. Wave-torn and pockmarked from exposure to open waters, the islands at the national lakeshore's north end, such as Devils Island, draw only the most adventurous and experienced kayakers. In calm weather, paddlers can weave in and out of tight passages and the hollow maw of caves.

If you're short on time, the Madeline Island Ferry *(715-747-2051)* will transport you and your car to its namesake island. The appealing state park here will give you a good feel for the region.

Visiting the Islands

Oak Island is the highest island in the Apostles, rising nearly 500 feet above the lake surface. It was the first to emerge as lake levels fell. Remnants of different lake stages can be seen in several places on the island. With more than 11 miles of maintained trails, it's one of the best destinations for hikers, who can explore ancient beach lines, steep hills, deep valleys, the area's highest cliffs, and Hole-in-the-Wall, an eroded sandstone arch along the northeast shore.

Another good hiking choice, **Stockton Island** offers 14 miles of delightful trails. It became the largest island in the Apostles about 5,000 years ago, when shifting sands linked it (via a sand bridge called a tombolo) with a small island to the south. Explore this area on the 3-mile-long **Tombolo Trail.** Other trails lead to an abandoned logging camp, an old sandstone quarry, and past bogs and beaches.

On **Sand** and **Raspberry Islands,** you can tour restored lighthouses and learn from naturalists about the life of a 19th-century lightkeeper. The 1881 sandstone lighthouse at the north end of Sand Island is one of Lake Superior's most picturesque. Both islands boast lovely beaches embracing crystal-clear bays.

With its year-round residents, resorts, restaurants, roads, and cars, **Madeline Island** seems downright urban compared with the rest of the Apostles. Still, it's a fine spot to explore, especially around **Big Bay State Park** *(715-747-6425)*. Here, trails skirt a lagoon, pass sandstone formations and sea caves, and wind through pine forest. The eponymous bay offers more than a mile of protected sand beach. ∎

Black River Waterfalls

■ Final 6-mile stretch of Black River ■ Michigan's Upper Peninsula, from Bessemer north via Cty. Rd. 513 ■ Best season spring ■ Hiking, wildlife viewing
■ Contact Ottawa National Forest, E6248 US 2, Ironwood, MI 49938; phone 906-932-1330. www.fs.fed.us/r9/ottawa/

THE HANDSOME BLACK RIVER ends its run with a flourish, tumbling and crashing over seven falls in 6 miles before bursting into Lake Superior. Given the large concentration of waterfalls here, it seems as though Mother Nature set out to create the perfect cataract display: plenty of drama, lots of variety, a lovely backdrop of whistling white pines, and the solitude necessary to enjoy it all.

Five of the seven falls lie north of US 2 and the town of Bessemer, accessible from the **Black River Road National Scenic Byway** (County Road 513), which parallels the river on its west side. The maples that line the road and extend into the forest seem to glow electric crimson and yellow in autumn. The waterfalls, too, are brilliantly backdropped in fall, but they're at their most spectacular in spring, when snowmelt turns them into raging torrents.

The first, **Chippewa Falls,** is on private land and inaccessible. **Algonquin** is next. Lying off the **North Country National Scenic Trail** at the north end of Copper Peak Road, it can be difficult to find. The next five falls are much more accessible, thanks to well-marked hiking trails, a few staircases, and basic observation decks added by Ottawa National Forest.

Great Conglomerate Falls takes its name from the pebbly rock fragments found here that are cemented together by finer sand and other material, called conglomerate or "pudding stone." In a wild, noisy show, water roars over this textured rock and squeezes into a gorge. Half a mile downstream (north) lies lovely **Potawatomi Falls,** its delicate fretwork of foam cascading over remnants of an ancient lava flow. Potawatomi is considered one of the prettiest of the falls. Continue downstream for 200 yards from Potawatomi to **Gorge Falls,** where the river narrows from 130 feet to just 29, churning the water into a torrent as it charges through the smooth-walled gorge.

The geology changes at **Sandstone Falls,** where the powerful erosive forces of the Black River are slowly sculpting and shaping the softer rock of the riverbed. Here sparkling water spills through bowls and potholes, while white pines lean out over the golden sandstone banks.

The final and largest cataract in the group is **Rainbow Falls.** This cascade plummets 40 feet, its rebounding spray sometimes revealing its luminous namesake rainbow. The east side of the river, accessed from a suspended footbridge near the mouth of the river at Black River Harbor, provides the best view. Pause on the bridge long enough to enjoy the sight of Lake Superior from this unique mid-river vantage point. ■

Potawatomi Falls, Black River Waterfalls

Shale deposits, Presque Isle River, Porcupine Mountains WSP

Porcupine Mountains Wilderness State Park

■ 63,000 acres ■ Michigan's Upper Peninsula, 25 miles west of Ontonagon via Mich. 64 and 107 ■ Year-round ■ Camping, hiking, backpacking, skiing, snowshoeing, wildlife viewing ■ Adm. fee ■ Contact the park, 412 South Boundary Rd., Ontonagon, MI 49953; phone 906-885-5275

As EARLY AS THE 1940s, the Porcupine Mountains were considered for national park status, an honor that tells you something about the awesome beauty and pristine nature of this gem anchored on the southern shore of Lake Superior. While the national park idea was wending its way through the federal government bureaucracy, loggers were preparing to strip the region of its virgin timber. Afraid the federal government would not act quickly enough, Michigan stepped in and preserved the area as a state park in 1944.

The result is the largest property in Michigan's excellent state park system. Porcupine Mountains Wilderness State Park preserves wild rivers, 23 miles of undeveloped Lake Superior shoreline, secluded lakes, and vast stands of virgin eastern hemlock, white pine, and maple—the largest tract of virgin timber between the Rocky Mountains and the Adirondacks. The Porcupines also represent one of the few true mountain ranges in the central United States, even though their highest point, Summit Peak, tops out at just 1,958 feet.

The Ojibwa named the range, deciding this rumpled landscape of low mountains and tall pines had the silhouette of a porcupine. Today "the Porkies," as they are affectionately called, remain largely unchanged from when the Ojibwa lived here, with the exception of 16 rustic trailside cabins *(call 906-885-5275 for reservations)* and a staggering network of more than 90 miles of well-maintained hiking trails. That's more than you'll find in many national parks—and certainly more than you'll find in most parks throughout the Great Lakes region.

Defying the notion of a state park, Porcupine Mountains encompasses an area large enough to convey a true sense of untrammeled wilderness.

What to See and Do

Hiking

Two different roads lead to the park's east and west ends; both deposit you near the shores of Lake Superior. South Boundary Road connects these roads (as you might expect) along the park's southern edge. And that's about it; to see the rest of the park, you'll need hiking boots (with one exception).

Begin your visit at the east end, where the visitor center offers interpretive displays, a multimedia presentation, and a gift shop with a good selection of nature guidebooks. From the visitor center, a 1-mile **interpretive nature trail** introduces you to the plants and animals commonly found in the park, looping through a mixed forest of hemlock, spruce, black ash, paper birch, white cedar, and sugar maple. The park's abundant wildlife includes bears, deer, coyotes, and a large array of birds from ruffed grouse to bald eagles.

The park's only interior road leads 7 miles west from the visitor center to the Porkies' marquee view, the **Lake of the Clouds Overlook.** Hundreds of feet below this 1,400-foot-high escarpment, the placid lake divides a thick mat of jade forest that extends for miles in three directions.

Some of the park's finest and most rugged trails begin at the overlook. **Big Carp River Trail** climbs and dips for 9 miles over

volcanic rock, lined with the wild roses and berries that manage to survive in the thin soil and parched southern exposure. After

Presque Isle River, Porcupine Mountains WSP

tracing the ridge for a mile or two, you can follow the trail north to 25-foot **Shining Cloud Falls** and Lake Superior, or descend into a forest of eastern hemlock and sugar maple, where ostrich ferns and blue beaded lilies share the cool understory.

Also leading away from the overlook is the 4-mile **Escarpment Trail,** which lets you absorb the Lake of the Clouds view in solitude. You will skim several peaks as you follow the north shoreline of the lake from high above. Both the Big Carp River Trail and the Escarpment Trail hook up with other routes that head south in-

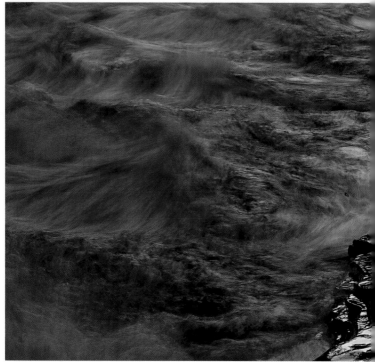
Presque Isle River, Porcupine Mountains WSP

to the heart of the state park.

Near the visitor center, 1-mile **Union Mine Trail** provides interpretive signs that chronicle the activities of the copper mine worked here in the 1840s. You can still see shafts and other diggings along this delightful trail as it loops through the Little Union Gorge, where the Union River flows clear and cold from a spring two miles upstream.

Two miles south of the visitor center off South Boundary Road, pick up **Union Spring Trail.** This 4-mile stroll brings you to a floating dock; beneath the surface you will see water bubbling forth at 700 gallons per minute from Michigan's largest spring.

At the park's south end, a short walk uphill from South Boundary Road leads through lustrous golden birches to **Summit Peak.** The park's highest point, the peak reaches almost 2,000 feet thanks to the 40-foot observation tower at its crest. This remarkably unobtrusive structure offers an inspiring view of the park, including the dark scribbled path of the Big Carp River and the Lake Superior horizon. On a clear day, you can see the Apostle Islands nearly 40 miles west. Trails from here lead to **Mirror Lake,** one of several secluded lakes that lie deep in the park's interior.

Five miles west of Summit Peak Road, **Little Carp River Trail** *(11 miles)* parallels the north bank of its namesake river, which tumbles over four waterfalls before pouring into Lake Superior. As you hike this lovely trail that burrows through fallen logs, over rocks, and along banks of ferns and massive white pines, notice the adjacent

river's tea-colored water (tinted by natural tannins in cedars).

The **East** and **West River Trails** depart from Presque Isle Campground at the park's west end. Hikers follow the turbulent Presque Isle River for a mile up one bank and back down the other, watching as the river roils and boils between narrow volcanic rock walls; finally, it tumbles into Lake Superior.

Lake Superior Trail likewise leaves from the campground, then winds for 16 miles along the shore. Above soar the occasional eagle, merganser, and merlin, while shorebirds skitter along the waterline. You may even glimpse deer or black bears wandering along the sand. Along this route stand several of the park's 16 trailside cabins—simple shelters with bunks, woodstoves, and cooking utensils that let you savor the solitude of the Porkies in comfort at day's end. They can be a godsend in June, when blackflies and mosquitoes traditionally make tent camping unpleasant.

Skiing

More than 25 miles of hiking trails at the east end of the park are groomed for cross-country skiers. Some lead to Lake Superior, where waves create dramatic ice sculptures along the shore. Rarely freezing over, Superior shines a deep cobalt blue beyond the shoreline ice pack.

Downhill skiers may be surprised to find a state-run ski hill within the park, with trails spanning a north-facing flank. Sweeping views of Lake Superior rimmed by white shore and dark forest make a winter foray here well worth the cost of a lift ticket. ■

Keweenaw Peninsula

■ 80-mile-long peninsula ■ Northwest Upper Peninsula of Michigan, around Houghton ■ Year-round ■ Camping, hiking, backpacking, fishing, mountain biking, skiing, snowshoeing, wildlife viewing ■ Contact Keweenaw Tourism Council, 326 Shelden Ave., Houghton, MI 49931; phone 906-482-5240 or 800-338-7982. www.keweenaw.org

RAKING OFF THE BACK of Michigan's Upper Peninsula like a dorsal fin, the Keweenaw Peninsula was the epicenter of the nation's copper mining industry in the mid-1800s. Today the Keweenaw's wealth is measured not in metals but in its mother lode of natural beauty.

One of the highest points of the uplifted Superior Basin, the Keweenaw contains the classic complement of Upper Peninsula landscapes: birch, aspen, and pockets of sugar maple clinging to corrugated ridgelines; white pine forests stretching 80 feet or more to the sky; and clear rivers coursing toward Lake Superior. Miles of deserted beaches—some sand, some rocky cliff—rim the peninsula.

Those interested primarily in relaxation on their visit to the peninsula will not find it wanting. Some pretty little tourist towns invite exploration, and nearly every paved road could be labeled a scenic drive. Even a casual walk or brief lakeside picnic lunch will leave you with fond memories of the area's beauty.

Many of the Keweenaw's loveliest spots, however, are hidden from view. The forests are filled with miles of trails that loop through groves of old-growth pines, passing unmarked waterfalls and fantastic stretches of otherwise inaccessible Lake Superior beach. Fair warning: Few of the trails are marked, much less maintained, and some simply peter out in the middle of nowhere.

To get a true taste of this remote area, then, you'll need a sense of adventure—and a good map, for you are entering territory almost as pristine as it was for the early copper miners. Today it remains a remarkable land of discovery.

What to See and Do

Though the Keweenaw Peninsula actually begins 25 miles or so to the south, the twin towns of Houghton and Hancock represent the psychological gateway to the Keweenaw. They are located on the Portage Lake Ship Canal, which severs the peninsula from the mainland. This 21-mile canal largely follows an old Indian paddle-and-portage route that spared travelers a time-consuming 100-mile trip around the peninsula.

Just north of the twin towns on US 41, the skeleton of the Quincy Mine shaft house lurches skyward, dwarfing even the super-steep bluffs of Hancock. The Quincy ranked as one of the world's richest copper mines in the late 1800s,

Eagle Harbor Light Station, Keweenaw Peninsula

Keweenaw Peninsula, between Copper Harbor and Eagle River

producing more than half a million tons of copper. The **Quincy Mining Company** *(201 Royce Rd., Hancock, MI 49930, 906-482-3101, Adm. fee)* is a key site in **Keweenaw National Historical Park** (see sidebar, p. 61). An excellent tour takes you through the world's largest steam hoist (used for hauling out miners and their equipment), down a steep bluff in a glass-enclosed tram, and then thousands of feet into the mine. Here you'll get a sense of what it was like to work in a damp, dark environment with only hand tools and candles.

Copper isn't the only notable mineral veining the Keweenaw. Its spine of Precambrian rock is one of the most geologically rich and fascinating regions in the world. The **A. E. Seaman Mineral Museum** *(5th Floor, Electrical Energy Resources Center, 1400 Towson Dr., 906-487-2572. www.geo.mtu. edu/museum),* on the campus of Michigan Technological University in Houghton, holds the premier collection of area minerals, including crystallized copper, silver, datolites, and agates.

Heading up the peninsula on US 41, you'll pass through Calumet, once the heart of Keweenaw copper mining. Much of the area, including the mine's industrial core and its once-glamorous downtown, now belongs to the Keweenaw historical park. The sturdy buildings have held up well; many of them were made from red sandstone quarried in nearby Jacobsville.

Nature has slowly reclaimed mining operations north of Calumet, where villages such as Cliff, Central, Delaware, and Mandan are little more than ghost towns surrounded by mine tailings and stamping plant residue.

Continuing up US 41, turn northwest at the town of Ahmeek, cross the Gratiot River, and head for Superior's shore. Well-hidden hiking and mountain biking trails lead along the river to beautiful **Upper** and **Lower Gratiot Falls.** The road traces a sandy stretch of shoreline to the town of Eagle River. Along with Eagle Harbor, 7 miles up the road, it served as an important mining port. The towns' names reflect the area's healthy population of bald eagles, often seen riding lakeshore updrafts.

From Eagle River, continue along the lake on **Sand Dunes Drive** (Mich. 26), which ascends through a dune landscape above Great Sand Bay. Beach peas, sand cherries, and wild roses cling to windswept mounds of sand. Like beach grasses, the plants' spreading root systems help trap sand, stabilizing and enlarging the dunes.

The Keweenaw's fault line tilts precipitously in this part of the peninsula. To the south rises the exposed basalt face of the Cliff Range, while to the north the fault line drops away so quickly that Great Sand Bay reaches depths of more than 1,000 feet. In between, deep ridges nurture microclimates. Along the south side of Sand Dunes Drive, watch for the faintly marked trails maintained by the Michigan Nature Association;

these dip into deep, dark forests, where lichen dangles from the pines and deep moss covers the rocky path.

North of Eagle Harbor, the road forks into two distinctly different drives. Mich. 26 continues to parallel the shoreline, now rocky with bony fingers of reddish volcanic rock reaching into the lake. Balsams grow gnarled and stunted like bonsai trees in this exposed and windswept environment. The coves here are littered with agates—banded rocks that formed as different minerals seeped into gas bubbles in cooling lava.

The other fork turns briefly inland, then up the steep backbone of Brockway Mountain. Deemed "the most beautiful road in Michigan" by some, the 10-mile **Brockway Mountain Drive** rises 726 feet above Lake Superior, making it the highest paved road between the

The Lake Effect

The Great Lakes are big insulators. Slow to warm up and slow to cool down, they create a notable temperature difference between the lakeshore and the interior. Five miles inland, you may be perfectly comfortable in shorts and a T-shirt; at the beach, meanwhile, folks shiver in sweatshirts. The reverse holds true during the winter months, when the lakes moderate cold air.

These massive bodies of water also have a dramatic effect on snowfall. Traveling on prevailing western winds, dry winter air moves over the lakes, soaking up moisture. When it hits land, the air dumps its load of precipitation as snow. Surprisingly localized, these snowfalls often target a narrow band along a lake's leeward shore. Meteorologists refer to this phenomenon as "lake-effect snow."

Jutting far out into Lake Superior, Keweenaw Peninsula often gets severely hit with lake-effect snow. Whereas Detroit averages less than 40 inches of snow a year, the Upper Peninsula receives 160 inches—300-inch years are not uncommon. A giant snow gauge on US 41 near Phoenix proudly marks Keweenaw's record snowfall—390.5 inches—in the winter of 1977-78.

In the shade of pine forests, patches of snow may last beyond Memorial Day.

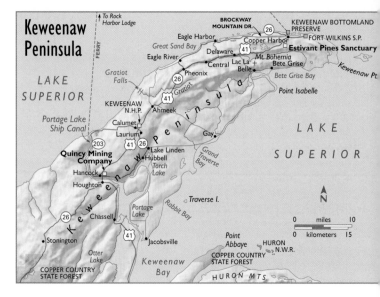

Rocky and Allegheny Mountains. A wide variety of plants thrive in the mountain's varied ecosystems. The list of several hundred flowers includes Indian pipe and several kinds of orchid, such as lady's slippers and swamp pinks. **Brockway Mountain Sanctuary** and **James H. Klipfel Memorial Nature Sanctuary** protect area plant life.

From **Brockway Mountain Lookout** (elevation 1,328 feet), you'll get an outstanding view of Superior's rocky shoreline, the town of Copper Harbor, a handful of inland lakes, and the Keweenaw interior as it narrows to a point. Watch for hawks and other raptors soaring below you. The area is a spring migration route for red-tailed, sharp-shinned, and other hawks, which effortlessly ride the thermals around the mountain before striking out across Lake Superior to points farther north.

One of Michigan's most appealing towns, **Copper Harbor** wedges between its namesake harbor and an inland lake named **Fanny Hooe.** When copper prospectors poured into the region in the mid-1800s, the federal government, fearing fights between the miners and local tribes, ordered the construction of a fort. Fortunately, it was never needed. Today the whitewashed structure is the highlight of **Fort Wilkins State Park** *(906-289-4215. Mid-May–mid-Oct.),* which also includes pleasant walking trails and campgrounds along Lake Fanny Hooe.

As it did throughout much of the Superior region, white pine once blanketed Keweenaw. Loggers were still felling old-growth stands near Copper Harbor—some of the last remaining in Michigan—when conservationists and the Michigan Nature Association stepped in. Now, just south of Copper Harbor, the **Estivant Pines Sanctuary** protects a 20-acre stand of these magnificent trees on its 377 acres.

Several trails wind through the sanctuary, with orchids and rare ferns thriving beneath a canopy of tamarack, spruce, and balsam. The majestic 1,000-year-old white pines are so out of scale—some are more than 20 feet around and ten stories tall—that they can escape notice. Just look for impossibly immense trunks, then look up, up, up.

The cold, fresh waters of Lake Superior and navigational hazards around Keweenaw seem to have colluded to provide outstanding opportunities for divers. Within the 103-square-mile **Keweenaw Bottomland Preserve,** experienced divers can explore several sunken vessels. Among them is the *John Jacob Astor,* which went down in 1844 off Copper Harbor. An underwater trail leads to the ship's rudder, anchor, and other remains.

The road may end at Copper Harbor, but the Keweenaw Peninsula continues another 10 miles or so. Here a 60-square-mile tract is veined with miles of trails that range from old logging and mining roads to single-track paths and deer trails. Mountain bikes and hiking boots offer the best means for exploring this undeveloped area, owned by a paper company and open to the public in exchange for a tax break. Black bears, deer, coyotes, pileated woodpeckers, warblers, and other wildlife far outnumber humans here.

At the north end of the tract, a deeply veined rocky spine forms **Horseshoe Harbor,** a narrow and picturesque sliver of water. Lichen splatter the bedrock beach, while ground-hugging shrubs and stunted trees bear witness to the weather off Lake Superior. More protected areas form a cool, moist environment that is ideal for a variety of plants, including butterwort, Indian paintbrush, rayless mountain ragwort, and several threatened species.

To access the southern half of this tract, which is blocked from the north by beaver dams and marshy areas, drive southwest on US 41, then south toward Lac La Belle. Here, 1,465-foot **Mount Bohemia** boasts a new ski area. East of Lac La Belle, **Bete Grise Bay** sweeps in a sickle of sand, a good spot for a chilly wade or dip in Lake Superior. Follow the shoreline drive to Gay for more views. ∎

Keweenaw National Historical Park

Not so much a place on a map as a place in time, Keweenaw National Historical Park was established in 1992 "to commemorate the heritage of copper mining on the Keweenaw Peninsula—its mines, its machinery and its people."

Rather than a park with simply defined boundaries, Keweenaw National Historical Park consists of cultural attractions throughout the peninsula. Two units anchor the park—the Quincy Unit at the Quincy Mine in Hancock, and the Calumet Unit in historic downtown Calumet.

Much of the park's 1,700 acres, surprisingly, remain in private hands. The park has also designated "cooperating sites" throughout the peninsula, including various mine tours and museums.

The park currently operates with a skeleton headquarters staff. For information, contact the Keweenaw Tourism Council (*56638 Calumet Ave., Calumet, MI 49913; 800-338-7982*).

Superior Riches

THE UPPER PENINSULA of Michigan has its roots in the rich veins of copper and iron that were laid down under thick layers of basalt millions of years ago. First discovered by Indians, mineral riches later lured prospectors north into the wilderness, then larger mining enterprises, then powerful 19th-century industries. The mineral wealth they extracted dwarfed the California Gold Rush—and left an indelible mark on land and culture.

A mere 5,000 years after the glaciers retreated, natives on Keweenaw Peninsula and Isle Royale had already discovered the area's mineral bounty. The Copper Culture Indians of about 5000-2000 B.C. dug thousands of mining pits—some as deep as 80 feet—into the brutally hard basalt (the best-preserved pits still exist on Isle Royale). Once they had exposed the copper, they built fires to heat the bedrock, then splashed the rock with water; the rock would break up, making it easier to extract the copper. The Copper Culture Indians used the metal extensively, trading it and pounding it into fishhooks and tools. Archaeologists believe they were the first to make metal tools in the Americas, and perhaps in the entire world.

The Indians extracted only a minuscule amount of the region's copper over the centuries, and its vast lodes remained unknown and nearly untouched. Then, in 1840, State Geologist Douglass Houghton returned from a survey of the Upper Peninsula (U.P.) and confirmed the presence there of vast deposits of copper, much of it near the surface. Houghton's find, it turns out, was better than gold: The young United States had an insatiable appetite for copper, first for new industrial machinery, then for Civil War armaments, electrical wiring, and other innovations.

The Copper Rush was on. Prospectors flooded the wild and remote Keweenaw. The lucky ones secured deck space on Great Lakes vessels. Hundreds of others straggled into the roadless wilderness, following rivers through thick forests in their quest to reach the fabled riches.

Amateur prospectors were soon replaced by more sophisticated mining operations, which had the financial backing to dig shafts. More than 400 mining companies operated in Keweenaw during the 19th century. The Quincy Mining Co. opened a mine above Hancock in 1856 and achieved almost instant success. Profits went to build schools, homes, and a hospital, and to expand the mine that eventually burrowed underground nearly 10,000 feet—deep enough to hold a stack of six Sears Towers.

During the Civil War, the Upper Peninsula supplied 90 percent of the nation's copper. The copper industry employed thousands of immigrant laborers, built cities, made millionaires, and prompted extravagant luxuries, such as rococo opera houses and "copper baron" mansions adorned with silver leaf and elephant-hide wallcoverings. The largest mine was based in Red Jacket, now Calumet, a boomtown that roared with the sound of 50 steam hoists and 11,000 laborers. Before it was over, King Copper generated more than $9.6 billion—10 times more than the California Gold Rush.

But even that paled compared with the wealth created by iron: A staggering $48 billion. Federal surveyors first

Quincy Mine, near Hancock, Michigan

discovered iron ore in 1844, near present-day Iron River. As workers surveyed the land, their compasses swung wildly near Negaunee, where iron ore was so plentiful it was visible on the surface, intertwined in the roots of a fallen tree.

In the 1870s, the arrival of the railroad allowed miners to haul ore to nearby shipping ports and on to industrial lakefront cities such as Chicago and Cleveland.

World War II and its demand for iron drove area mines to peak production, eventually depleting some. After shipping out nearly two billion tons of ore, all underground iron mines in the U.P. had closed by 1978, hurt by competition from abroad and the growing use of plastics in manufacturing.

Copper mining faced a similar fate. Virtually all the big mines disappeared in the mid-1900s. The easiest-to-reach copper was gone, and newer mines in the southwestern U.S. and South America proved more cost-effective.

The loss of mining devastated the U.P.'s economy and left behind an array of environmental scars.

Keweenaw National Historical Park (see sidebar, p. 61) now preserves some of that boom-and-bust mining heritage, including the Quincy Mine and most of downtown Calumet. Also well worth a visit is the state-run **Iron Industry Museum** (906-475-7857) outside Negaunee, on the site of one of the area's earliest iron forges. ■

Isle Royale National Park

■ 572,000 acres (134,000 land acres, 438,000 water acres) ■ Accessible by boat or seaplane from Copper Harbor, MI; plan for possible weather-related delays ■ Closed Oct.–mid-April; best months late June–mid-Sept. ■ Backpacking, hiking, kayaking, canoeing, fishing, bird-watching, wildlife viewing ■ Adm. fee ■ Only experienced boaters in craft longer than 20 feet should attempt to cross Lake Superior; permit required ■ Contact the park, 87 N. Ripley St., Houghton, MI 49931; phone 906-482-0984. www.nps.gov/isro

MAROONED IN THE VAST WATERS of Lake Superior, Isle Royale is a model of what a national park should be: wild, rugged, remote, and buffered from the outside world. The park encompasses the entire 45-mile-long island, untouched by roads and most modern conveniences. Among the least-visited national parks in the lower 48 states, Isle Royale attracts just 17,000 visitors a year—fewer than California's Yosemite National Park sometimes hosts in a single weekend.

Isle Royale (pronounced ROY-al) lies in northwest Lake Superior. Although just 18 miles of open water separate it from its nearest mainland shore on the Minnesota-Ontario border, it is considered part of the state of Michigan, 56 miles across the lake to the south.

Those who make the trek to Isle Royale by boat or seaplane come to hike its 165 miles of trails, fish its 46 inland lakes, and paddle along its saw-toothed shoreline. **Rock Harbor Lodge,** at the island's east end, offers simple motel-style rooms, a handful of cabins, a dining room, camp store, and marina. The rest of the island is backcountry—mile after mile of forested foot trails, rocky bluffs, quiet lakes, and rustic campsites.

A key draw for visitors is the island's wildlife, especially the moose that swam across from Ontario in the early 1900s, and the eastern timber wolves that followed them across on pack ice a couple of decades later. Scientists carefully study the predator/prey cycle between these two animals (see sidebar, p. 73). The island's wolves are shy and stealthy creatures, and rarely will the backpacker see one. Moose are a different story. Hikers have an excellent chance of spotting moose, which often feed in ponds and lowlands, or along lakeshores. Give wide berth to these 1,000-pound animals: They can be exceptionally dangerous—especially cows with calves, or bulls during fall rutting season.

Some of the other large mammals common in the northern Great Lakes are notably absent on Isle Royale. Black bears never made it here, and white-tailed deer vanished early in the 20th century. Caribou, lynx, and coyote also disappeared. Instead, hikers are likely to spot the small-scale rodents and other mammals that thrive here: beaver, red fox, otter, mink, and muskrat. Bird-watchers scour the waters for the common loon, bufflehead, black duck, cormorant, merganser, and mallard. Smaller birds inhabiting the island include kingfishers, woodpeckers, warblers, thrushes, and chickadees. Both bald eagles and ospreys nest in the park.

Rock Harbor Lighthouse, Isle Royale National Park

Rock Harbor Trail, Isle Royale National Park

Moose ravaged the yew and mountain ash that once flourished on Isle Royale, and their heavy browsing continues to affect the island's plant life today. Beaver mitigate the damage by building dams and creating ponds that support water plants, a staple in the moose's diet. Boggy lowlands harbor wild irises, calla lilies, and yellow pond lilies. Some two dozen varieties of orchid bloom on Isle Royale, under a canopy of spruce, fir, and aspen that represents the island's primary forest. Pockets of sugar maple and yellow birch dominate the more protected interior. Planted by early island residents to feed their horses, non-native clover still blankets some forest clearings. In July and August, blueberries and thimbleberries ripen on dry, exposed terrain.

Along with its namesake island, Isle Royale National Park actually consists of more than 200 islands, all of them remnants of the same landmass. The Precambrian lava flows that formed Keweenaw Peninsula 1.2 billion years ago also gave rise to the Isle Royale archipelago. Between lava flows, rain and streams carried away pebbles, sand, and silt from the surrounding basin. As a result, slabs of softer rock are sandwiched between the tough basalt layers, creating the island's characteristic ridge-and-trough pattern.

About 30 million years later, faulting occurred, thrusting the Earth's crust upward at an angle. On one side of the fault rose Isle Royale, with a northwest side of steep ridges and bluffs and a southeastern shore that slopes gradually to the water, embracing lowlands and bogs. On the other side of the fault rose Keweenaw Peninsula, its topography a near mirror image of Isle Royale, with a gradual northern shore and a more steeply angled southern flank.

Hikers are usually quick to notice Isle Royale's washboard topography. North-south trails continually rise and fall as they traverse the folded terrain of each corrugated ridge. The Greenstone Ridge Trail, on the other hand, remains relatively level as it traces a high east-west ridgeline across the island.

What to See and Do

Travel to Isle Royale is both challenging and expensive, which accounts for average visitor stays of more than three days. Overall, the average stay during a visit to most national parks in the U.S. is four hours.

Backpacking is the best way to experience Isle Royale, hiking from campground to campground strung along the park's network of trails. Paddling is another excellent option. A day trip, however, will give you only a cursory look at Isle Royale—much of your day will be spent getting to and from the island. (If you have just one day, take the ferry from Windigo, the shortest route.) Noncampers can get a taste of the island by lodging at Rock Harbor, then taking day hikes and park tour boats to various island attractions.

Accessing the Island

The majority of visitors arrive by ferry from Houghton, Michigan *(906-482-0984)*, Copper Harbor, Michigan *(906-289-4437)*, or Grand Portage, Minnesota *(715-392-2100)*. Make reservations well in advance. Seaplane service is available from Houghton *(906-482-8850)* as well. Another option is to arrive by private boat and rent a slip at Rock Harbor or Windigo marina, or drop anchor in a protected bay. Upon arrival, all boaters must obtain a permit at a ranger station. Only experienced boaters with strong navigational skills and radio equipment should attempt a Lake Superior crossing. Small, open vessels are highly discouraged. Sudden squalls make Lake Superior life-threatening.

Day Hikes from Rock Harbor

If you have time for just one hike, walk the **Stoll Trail** to Scoville Point. This 4.2-mile loop with interpretive signs traces a rocky finger of land east of Rock Harbor. Scoville Point describes a water-logged version of Isle Royale's ridge-and-valley topography: The ridges are the point's long, rocky fingers, while the valleys are slivers of water wedged between them.

Return from Scoville Point via the **Tobin Harbor Trail,** which follows a lovely slivered cove. Across

Following pages: Sunset, Tobin Harbor, Isle Royale National Park

Blue flag

Fireweed

Tobin Harbor lies **Lookout Louise Trail.** Rent a canoe to cross the harbor, then hike 2 miles for one of the island's most spectacular views, looking out over its ragged northeastern shoreline. High along the ridge, wild roses and blueberries cling to the thin, dry soil. On the way to Lookout Louise, the trail skirts **Hidden Lake,** a natural salt lick that is frequented by moose. You're likely to spot their hoofprints along the trail, and their wide paths cut through the trillium and thimbleberries.

Another popular short hike is the 3.8-mile loop to **Suzy's Cave,** formed by the wave action of a once much-deeper Lake Superior. Along the lakeshore, low junipers spread across the rocks, which are speckled with patches of gray-green reindeer moss. For a longer trek (about 10 miles round-trip), continue on to **Mt. Franklin Trail,** which heads north and brings you high up on **Greenstone Ridge.** From this vantage point, enjoy a sweeping view of the island's interior and the distant shore of Ontario to the north.

Boat Tours

The Park Service shuttles visitors from Rock Harbor Lodge to various island attractions on its 25-passenger boat the *Sandy (fare).* Two or three times a week, the *Sandy* makes the short trip across the mouth of Moskey Basin to historic **Edisen Fishery,** restored to show what life was like for the commercial fishermen who once made their living on Isle Royale. Today, in an embrace by Mother Nature and a nod to the inevitability of time, wild daisies grow

Wood lily

among the oars and nets. From Edisen Fishery, it's a short quarter-mile walk to the stout, simple **Rock Harbor Lighthouse,** built in 1855 to guide ships to Isle Royale's busy copper ports.

The *Sandy* also shuttles the half-mile to **Raspberry Island,** where a self-guided boardwalk trail leads through spruce bog and Isle Royale's classic boreal forest of white spruce, balsam fir, birch, and aspen. Unusual plants—notably the insect-eating sundew and pitcher plants—thrive in the acidic environment of the bog.

Once a week, weather permitting, the *Sandy* departs on an all-day cruise to the remote north side of Isle Royale, indented with deep, narrow coves. A park guide leads the 2-mile round-trip walk to **Minong Mine,** site of the island's largest copper mining operation in the 1870s. Old ore cars and rails remain visible. Ancient copper mining pits dug by natives still pockmark the area; it's probable these tipped off later miners to the area's underground wealth.

Backpacking

Greenstone Ridge Trail traverses the island along its backbone for 42 miles through mostly high, dry terrain. Many of the park's trails cross Greenstone Ridge, allowing you to create your own loop routes. Along the eastern half of the trail, you'll pass the **Ojibway Tower,** an atmosphere-monitoring station that marks the highest spot on the eastern end of the island. You are welcome to climb its steps (but not enter the tower room) for an unmatched view of Isle Royale's interior lakes, as well as the bays

that embrace its northern and southern shores.

A lightly used route that continues for 22 miles, the **Feldtmann Ridge Trail** loops along Isle Royale's southwestern shore. The trail offers outstanding variety, from the shoreline of Washington Harbor, through trickling creeks and lily ponds, up the high Feldtmann Ridge itself, and finally to the open wildflower meadows and waters of Siskiwit Bay.

The 26-mile **Minong Ridge Trail** traverses the north end of the island from near Windigo to McCargoe Cove. This rough and lightly used trail hobbyhorses over a rocky ridge and disappears through bogs. If you like primitive and peaceful—and are not rattled by poorly marked stretches—this is the trail for you.

Paddling

Isle Royale is about as close to a dream destination for paddlers as

---

Royale Gems

Scour the beaches of Isle Royale and you may discover the greenstone, a lustrous pebble with a distinctive segmented turtle-shell pattern. More properly called chlorastrolite, it was formed in the gas cavities of lava flows.

Not to be confused with the greenish volcanic rock found on Greenstone Ridge and elsewhere on the island, chlorastrolite has been unearthed on certain islands in the South Pacific as well. In 1972, the governor of Michigan declared the stone as the official state gem.

Cow moose and calf, Hidden Lake, Isle Royale National Park

you can get. It's a nook-and-cranny wilderness of rocky islands, secluded coves, and undisturbed inland lakes.

Sea kayakers can explore the Isle Royale shoreline or slither among its adjacent islands. A prime example is **Five Finger Bay,** a collection of fjordlike harbors and rocky promontories that crenellate the east end of the island. If you're a canoeist, take note: Although canoes can handle some of Lake Superior's more protected waters during calm weather, the open craft truly find their niche in the routes that lace the island's eastern side. If you can stand a few trudging portages, you will be able to hopscotch your way across Isle Royale on the dozens of lakes that sprinkle the island's interior.

Ferry services from the mainland will transport your kayak or canoe for a fee. Additional services allow you to arrange for a water taxi to drop you off or pick you up at predetermined points around the island. ■

Superior Symbiosis on Isle Royale

Insulated from civilization's effects, Isle Royale serves as an ideal living laboratory of how plants and animals interrelate in nature's cycles. Because of its uniquely isolated habitat, Isle Royale was declared an International Biosphere Reserve in 1980 by the United Nations.

The world's longest running wildlife research project involves Isle Royale's moose and wolf populations. Since 1958, biologists have been monitoring their numbers, tracking them by plane during the winter months when they are easier to see. Many of the wolves have been fitted with radio collars.

When moose first swam to the island in the early 1900s, they found an ample food supply in the vegetation and no natural predators. By the 1920s, their population had soared to between 1,000 and 3,000. But the moose ravaged their food source, and their numbers dropped. A fire in the 1930s spurred a lush regrowth of vegetation, which in turn boosted their numbers again.

This cycle might have continued in perpetuity had it not been for the arrival of the eastern timber wolf. During the frigid winter of 1948-49, an ice bridge formed on Lake Superior between Ontario and Isle Royale, allowing a small pack of wolves to cross to the island. The terrain suited them, as did the bountiful food source: moose. In response, the wolf population began burgeoning.

Thus began an interdependent cycle. With a large moose herd, wolves prevent overpopulation by culling the sick, the old, and the young. A smaller, stronger herd, by contrast, means difficult hunting for the wolves, curtailing their breeding rate. The wolf population peaked at about 50 animals in 1970, but the number fell to just 14 in 1998. The winter 2000 count recorded 29 wolves; the 2001 count, only 19. Meanwhile the moose herd has grown from about 850 to 900 animals; in a dance as old as time, the wolf numbers may follow suit.

Sturgeon River Gorge Wilderness Area

■ 14,159 acres ■ Houghton County, north of Mich. 28, west of US 41 ■ Road passable spring through fall, except in wet weather; excellent colors in fall ■ Camping, hiking, bird-watching ■ Contact Kenton District, Ottawa National Forest, Kenton, MI 49967; 906-852-3500. www.fs.fed.us/r9/ottawa/

A WEB OF FREE-FLOWING rivers stitches across the Upper Peninsula of Michigan, each with its own inviting picnic rock or casting spot, each a bit lovelier than the last. As you cross river after river on the highway, the enticement of natural riches becomes almost too much: Which do you pass up, and which do you explore?

Put the Sturgeon River on your explore list. The river travels a circuitous route through one of three wilderness areas in Ottawa National Forest, cutting and tumbling through a 300-foot-high basalt gorge—one of the deepest and most scenic in the Midwest. From the eastern lip of the gorge, you get an eagle's-eye view of the river's frothing rapids and its dark, curlicue path squiggling off through the forest. **Sturgeon Falls Trail** leads half a mile or so from the gorge down to the river's edge, where it pours over a series of small cascades, then plummets over 22-foot-high **Sturgeon Falls.**

The isolation of the gorge adds to its appeal. From Mich. 28 near Sidnaw, follow Forest Road 2200 north to Forest Road 2270, which wanders along the eastern boundary of the 14,000-acre wilderness that encompasses the Sturgeon River and its tributaries. Several unmarked, overgrown logging roads cut through the region, beckoning hikers and backpackers who wish to explore on their own. (A topographic map is an absolute necessity.) Black bears are common in this area, so be sure to follow safe backpacking practices and always hang food well out of reach.

Several unmarked footpaths on the left side of the road will eventually bring you to the river. (If you're not in the mood for that challenge, you can drive until you reach a small marked parking area.) Once you've viewed the gorge, continue on Forest Road 2270 to **Silver Mountain,** a 1,312-foot peak that once was the site of a fire tower. Climb the wooden steps for a fine view of this wilderness of wavelike ridges forested in pine, hemlock, birch, and sugar maple falling away in the distance.

To experience the river as it manifests a completely different character, follow US 41 north to the **Sturgeon River Sloughs Wildlife Area** outside the national forest near Chassell, where the river bleeds through lowlands before emptying into Portage Lake. The 1.5-mile **De Vriendt Nature Trail** follows dikes and boardwalks back into the slough. Interpretive signs at intervals along the trail discuss the herons, ospreys, eagles, and duck species that frequent the area. ■

Sturgeon River Gorge, north of Sidnaw, Michigan

Fritillary on orange hawkweed, White Deer Lake Trail, McCormick Wilderness Area

Huron Mountains

■ 700 square miles ■ Upper Peninsula of Michigan, northwest of Marquette via Cty. Rd. 550 ■ Year-round ■ Backcountry camping, hiking, paddling, fishing, mountain biking, cross-country skiing, snowshoeing, wildlife viewing ■ Adm. fee for state parks ■ Contact Marquette Country Visitors Bureau, 2552 US 41, Marquette, MI 49855; phone 800-544-4321. www.marquettecountry.org

IT DOESN'T GET ANY WILDER THAN THIS: Created by volcanoes and scoured by glaciers, the vast humpback of the Huron Mountains rears up from the north shore of Michigan's Upper Peninsula, covered with washboard peaks and valleys, virgin white pine forests, hundreds of lakes, dazzling waterfalls, and the headwaters of half a dozen classic wilderness rivers. Virtually devoid of roads, much less towns, the Huron Mountains instead harbor wildness: Wolves, moose, loons, and other animals all seek the solitude of these remote mountain fastnesses.

Preservation did not occur by happenstance. Beginning around 1880, the Huron Mountains became the wilderness retreat of choice for several ultrawealthy downstate industrialists. While some—such as Cyrus McCormick, head of the farm implement company that would become International Harvester—amassed their own wilderness holdings, dozens of others owned camps at the exclusive Huron Mountain Club. The powerful club members easily stopped construction of a road that was to link Marquette with L'Anse to the west: County Road 550 ends abruptly just west of Big Bay at a security-patrolled gate.

For more than a century now, the Huron Mountain Club has kept away miners, loggers, and developers. As a result, this 25,000-acre enclave is a magnificent specimen of untouched Upper Peninsula: blue-ribbon trout streams, 80-foot white pines, carpets of orchids, miles of untouched Lake Superior beach, hidden waterfalls that appear on no map. Today, descendants of the original families still protect and preserve this spectacular landholding as a private club.

But not to worry—the Huron Mountains and plenty of near-pristine wilderness extend far beyond the club's boundaries. Though every local has an opinion about where the Huron Mountains begin and end, it's safe to say they fall within the fuzzy boundaries of Lake Superior to the north and US 41 to the south and west. That's a chunk of land roughly 30 miles wide by 25 miles long, with plenty of protected terrain—including state parks and federal wilderness areas that once formed pieces of those millionaire estates—open to a public willing to get off the pavement.

First, get yourself some maps, such as a venerable USGS topographical map or the local map (also known as the waterfall map) produced by the Marquette Country Visitors Bureau. Next, gas up and check the spare. You're not heading into impenetrable backcountry, but you're not going to pass many service stations, either. A dusty car and tired feet are about the only price you'll have to pay for exploring one of the most rugged and remarkable places in the Midwest.

What to See and Do

Big Bay Environs

County Road 550 links Marquette with the tiny town of Big Bay. This 30-mile paved route offers plenty of good jumping-off points into the Huron Mountains. Dozens of old logging roads and single-track trails spin off 550 to the west; you'll find them perfect for mountain biking and visiting the falls of the **Little Garlic River,** halfway between Marquette and Big Bay.

From Big Bay, your best bets for venturing into the backcountry

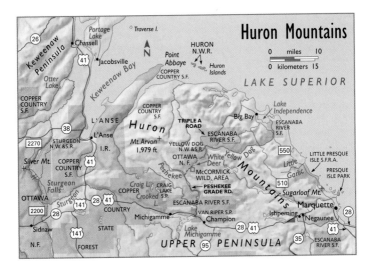

Craig Lake State Park

are County Road 510, which branches off 550 southeast of town, and the Triple A Road, off 510. Both are well-maintained (but slow-going) dirt roads. County Road 510 leads to **Yellow Dog River,** a crystalline trout stream that splashes and tumbles over cliffs and through canyons from Yellow Dog Plains to Lake Independence. (It's also a nationally designated wild and scenic river.)

Seek out **Hills, Bushy Creek,** and **Big Pup Falls,** some of the loveliest cascades in the region.

McCormick Wilderness Area

Ottawa National Forest *(Kenton Ranger Station 906-852-3500)* manages this isolated 16,850-acre unit at the southern flank of the Huron Mountains, accessible from US 41 near the town of Champion. Undeveloped and little used, the

McCormick Wilderness Area hides a trove of natural beauty. You won't find well-worn trails leading to scenic overlooks here. And frankly, at first glance, the area doesn't hold that much promise— just a landscape of scrubby jack pines, high hills, vast muskegs, and bedrock outcroppings.

But anyone with the skills and interest to do a little cross-country exploring will be amply rewarded. Within the McCormick tract, you may discover the headwaters of four rivers, a stretch of the beautiful Yellow Dog River, 18 undeveloped lakes, waterfalls, impressive stands of century-old white pines, and, possibly, some memorable wildlife sightings. This remote location of mixed forest and bog is perfect moose habitat. Thanks to reintroduction programs (see sidebar, p. 80), the state's largest moose herd roams here, attracting predators such as the eastern timber wolf.

Trails are unmarked or faintly marked at best. You'll need a good map, a compass—and experience —even for day hiking. One exception is the clearly delineated path that leads from the Peshekee Grade Road 3 miles northeast to **White Deer Lake.** Cyrus McCormick, whose father invented the reaping machine, loved to hunt and fish in the Huron Mountains, and chose this spot for his retreat. In 1902, he built a lodge and guest cabins on an island in White Deer Lake (supposedly to protect it from forest fires) and constructed the dining room on the mainland shore. McCormick's estate and the vast property around it were donated to the Forest Service in 1967.

Today, the wilderness area is open to a wide range of recreational activities, from camping and fishing (check local regulations) to skiing and snowshoeing.

Craig Lake State Park

This remote park *(906-339-4461)* protects another parcel on the south side of the Huron Mountains, encompassing half a dozen gorgeous wilderness lakes. Like the McCormick tract, it was a millionaire's estate, once owned by Frederick Miller of the Miller Brewing Company.

An avid fisherman, Miller picked a gem of a spot. Craig is the park's largest lake, a 374-acre body of water studded with rocky islands and hemmed in by towering granite bluffs, thin ribbons of sand beach, and a loopy wooded shoreline that supports aspen, hemlock, and pine. Muskellunge, walleye, northern pike, and bass all inhabit lake waters; their populations remain healthy thanks to catch-and-release policies and regulations that restrict anglers to artificial lures. Loons also frequent the area, riding low in the water and filling the air with their eerie, haunting whistles.

Getting to Craig Lake State Park involves a slow, bumpy trip down a 7-mile dirt road with a surface that alternates between sharp rock and washboard. The route tends to be confusing, so pick up a map at nearby Van Riper State Park before setting out. Once you reach the small parking area at the south end of Craig Lake, your only access into the vast 7,000-acre park will be by foot or paddle, since the use of boat motors and any kind of wheeled vehicles is prohibited.

A canoe or kayak is the best way to experience the park. After exploring Craig Lake and its islands, try the short but hilly portage at the north end of the lake to reach **Clair Lake,** or at the east side to reach **Crooked Lake.** Paddlers will enjoy the serenity of all the lakes, but Crooked Lake is perhaps the most appealing, with lots of interesting bays and inlets. Because you can access it only by portaging from Craig Lake, you'll find it lightly traveled. Other good paddling lakes, **Teddy** and **Keewaydin,** have separate boat launches off the main road.

Old logging roads form **Craig Lake Trail.** The well-marked 7-mile path circles the lake, crosses the Peshekee River, dips through ferny ravines, and offers plenty of lake views through the pines.

Operation Moose Lift

How do you boost a moose? Though it sounds like the lead-in to a corny joke, two "moose lifts" in the 1980s successfully transported 59 of the mammals from Ontario to the lightly traveled wilderness north of Van Riper State Park. Wildlife biologists tranquilized the moose, trucked them to a helicopter, and airlifted them one at a time—swaying below the chopper in a sling—to trucks that carried them 600 miles to their new home. The Moose Information Center at Van Riper State Park displays photos of the event that must have prompted a few double takes from uninformed passersby.

Van Riper State Park

Situated on busy US 41 and the shores of **Lake Michigamme,** a popular fishing and swimming spot, this park (906-339-4461) looks unappealing to those seeking solitude. But many people don't realize that the park extends north of the highway, too. Four miles of hiking trails penetrate this area bordering the Peshekee River. The **River Trail** (1.5 miles) loops up a rocky outcrop for a great view of rolling hardwood forest and Lake Michigamme.

Moose were reintroduced just a few miles northwest of here in the mid-1980s (see sidebar at left). Once plentiful in the Upper Peninsula, moose populations plummeted in the 1880s, when settlers killed them for food and loggers felled the deep pine forests where they roamed. The clear-cuts created ideal habitat for white-tailed deer, which carried brainworm, a parasite that is usually harmless to deer but fatal to moose. As deer populations skyrocketed, the moose all but disappeared.

Thankfully, the reintroduction program worked, and today the local moose herd numbers between 200 and 300. Primarily browsing animals, moose eat aquatic plants and woody vegetation such as leaves and twigs. Your best bets for spotting them are near dawn or dusk in open, low-lying wet areas, such as those found along the **Peshekee Grade** (also called Huron Bay Road) near the park's western boundary. The largest member of the deer family, moose can stand more than six feet tall and weigh thousands of pounds. Keep your distance. ■

Crooked Lake, Ottawa National Forest

Little Presque Isle State Forest Recreation Area

■ 3,000 acres ■ Michigan's Upper Peninsula, 7 miles north of Marquette via Cty. Rd. 550 ■ Hiking, mountain biking, beachcombing, bird-watching ■ Contact Marquette Operations Service Center, 1990 US 41 South, Marquette, MI 49855; phone 906-228-6561

THIS LOVELY PATCH OF STATE forest demonstrates what makes the Upper Peninsula of Michigan so special: Just 10 minutes from the city of Marquette, you can hike a few more minutes into red pine forest and be alone among the woods, water, and wildlife.

A favorite among locals, the area otherwise has remained relatively unknown, perhaps due to simple confusion: All kinds of locations—towns, rivers, parks, bays—in Michigan and Wisconsin are named Presque Isle, French for "peninsula." Just a few miles away, in fact, 328-acre **Presque Isle Park**—a municipal park with walking trails, picnic grounds, and even a few resident albino deer—juts out into Lake Superior from the north end of Marquette.

To explore the **Little Presque Isle** tract, drive north from town up County Road 550, also known as the Big Bay Road. Start with a climb—a tiring walk, really, up a long series of steps—to the crest of **Sugarloaf Mountain,** a bald granite knob that peeks out above the surrounding forest. Though Sugar Loaf is urban by Upper Peninsula standards, the view is anything but: With Marquette's smattering of civilization at your back, you'll gaze out over a rocky red shoreline and the endless blue sea of Lake Superior in one direction, and a forest that rolls off to the rumpled horizon of the Huron Mountains in the other.

A mile or two north of Sugar Loaf, **Little Presque Isle Point** pinches out into Lake Superior, ending just 100 yards short of **Little Presque Isle,** a picture-perfect hump of rock riddled with tiny inlets. The mainland point is forested in girthy old-growth hemlocks and red pine, then opens to a curve of soft sand. On either end of the beach, like bookends, red bands of rock reach out into the lake, forming fluted cliffs and coves. It's a fine spot to wade, take a (brisk!) swim, or launch a kayak.

At the north end of the point, the **Songbird Trail** forms a one-mile loop between **Harlow Creek** and Lake Superior. The mixed habitat of pines, hardwoods, berry bushes, and water attracts a diversity of songbirds, especially in spring. Interpretive signs along the trail describe some of the species found here, including pileated and hairy woodpeckers, thrushes, merlins, and several kinds of warblers.

Nearly 20 miles of trails wind through the Little Presque Isle Tract, most of them west of County Road 550. Follow Harlow Creek upstream to horseshoe-shaped **Harlow Lake,** surrounded by pines and huge granite boulders. Several trails spin off the main route that curls around the

Deer, Little Presque Isle SFRA

lake's west end. It's best to equip yourself with a state forest trail map (*available from Department of Natural Resources office in Marquette*) before wandering too far: These trails are poorly marked, and the readily available cross-country ski map is confusing at best.

From Harlow Lake, follow an old railroad grade south to **Wetmore Pond,** where an observation platform surveys a bog carpeted with thick mats of sphagnum moss. Decaying plants raise the acid levels of the water, which allows acid-loving sphagnum and pitcher's plant to thrive.

Almost due west of the pond lies the arching ridge of **Hogsback Mountain,** the area's highest point. Like Sugarloaf, Hogsback offers great vistas of the surrounding forest and Lake Superior, but it lies a bit farther off the beaten path. From the parking lot on County Road 550 near Wetmore Pond, a 1.5-mile trail lumbers up a steep ridgeline to the top. ■

Northern Highlands

Shoreline near Two Hearted River, Lake Superior State Forest

UP NORTH: THOSE TWO WORDS, tossed about in casual conversation as a well-understood watchword, speak volumes to someone from the Great Lakes region. Announce "I'm going Up North" and everyone smiles and nods with understanding.

Up North is verbal shorthand for liberation: An escape from hot, sticky summers. An escape to reliably snowy winters. An escape to piney lakes and pea-gravel trout streams, to waters teeming with trophy muskie and forests filled with white-tailed bucks sporting 10-point racks. For many, the words signal a getaway to a weekend cottage or canoe campsite beneath the smear of the Milky Way.

More often than not, *Up North* describes the Northern Highlands— one of the predominant natural landscapes of the Great Lakes region. The highlands are characterized by a mixed forest of maple, hemlock, and birch, interspersed with extensive stands of red and white pine; thousands upon thousands of glacial lakes; and some peat bog lowlands dotted with black spruce, tamarack, and white cedar. They are the quintessential North Woods, celebrated in every cultural artifact from Ernest Hemingway short stories to male-bonding beer commercials.

The Northern Highlands cover a broad band between the boreal forests and ancient volcanic rock of the Canadian Shield to the north and the great till plain scrubbed and scoured by glaciers to the south. They extend across the northern half of Wisconsin (except for the extreme northern portion along Lake Superior), the northern half of Michigan's

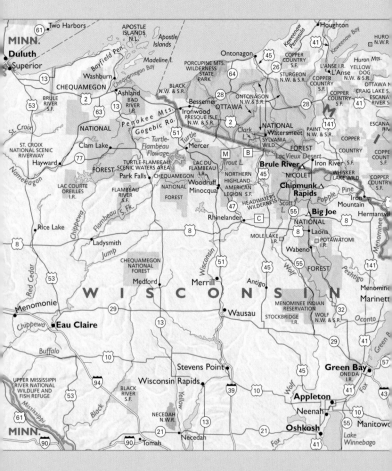

Lower Peninsula, the eastern half of Michigan's Upper Peninsula, and the islands that scatter off into Lake Huron.

None of these boundaries are precise, of course; all were determined by the uplift of an ancient fault and the whim of an advancing glacier. As a result, the Northern Highlands are a crossroads, a melting pot of flora, fauna, and geology found both north and south of here. Like the Superior Uplands, the Northern Highlands contain endless braids of rivers and lands riddled with glacial lakes. Like the Great Lakes Plains, they include sand dunes and sandstone, but on a grandiose scale: The 460-foot-high perched dunes of Sleeping Bear—among the world's largest freshwater dunes—and the 200-foot-high sandstone cliffs of Pictured Rocks. It's as if the Northern Highlands took cues from the surrounding regions and tried to best them all.

Lakes Michigan and Huron began forming in the Paleozoic era, some 500 million to 185 million years ago, when the region was awash under ancient tropical seas. Layer upon layer of marine-life skeletons and shells

were compacted for millions upon millions of years, eventually forming limestone and dolomite bedrock thousands of feet thick. At some point, the land sank, creating the beginning of the lake basins. Other areas were uplifted to form the limestone escarpments that arc across the region today, visible in Door County, Wisconsin; the Garden Peninsula of Michigan; the islands and points around the Straits of Mackinac; and Drummond Island off the eastern end of the Upper Peninsula. Rogers City, just east of the Straits of Mackinac, is home to the largest limestone quarry in the world.

As the tropical seas began draining away, rock, sand, and other debris were compacted into sandstone. These falling water levels also helped sculpt the lakes. Lake Michigan gained its long and leggy shape when waters were unable to cut through the hard limestone along its southern shore; instead, they were forced to drain through the Straits of Mackinac.

The Pleistocene glacial epoch followed. Four ice ages, from nearly 2 million years ago to just 10,000 years ago, scrubbed their way across the landscape. They shaped the Michigan and Huron basins, gouged out thousands of smaller lakes, fashioned sandstone outcroppings, ground other shores into fine sand, and left behind a soil well-suited to pine and hardwood forest.

Seemingly endless tracts of towering white and red pine once blanketed much of Wisconsin and Michigan. But as industrious loggers would prove in just a few short decades, the vast stands were not infinite. A young nation expanding westward into the treeless plains in the mid-19th century, the United States cultivated an insatiable appetite for wood. Acre by acre, the great trees were felled, fed into rivers, and floated downstream to sawmills.

The logging industry made "timber baron" millionaires and gave rise to lumbering boomtowns from Menomonie in western Wisconsin to Alpena, Michigan, on the shores of Lake Huron. By 1880, Lake Michigan cities such as Muskegon, Michigan, had grown into lumbering metropolises, buzzing with 47 sawmills—and at least that many saloons, dance halls, and gambling joints.

Twenty years later, nearly all the big trees were gone. Although scattered stands were left behind—you can marvel at 500-year-old cedars on South Manitou Island, for example, and magnificent hemlocks and white pines in the Sylvania Wilderness and other protected areas—the legacy of the lumberjack was for the most part a scarred, barren landscape of stump prairies and burned soil.

Enterprising entrepreneurs tried to reinvent the cutover land, selling it as farmland or resort property. But it required the intervention of the federal government and a Depression-era New Deal program, the Civilian Conservation Corps (CCC), to turn things around and truly begin healing the land. Employing otherwise out-of-work youth during the Great Depression, the CCC went to work planting trees, fighting fires, and restoring wetlands. Between 1933 and 1942, young men in Michigan alone planted 484 million tree seedlings.

Antique boat show, Hessel, Michigan

Largely thanks to the CCC's work, the Northern Highlands have now come full circle. No, it isn't the same landscape it was two centuries ago; several more centuries will have to pass before the big pines genuinely bounce back. More sophisticated logging practices have since replaced ravaging clear-cuts, however, and the belching sawmill boomtowns have all but disappeared.

Nature itself, meanwhile, is slowly erasing the scars. Forests once again grow thick and tall with hardwoods and pines. Native animals such as white-tailed deer, black bear, coyote, and fox find plenty of habitat, as do moose, wolf, and even elk. The state of Michigan, which reintroduced the elk in 1918, today boasts the largest free-roaming herd east of the Mississippi River; Wisconsin's reintroduction program, just a few years old, is likewise doing well.

Tourism has replaced logging as the economic mainstay of the Northern Highlands. That transition can bring its own perils, of course. Popular destinations such as Door County, Wisconsin, and Traverse City, Michigan, are exceedingly lovely, but care must be taken to ensure they are not loved to death. As visitors enjoy their boats and mountain bikes and waterfront resorts, knotty issues such as water quality, shoreline erosion, and overdevelopment will all have to be tackled and resolved.

Despite their justifiable popularity, the Northern Highlands encompass plenty of areas where you're likely to see not a soul. Millions of acres in the region have been protected as national lakeshores, national forests, wilderness areas, and other public lands. This guarantees that future generations, too, will be able to enjoy the simple but sublime pleasure of heading *Up North*. ▪

Chequamegon National Forest

■ 857,000 acres ■ Northern Wisconsin, in Bayfield, Ashland, Sawyer, Price, and Taylor Counties ■ Year-round ■ Camping, hiking, boating, fishing, mountain biking, horseback riding, cross-country skiing, snowshoeing, wildlife viewing, scenic drives ■ Contact the Great Divide Ranger District, Hayward Office, P.O. Box 896, 10650 Nyman Ave., Hayward, WI 54843, phone 715-634-4821; or Glidden Office, P.O. Box 126, Glidden, WI 54527, phone 715-264-2511. www.fs.fed.us/r9/cnnf

THE TONGUE-TWISTER TITLE of this national forest (pronounced shuh-WAH-mi-gun) is derived from the Ojibwa phrase for "land of shallow water," a reference to the nearby bay on Lake Superior that dips inland to Ashland. But that sobriquet could just as easily describe the national forest itself, peppered as it is with 800 or so lakes and etched with more than 600 miles of navigable rivers.

Chequamegon National Forest lies near the western end of the Northern Highlands region, which stretches across much of northern Wisconsin and Michigan. It typifies much of the region—a landscape of glacial lakes and rivers surrounded by forests of hemlock, birch, and maple, spruce and cedar bogs, and thin soils. At its northern reaches, though, the Chequamegon segues into Superior Uplands terrain, evidenced by the volcanic rock of the ancient Penokee Mountains.

Part of what makes the Chequamegon special is its sheer volume: Four large blocks of national forest stretch south from the Bayfield Peninsula for nearly 150 miles. The largest block lies between Hayward and Glidden; if you have limited time or are looking for an introduction to the area, it offers an excellent cross-section of wilderness areas, short hikes, accessible lakes, mountain-bike trails, and scenic drives. (The following pages focus largely on this area.) Other ranger district offices are located to the north in Washburn and to the south in Park Falls (the Forest Service headquarters) and Medford. Contact these local offices for maps and specifics on hiking, camping, and other activities in their surrounding areas.

Like many national forests in the Great Lakes region, the Chequamegon was set aside in the wake of logging's heyday. As a result, only isolated tracts of big, old-growth pines remain. Established in 1933 to conserve timber and protect the local waters, the forest has a more complex task today: It is now managed for timber, hunting, fishing, and other forms of recreation.

A variety of wildlife thrives in the vast expanse of the Chequamegon National Forest. Especially notable is the population of ruffed grouse—a popular upland game bird that the Forest Service encourages by seeding old logging trails with clover. Glidden also proclaims itself the "black bear capital," no idle boast; it has the state's highest concentration of the creatures.

Fall color, Chequamegon National Forest

The most unusual mammal inhabiting the national forest is the elk. Once found throughout Wisconsin, elk were wiped out more than 130 years ago. In 1995, some 25 of the animals were reintroduced to the state in the area around Clam Lake. As of 2001 the herd was doing quite well, with several calves and a population estimated at 80 to 85.

Elk stand four to five feet high at the shoulder, with a black neck, black legs, and tan rump. Males grow spectacular racks of antlers, often stretching several feet across. Elk tend to browse in areas of balsam, fir, spruce, and aspen. Like deer, they are most active at dawn and dusk. Lucky visitors may spot one or hear its magnificent bugling call—a memorable souvenir of a North Woods visit.

What to See and Do

Hiking

With more than 200 miles of marked trails, Chequamegon National Forest offers a wide range of trekking options.

Three miles west of Mellen on County Road GG, the **Penokee trail system** gives a good overview of the forest. An observation platform faces south toward the Penokees, a mountain range that was formed by volcanoes, then tilted and faulted. The Penokees were once higher than today's Rockies; eons of wind, water, and glacial ice have reduced them to the 80-mile-long rocky ridge visible today.

The Penokee trails include three loops totaling 7.6 miles, winding up and down the rock outcrops of the Penokees' foothills. The trailhead for all three loops is adjacent to the viewing platform. The trails are groomed for cross-country skiing.

West of the Penokee trails near the western end of the range, **St. Peters Dome** rises 1,565 feet above sea level to loom high above the surrounding forest. This knob of red granite is the second-highest point in Wisconsin. On a clear day, Lake Superior and the Apostle Islands are visible to the north. The view is particularly beautiful in fall, when the ocean of treetops brightens into a brilliant tableau of crimson and fiery orange.

A 1.8-mile trail leads up to St. Peters Dome from the parking lot on Forest Road 199. Where the trail splits, take the right fork and follow Morgan Creek upstream. That faint splashing resonates deeper until you reach **Morgan Falls,** where the creek tumbles 80 feet over a bed of black granite. Retrace your steps to the main trail and follow it on its switchback route up St. Peters Dome.

The Chequamegon includes two wilderness areas near the western end of the forest boundary. The 4,446-acre **Porcupine Lake Wilderness** lies south of Grand View off County Road D. Most of this area is an old glacial drainage, a flat, sandy delta favored by balsam, oak, and aspen. A 65-mile segment of the **North Country National Scenic Trail** runs through the forest; it's one of the longest legs in this seven-state route. A 7-mile stretch of the trail *(trailhead 5 miles S of Grand View on Cty. Rd. D)* passes through the

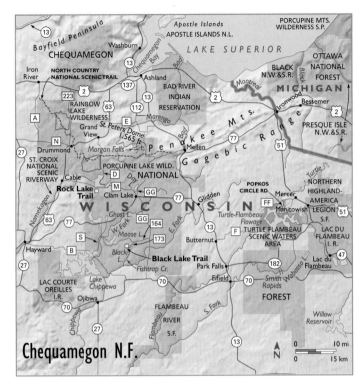

Chequamegon N.F.

wilderness, crossing several trout streams and ponds created by active beavers.

The 6,583-acre **Rainbow Lake Wilderness** lies north of Drummond off Forest Road 223. The north and east ends are delineated by glacial moraines—long ridges of gravel and other debris left behind by retreating glaciers. Much of the rest of the terrain is gently rolling, cloaked in hemlock, white pine, oak, and maple, and dotted with dozens of placid lakes. A 6.4-mile stretch of the North Country NST runs the length of the wilderness area, in many places tracing the beds of narrow-gauge railroads used by loggers. To reach the trail, drive west from County Road H for 2 miles on the Great Divide Scenic Drive, then south on Forest Road 228 for about 2.5 miles to the trailhead.

Mountain Biking

The national forest's mountain biking trails are among the best in the Midwest. The Chequamegon Area Mountain Bike Association (CAMBA) maintains several trail "clusters," each with 15 to 30 miles of single- and double-track routes designed to appeal to a variety of skill levels. One of the nation's top mountain bike races, the Chequamegon Fat Tire Festival, is held on the **Cable Cluster** south of Cable, Wisconsin; it follows the 33-mile route used by the American Birkebeiner, an equally renowned Nordic ski race.

Wabasso Lake, Chequamegon National Forest

West of Clam Lake off County Road M, the **Rock Lake Cluster** offers six interconnecting loops from 1.2 to 10 miles long. Open to hikers and bikers, the trails twist around several small lakes, threading stands of paper birch and aspen and groves of mature white pine. As you click through your gears, woodpeckers drum on the trees with a *rat-a-tat-tat.*

For more information on area biking trails, contact the nearest ranger district or CAMBA *(800-533-7454).*

Canoeing

Along with its hundreds of lakes, the Chequamegon includes hundreds of miles of canoeable rivers. The most notable is the **Namek-agon,** which begins in the national forest and flows into the St. Croix, part of the St. Croix National Scenic Riverway.

Two other rivers within the national forest—the **Flambeau** and the **Chippewa**—are being considered for national scenic river status. Both flow clean and clear

between banks shrouded in boreal forest—a mix of red and white pine with an understory of balsam fir, white cedar, and spruce. Native game fish, including the increasingly rare lake sturgeon, inhabit these waterways.

Depending on water levels, the Flambeau can generate Class II and III rapids that require skill to navigate. Inquire with a forest service office about river levels before setting out. Smith Rapids Campground has a put-in and takeout on the South Fork of the Flambeau.

Great Divide Scenic Drive

This 29-mile route in the heart of Chequamegon National Forest traces the high ridge formed by the Penokees. Waters on the north side of the divide flow into Lake Superior; waters on the south side flow into the Mississippi River and the Gulf of Mexico. By following the scenic drive you can link together many of the national forest's most interesting spots.

From Mellen, follow County

Road GG west: This is the Great Divide Scenic Drive. You'll pass the Penokee trailhead on the right. The Penokee trails mark the east end of the North Country National Scenic Trail segment within the Chequamegon; you can begin here and hike uninterrupted through nearly 60 miles of forest.

As you continue west on County Road GG, you'll pass several lakes, boat launches, and campgrounds. At the **Day Lake Recreation Area,** a half-mile interpretive trail and viewing platform overlook the lake and a surrounding bog. This is a good spot to watch for wildlife, especially at dawn and dusk. Lucky visitors may even spot an elk. Originally relocated from the northern Lower Peninsula of Michigan, the Clam Lake herd roams this general area.

At Clam Lake, follow Wis. 77 southwest out of town. Along with the elk crossing signs, you'll see a sign for the Ghost Lake CCC camp, where a small exhibit tells the story of the Civilian Conservation Corps crews who worked the North Woods in the 1930s.

Just past the Chippewa River, follow County Road S south, then turn left (east) on Moose Lake Road (FR 164), which jigs and jogs around the south end of horseshoe-shaped Moose Lake. Just beyond the Sawyer/Ashland county line, turn south on Forest Road 173 to the **Black Lake Trail.** This 4-mile interpretive trail rings Black Lake; a brochure keyed to trailside signs tells the story of the area's logging history. Loggers first took the valuable white pine from this area in the 1880s to early 1900s. In the 1910s, they returned for the hemlocks and some hardwoods. Although these trees were not as valuable as white pine, felling them brought the added benefit of clearing the land so it could be sold as farmland. The thin soils proved inadequate, however; by the time of the Great Depression, most farms had failed.

From Black Lake, backtrack to Forest Road 164 and follow it east to County Road GG, where you turn north to head back to Clam Lake and Mellen. ∎

Wolf or Coyote?

Though the eastern timber wolf inhabits Chequamegon National Forest, your chances of seeing this shy and stealthy creature are slight. You're far more likely to spot a coyote, a smaller canine relative common in the area. The two animals do have similarities: Both are doglike, and both tend to be shades of gray and brown with whitish bellies. However, they can be distinguished from each other in these key ways:

Face
Wolf: round ears, broad snout
Coyote: pointed ears, pointed snout

Shoulder height
Wolf: 28 to 34 inches
Coyote: 18 to 20 inches

Length (nose to tip of tail)
Wolf: 5 to 6.5 feet
Coyote: 4 to 4.5 feet

Weight
Wolf: 40 to 175 pounds
Coyote: 20 to 50 pounds

Tracks
Wolf: 4 to 5 inches long
Coyote: 2 to 3 inches long

Turtle-Flambeau Scenic Waters Area

■ 14,300 acres ■ Iron County in north-central Wisconsin ■ Year-round
■ Camping, hiking, boating, fishing, snowmobiling, wildlife viewing, scenic drive
■ Contact DNR Ranger Station, 5291 State House Circle, Mercer, WI 54547;
phone 715-476-7846

THE TURTLE-FLAMBEAU FLOWAGE sprawls like a giant amoeba across
north-central Wisconsin, a watery paradise comprising more than 300
miles of untrammeled shoreline, hundreds of islands, and endless bays
and backwaters.

Though surrounded by natural lakes, this body of water was the work
of humans: In 1926, a dam was built across the Flambeau River to control
water flows for paper mills and small hydroelectric plants. The project
consumed 16 natural lakes, several streams, and thousands of acres of
woods and wetlands.

Although it once must have looked like a swampy drowned forest, the
flowage has matured gracefully. All that's left of the flooded woods are
submerged stumps and downed logs, providing ideal habitat for fish and
the animals that feed on them. The shoreline, at one time intensely man-

Turtle-Flambeau Scenic Waters Area

aged, has now reverted to a natural-looking mix of pines, hardwoods, grass-sedge openings, and bogs and other wetlands.

Turtle-Flambeau supports a rich diversity of wildlife. It is home to the state's highest densities of bald eagles, common loons, and ospreys. Merlin, heron, and black tern live among these waters, while several other shorebirds and migratory waterfowl use the flowage as a staging area. A number of fur-bearing mammals do well here, including beavers, otters, minks, muskrats, and fishers. Some, like the mink and otter, feed on the small panfish that dart among the shallows.

The flowage is unsurpassed as a fishery. Its relatively warm waters support native populations of northern pike, smallmouth and largemouth bass, crappie, bluegill, rock bass, and muskellunge. Turtle-Flambeau is best known for walleye, a game fish prized for its taste, and muskie, known for its fighting spirit, menacing look, and substantial heft: Lunkers of 50 pounds have been hooked here.

Though the Turtle-Flambeau is a mapmaker's nightmare, it is also a quiet boater's dream. The shallows, submerged stumps, and rock bars keep away everyone but paddlers and puttering fishing boats. You could poke around for days, exploring nooks and crannies, without ever passing the same stretch of shoreline twice.

The state maintains 60 campsites accessible by water only, making Turtle-Flambeau an ideal canoe-camping destination. Because of the wandering shape of the flowage, it's almost like paddling a chain of lakes minus the hassles of portaging. Several boat launches are on the flowage: off US 51 from the east, near Manitowish; off Wis. 182 from the south; and off County Road FF, which winds along the north and west shores.

Looping south off County Road FF, the **North Woods Auto Tour** follows Popko Circle Drive. Pick up a guide booklet at the Department of Natural Resources (DNR) office in Mercer to make the most of this 24-mile route. It winds over and alongside bays, rolling through grassy uplands, a sedge-cattail marsh, a large bog, and managed forests of red pine, hemlock, and hardwoods.

One stop along the auto tour is the **Dead Horse-Ruffed Grouse Management Demonstration Area,** which is located near Dead Horse Lake on the northern edge of the flowage. The area has an information kiosk and a 3-mile loop walking trail that highlights management techniques for supporting ruffed grouse habitats.

The bog habitat is particularly lush. A bog forms when an open wetland fills in with floating vegetation that prefers acidic and anaerobic (low oxygen) growing conditions. Labrador tea, bog laurel, leatherleaf, blueberry, and wild cranberry thrive here. Because it's relatively dry, the bog also supports trees such as black spruce and tamarack.

Though the bog environment is too acidic for most amphibians, several species of frogs live elsewhere in Turtle-Flambeau, including green, bull, leopard, chorus, wood, mink, and gray tree frogs, as well as spring peepers. They begin calling in spring when the water warms to a certain temperature, usually above 60 or 70 degrees Fahrenheit. ■

Northern Highland-American Legion State Forest

■ 223,000 acres ■ North-central Wisconsin, near border with Upper Peninsula of Michigan ■ Year-round ■ Camping, hiking, canoeing, fishing, mountain biking, wildlife viewing ■ Fee for mountain biking and camping ■ Contact Trout Lake Forestry Headquarters, 4125 County Rd. M, Boulder Junction, WI 54512; phone 715-385-2727. www.dnr.state.wi.us/org/land/forestry/StateForests/meet .htm#NHAL

ALTHOUGH ESTABLISHED IN 1925 TO PROTECT the headwaters of several North Woods rivers, Northern Highland-American Legion (NHAL) State Forest is really defined by its glacial lakes. The pine and hardwood forests here are pitted with hundreds of them—one of the greatest concentrations of lakes in the world.

The NHAL encompasses 930 lakes, classic North Woods beauties encircled by pines and rocky shores, as well as several hundred miles of rivers and streams. This is one of the Midwest's most popular vacation areas, drawing campers, hikers, and especially anglers, who come with hopes of snagging a trophy muskie or northern pike. You won't find true wilderness here; the forest is a patchwork of public and private land, and vacation homes and mom-and-pop resorts dot many lakeshores. But you will find plenty of quiet corners in this landscape of woods and water, whether hiking under the evergreens or drifting over a glittering lake.

What to See and Do

Hiking

Nearly 80 miles of marked hiking trails stitch through the NHAL, along with countless old logging roads and abandoned railroad grades. The **Escanaba-Pallette Lakes trail system** (*E of Cty. Rd. M on Nebish Rd.*) is a particularly scenic hiking choice. Part of a popular cross-country skiing area in winter, the trails wind around and among five lakes, with loops from 2 to 8 miles.

The outer **red loop** (*trailhead on Nebish Rd.*) is the longest; it also gives views of all the lakes. The loop climbs a few rolling hills, passes through stands of maple and balsam, and traverses a wetland between Escanaba and Lost Canoe Lakes.

Hiking options within the state forest include four nature trails, all of them keyed to interpretive booklets or clearly marked with signs. The **Raven Trail** network (*off Wis. 47, SE of Woodruff*) scrambles over steep hills along the north shore of Clear Lake, with loops of 1.5 to 5 miles.

In spring and summer, the forest is a chorus of bird songs, from the endless singsong refrain of the red-eyed vireo to the *zee-zee-zee-zoop-zee* of the tiny black-throated green warbler. Yellow-bellied sapsuckers favor stands of aspen, where they drill small holes in the

Along Fallison Lake Nature Trail, Northern Highland-American Legion State Forest

soft trunks and lap up the sap with their long tongues. Hummingbirds, woodpeckers, and other birds with long beaks often take advantage of the sapsucker's work after the fact, probing the holes for sap or insects.

The **Fallison Lake Nature Trail** (E of Cty. Rd. M on Cty. Rd. N) is one of the forest's prettiest walks. The 2.5-mile hilly route rings Fallison Lake, wandering over spongy carpets of needles beneath groves of red pine and hemlock, and passing sphagnum hummocks and bogs.

Along the way, you'll see evidence of beavers at work. One beaver can fell four 6-inch-diameter aspen trees in an hour, gnawing through their trunks with its chisel-like incisors. Beavers dug a channel from Fallison Lake and logged an entire hillside along the trail, using the wood both for food (they eat the soft layer just under

the bark) and as a building material for dams and lodges.

Beaver lodges are marvels of engineering. Their thick wood-and-mud walls provide a warm shelter in winter, keeping the interior well above freezing even in the harsh north Wisconsin climate. The lodges also help flood surrounding lands, ensuring access to more wood. Most active at dusk, beavers can often be spotted on Fallison Lake.

Fallison Lake is one of the NHAL's 19 designated "wilderness" lakes. There is no direct road access to the lake, and no motors are permitted on its waters.

The Wisconsin Department of Natural Resources maintains a quarter-mile development-free buffer zone around the lake. Rather than managing this swath with planting or prescribed burns, the DNR allows the shoreline to evolve naturally.

Fishing on lake near Boulder Junction, NHAL State Forest

Boating

Comprising nearly 1,000 lakes, the NHAL offers a lifetime of boating options. Fishing can be excellent on most of these waters, with anglers vying for game fish such as muskie, northern pike, walleye, and largemouth and smallmouth bass. **Trout Lake,** the forest's biggest at 4,000 acres, also harbors lake trout, whitefish, and cisco— species associated with larger, deeper waters.

Paddlers may be happiest on one of the forest's 19 wilderness (and motorboat-free) lakes, such as **Nebish Lake** in the **Frank Lake Wild Area** or those in the **Partridge Lake Wild Area** (both areas lie east of Trout Lake). The Wisconsin Department of Natural Resources has also designated 41 "wild" lakes; these allow motorboats but are free of shoreline development. Many lakes have primitive canoe campsites *(maps showing designated landings available at ranger station).*

In **Allequash Lake** *(E of Trout Lake, on Cty. Rd. M),* wild rice bends in the breeze, nearly filling the narrow channel between the lake's two main lobes. Watch for ospreys circling high above, scanning for panfish such as bluegill, perch, and crappie. When it spots a fish, the osprey will hover, then fold its wings and plunge, talons first, into the water. If it succeeds in nabbing a fish, the bird heads for its nest to enjoy its meal.

Flowing languidly for 44 miles from High Lake to the Turtle-Flambeau Flowage (see pp. 96-97), the **Manitowish River** is another popular canoeing option. The state forest prints a brochure describing four different sections and showing campsites. The section from US 51 to **Murray's Landing** is the largest and most beautiful. Canoeists can also create paddle-and-portage loop routes using several state forest lakes and rivers, such as Escanaba Lake and the **Lost Canoe Lake** systems.

Biking

Mountain bikes are allowed on most forest trails (except nature trails) and on the many logging roads within the state forest. In addition, the DNR maintains three trail networks for mountain bikes: the 9.5-mile **Madeline Lake Trail;** the 10-mile **McNaughton Lake Trail,** a gently rolling route around McNaughton Lake; and the 12.5-mile **Lumberjack Trail,** which winds along the Manitowish River and White Sand Lake, skirting wetlands and passing through a recently logged area. The Lumberjack is a good place to see bear and white-tailed deer, which browse in the new, sunny clearings. Though scenic, none of the designated trails can be considered particularly challenging for avid mountain bikers. All three are groomed for cross-country skiing in winter.

Just west of the NHAL, the **Bearskin State Trail** is a favorite among cyclists; an abandoned railroad grade, it stretches 18 miles from Minocqua *(trailhead behind post office)* to County Road K west of Rhinelander. This relatively flat route slaloms between a dozen lakes and crosses Bearskin Creek nine times. Paved with crushed limestone, it is most appropriate for fat-tire bikes. ■

Sylvania Wilderness

■ 18,327 acres ■ Michigan's Upper Peninsula, east of Watersmeet near Wisconsin border ■ Best months May-Oct. ■ Camping, hiking, canoeing, swimming, fishing, cross-country skiing, snowshoeing, wildlife viewing ■ Adm. fee ■ Contact the Ottawa Visitor Center, Ottawa National Forest, P.O. Box 276, Watersmeet, MI 49969; phone 906-358-4724. www.fs.fed.us/r9/ottawa

OLD MONEY IS PARTLY TO THANK for the condition of the Sylvania Wilderness today: 36 crystalline glacial lakes hidden among thick stands of massive, old-growth trees. For anglers who dream of landing (and then releasing) that once-in-a-lifetime smallmouth bass; for paddlers who yearn to glide across deep, quiet waters and along undeveloped shorelines; for hikers who wish to trek beneath a towering canopy of trees and hear nothing more than the haunting whistle of a loon, Sylvania can be a truly magical place.

Though Sylvania was once viewed as just another tract of good timber, its fate turned in the late 1890s, when a lumberman purchased 80 acres near the south end of **Clark Lake.** He decided it was too lovely to cut and instead kept it as his personal fishing retreat. The lumberman hosted his wealthy buddies—some of them executives of U.S. Steel—who were likewise captivated by the land. Together they purchased several thousand additional acres and formed the private Sylvania Club.

Like other upscale Upper Peninsula "great camps," the Sylvania Club soon had grand log lodges along its shores, guards to keep trespassing anglers away from its bountiful lakes, and caretakers to squelch forest fires as they cropped up. Ownership changed hands a few times over the decades, eventually ending up in those of Lawrence Fisher of Fisher Auto Body. When he died, his heirs sold the property to the federal government. It was operated as a recreation area from the late 1960s to 1987, when the bulk of it was designated wilderness by the 1987 Michigan Wilderness Act.

Sylvania's lakes provide some epic fishing, especially for bass. Its waters remain pristine, thanks to the lack of development, a ban on powerboats (except on **Crooked Lake**), and the area's particular topography: Located on the divide between Lake Superior and the Mississippi, Sylvania doesn't suffer from the runoff of nearby farmlands. Decades of fire protection mean visitors can marvel at a virgin forest of white pines, hemlock, maple, and basswood trees more than 200 years old.

One of three wilderness areas within Ottawa National Forest, Sylvania stretches across 18,000 acres near Watersmeet, an area roughly bordered by US 2 to the north, US 45 to the east, and the Wisconsin border to the south. Acting as a buffer is the adjacent **Sylvania Recreation Area—** an additional 3,000 acres of lakes, soft sand beaches, and woodlands with a few developed services such as a drive-in campground, flush toilets, and running water.

What to See and Do

Begin a trip to Sylvania with a visit to the Ottawa Visitor Center at the intersection of US 2 and US 45. The staff can help you with maps, regulations, campsite reservations, and other information. Sylvania's rules—especially its fishing regulations—can be quite particular, so take time to ask questions and read through the materials provided. To reach Sylvania itself, follow US 2 west about 4 miles from the visitor center and turn south on **Thousand Island Lake Road.** Travel about 3.5 miles, following signs to reach the entrance building. All visitors are required to register upon arrival.

For hikers, Sylvania maintains a 7-mile **trail** around **Clark Lake,** the tract's largest lake. This main trail also provides access to campsites and trails to other lakes. Coralroot and other orchids, Indian pipe, orange jewelweed, and club mosses grow under the high canopy of red and white pines, sprouting among a bed of spongy needles. Most of Sylvania's trails are old roads left over from its days as a fishing camp; though not marked, they are quite easy to follow. These same roads become a great cross-country ski network in the winter months.

Birch bark

Fishermen and spotter, Crooked Lake, Sylvania Wilderness

As in the Boundary Waters Canoe Area Wilderness in Minnesota (see pp. 28-34), paddling is the best way to explore the Sylvania Wilderness. Most lakes are linked by water or by relatively easy portages, though a couple of them are "grunt portages" of 1.5 miles. Many campsites are accessible only by water. Motors and other "mechanized equipment" (including sailboats!) are forbidden. (The exception is Crooked Lake, which allows electric motors of up to 4 horsepower.)

Don't forget a bathing suit: Several slivers of inviting sand beach—and water that's as clear as a swimming pool—will lure you in for a dip. Indeed, the water visibility is so good that you may want to bring along snorkel gear to plunge deeper into the chilly waters, where you may spot huge bass gliding past.

From the entrance road, you can launch at Crooked or Clark Lake. Some of the smaller lakes—among them Mountain and High, both accessible from Crooked—see less traffic and lie just a short portage away. Quietly cruise the shorelines and you may spot signs of black bear, white-tailed deer, red fox, porcupine, and mink.

The loon is quite common in Sylvania, nesting on nearly every lake. Watch for the distinctive profile of this dramatic black-and-white bird, which rides low in the water, then suddenly dives for food or safety. Superb divers, loons can remain under water for as much as 15 minutes at a stretch; they are known to descend to depths of more than 150 feet.

The loon's anatomy is perfectly suited for diving and swimming underwater. Its wings are relatively small, its webbed feet relatively large, and its legs—positioned far back on its body—extend laterally like oars when swimming. Unlike most birds, which have hollow bones, the loon has heavy, marrow-filled bones that decrease its buoyancy, making it easier to swim underwater.

These characteristics are wasted off the water. The loon's leg placement renders it nearly helpless on land, and its heavy bones and small wings make taking off a laborious prospect. Loons therefore nest right along the water's edge, building large masses of mud, matted grass, and twigs. Give the nests a wide berth: Even slight disturbances can cause adult birds to abandon nests. ∎

A Dynasty of Pine

IN THE MID-1800S, a young and grow- ing United States suddenly developed a huge demand for lumber. Settlers were moving west into the treeless plains, and they needed lumber to build their new towns. Burgeoning cities required lumber to build more homes and businesses. And railroads had to have lumber as they laid mile after mile of track to connect it all.

The natural resources of the north- ern Great Lakes region proved the perfect mix to fuel the hungry nation. Immense white pines and other coni- fers grew thick and tall across north- ern Wisconsin, the Upper Peninsula of

A load of Minnesota timber, circa 1895

Michigan, and more than half of the Lower Peninsula. Rivers honeycombed these vast forests, providing a route to the Great Lakes, which in turn con- nected the northern wilderness to Chicago and other railroad centers. Mother Nature, in effect, had created the perfect delivery system for the logging industry.

Around 1850, logging camps began springing up deep in the woods, from western Wisconsin's Chippewa Valley

to the shores of Lake Huron. It was not easy work. The lumberjacks worked by hand, with ax and saw, tree after tree, acre after acre. To shouts of "Timber!" the old pines (some of them 20 feet in circumference and 100 feet tall) came crashing down with earthshaking thuds.

The logging camps operated primar- ily in the winter months, when it was easier to transport the huge logs. With horses and sleighs, workers hauled the logs from the woods to the river's edge, branded the ends with the lumber company's mark, and stacked them there until spring.

In spring, when the ice melted and the waters rose, the colorful and chaotic log drives began. Thousands of logs were shoved into North Woods rivers, then guided downstream by daredevil workers known as "river pigs." They danced across the shifting and dangerous mass of moving wood, using hooks, poles, and sometimes dynamite to dislodge logjams.

Once at the sawmills, the jumble of logs was sorted according to their brands and floated into mill storage ponds. From there, buzzing mills sliced the logs into lumber and loaded it on- to lumber schooners—and, later on, barges and steamers—for transporta- tion to Chicago.

In its heyday, the logging industry generated billions of board feet of lumber worth billions of dollars, the actual numbers almost incalculable. Lumber companies made all sorts of proclamations: The 20 million board feet milled in the Green Bay region, someone once estimated, would form a one-foot-wide walkway that would stretch around the globe 14 times. Michigan mills claimed they produced

Logjam in northern Michigan, circa 1910

enough lumber to lay an inch-thick plank across the entire state.

Success stories were everywhere. Menomonie, Wisconsin, home of the wildly profitable Knapp-Stout lumber company, was the first city in the Midwest to have electricity, city water, and sewer service—preceding even Chicago. The sawmill in Hermansville, Michigan, that came up with the idea of tongue-and-groove flooring quickly became the largest flooring plant in the country.

The era that everyone thought would last forever actually endured less than 50 years. By 1900, nearly all the big trees were gone. In their places was a scorched, denuded landscape of stump prairies. When farmers succeeded in converting some of the southernmost pineries into useful crop land, ambitious entrepreneurs sought to do the same in the north. Extolling the virtues of Upper Peninsula cutover land for farming or ranching, one local newspaper publisher declared, "No matter where the first Garden of Eden was located, the present one is in the Upper Peninsula."

Thousands of hardworking folks were lured north by the promise of cheap land in exchange for the back-breaking labor of removing pine stumps and tilling soil. But by the late 1920s, their work proved futile. Most ranches and farms had failed. Nearly half the Upper Peninsula was tax-delinquent cutover land.

In 1925, Wisconsin created Northern Highland State Forest in the area around Trout Lake, the nation's first state forest. The same year, the first national forests in the U.S. were established in Wisconsin and Michigan. The Civilian Conservation Corps continued the reforestation efforts, planting trees, fighting fires, and slowly nursing the great forests back to health.

Today, pines once again stretch skyward across the Northern Highlands. Logging continues, too, though with sophisticated forest management and reforestation practices. Throughout northern Michigan and Wisconsin, the lumber and paper industries have become slightly more enlightened monarchs in the modern-day dynasty of pine. ■

Nicolet National Forest

■ 669,000 acres ■ Northeast Wisconsin ■ Year-round; canoeing best in spring and early summer ■ Camping, hiking, fishing, canoeing, kayaking, mountain biking, cross-country skiing, snowshoeing, wildlife viewing, scenic drives ■ Contact the national forest, 68 S. Stevens St., Rhinelander, WI 54501; phone 715-362-1300. www.fs.fed.us/r9/cnnf

SEVEN OF WISCONSIN'S MOST RENOWNED North Woods rivers originate within Nicolet National Forest, earning it the nickname "The Cradle of Rivers." The Brule, Wolf, Peshtigo, Pine, Popple, Oconto, and even the mighty Wisconsin all have their headwaters here, part of a watery network of more than a thousand miles of rivers and streams that course through the national forest.

These waterways meander through groves of tall white pines and thick hardwoods, and slalom past more than 1,200 lakes. Trout fishing is excellent throughout the national forest. Paddlers also gravitate to the Nicolet, where they can find both stretches of quiet water and some of the state's best white-water runs.

At the forest's northernmost point, **Lac Vieux Desert** straddles the border of Wisconsin and Michigan's Upper Peninsula. This large lake is the headwaters of the Wisconsin River, which winds through the state for 400 miles before emptying into the Mississippi.

Lac Vieux Desert is also known far and wide among anglers as one of the state's prime muskellunge lakes. The muskie is the undisputed king of fighting game fish: Growing to 50 inches or more, it's shaped like a torpedo and possesses a menacing set of teeth, with a personality to match. Muskie stories—in which they feed on very small mammals, fight like marlins, and outsmart anglers—are the stuff of legend. Muskies were in decline for years, threatened by sediment-filled lakes, shoreline development, and overfishing. Stocking programs and stricter fishing limits have helped buoy the population.

East of Lac Vieux Desert, the sinewy **Brule River** flows for 30 miles along the northern edge of the forest and forms part of the meandering Wisconsin-Michigan border. Most years it's suitable for paddling, with reliable water levels and primarily Class I and II rapids. The river flows along the Nicolet's 7,500-acre Whisker Lake Wilderness, named for the "whiskers" on the area's white pines and hemlocks. The best put-in is at the Brule River Campground on Wis. 55; below that, primitive camping is allowed in the national forest.

South of the Whisker Lake Wilderness, the 9-mile **Lauterman National Recreation Trail** stretches between Lauterman and Lost Lakes, a hilly route that's a favorite among hikers, mountain bikers, and cross-country skiers. It links up with the **Ridge, Perch Lake,** and **Assessor's Trails,** one of the best trail networks in the national forest. The Ridge Trail, a 3-mile loop, skirts the Pine River at its northern end; access is via Chipmunk Rapids, Lost Lake Campgrounds, or the Assessor's Trail.

The **Pine River,** a designated state wild river, may be one of Wisconsin's loveliest. It flows cold and clear between shores heavily wooded in sugar maple, birch, hemlock, and white cedar, with occasional rocky riffles and water-falls. Muskrat, mink, otter, and fisher patrol its waters, which support native populations of brook and brown trout.

The Pine begins at the western end of the Nicolet in the **Headwaters Wilderness.** These 20,000 acres preserve fine stands of 300-year-old hemlock and white pine. The **Scott Lake Trail** *(trailhead on FR 2183, 4 miles E of intersection with Wis. 32)* loops through the old conifers and follows a wetland around Scott Lake, where the chirp of boreal chickadees com-

White birch and shelf mushrooms

petes with the buzz of mosquitoes. Pick up the short (less than a quarter mile) side trail to **Shelp Lake** and a well-preserved bog.

From here, the Pine River winds east and north through the national forest, a 56-mile stretch spilling over Class I and II rapids. Popular access points for paddlers include Wis. 55 and Chipmunk Rapids Campground, just east of Wis. 139. (Check with the Florence Ranger District for information on river conditions before setting out.) After it exits the Nicolet, the Pine continues largely through protected, undeveloped land, part of a state wild river project area. Within the project area, the Pine merges with the Popple, another state wild river with several Class II and III rapids. Just downstream from their confluence, the Pine pours over 15-foot **La Salle Falls** and squeezes through a 100-foot-high gorge.

The **Peshtigo River** ranks as one of the North Wood's classic paddling venues. Its upper stretches of Class I and II rapids are perfect for canoeists, while its lower runs of Class III and IV are a favorite among white-water kayakers. Put-in at **Big Joe Landing** on Wis. 139, where the river rolls lazily through the forest for 10 miles to the takeout at Burnt Bridge on Forest Road 2134. Bald eagles often soar overhead, and wood ducks and mergansers mutter alongside the shrubby banks. Contact Kosir's Rapid Rafts *(715-757-3431)* for canoe and kayak rentals.

Hikers can enjoy the tea-colored Peshtigo from the **Michigan Rapids Trail,** a 2-mile loop near Burnt Bridge that follows the river past rapids and rock formations, and the **Dendro-Eco Trail,** a 0.6-mile interpretive nature trail on Forest Road 2131, about 3 miles north of Laona. ▪

Following pages: Nicolet Bay from Eagle Tower, Peninsula State Park

The Door Peninsula

■ 70-mile-long peninsula ■ Northeast Wisconsin ■ Year-round ■ Camping, hiking, boating, swimming, fishing, biking, cross-country skiing, snowshoeing, wildlife viewing ■ Adm. fee for state parks and private attractions ■ Contact Door County Chamber of Commerce, Box 406, Sturgeon Bay, WI 54235; phone 920-743-4456. www.doorcountyvacations.com

WAGGING LIKE A JAGGED, ARTHRITIC FINGER from the northeastern corner of Wisconsin, the Door Peninsula is a limestone digit jutting 70 miles into Lake Michigan. The peninsula is part of the Niagara Escarpment, an ancient limestone ledge stretching from western Lake Michigan across to New York State, where it forms the riverbed under the torrent of Niagara Falls.

Glaciers have stirred up the landscape, too. Behind them they left a ramshackle mix of high ridges, till plains, sheared-off bluffs, flattened

Sunset, Peninsula State Park

moraines, saw-toothed shorelines, estuaries, and a scattering of limestone shoals and islands.

Although three counties occupy the Door Peninsula, most visitors associate the peninsula with its northern half and therefore simply refer to the whole thing as Door County. One of the Midwest's most popular vacation areas, Door County boasts 250 miles of shoreline; no matter where you stand on this narrow backbone, you're never more than a few minutes from a water view: To the west lies Green Bay and its long sliver of protected waters; to the east stretches the vast, open expanse of Lake Michigan.

Door County, then, is a landmass defined by water. Just as Florida has its Gulf coast and its Atlantic coast, Door County has its "bay side" and its "lake side": They are half a dozen miles and one world apart. Bayside towns, with their shops and cafés huddled around protected little harbors, provide the main tourism draw. Lakeside towns are fewer, the land a mix of forests, wetlands, rocky ledges, and beaches stretching to the water's edge.

What to See and Do

Protecting the finest of the bay side's beauty, **Peninsula State Park** *(920-868-3258)* is a spectacular 3,776-acre rocky headland that sticks out into Green Bay between Ephraim and Fish Creek. The park's Shore Road snakes along its watery boundary, rising and falling with the whim of the glaciers. On the park's western end, the 5.1-mile gravel **Sunset cycling trail** dips among birches, pines, and tranquil Tennison Bay, its shore blanketed in cobblestones worn smooth by the lapping waters.

At Eagle Bluff, an observation tower pokes above the treetops, awkward as a circus clown on stilts. From 250 feet above the water, it offers views of the half-dozen islands sprinkled offshore, from forested Horseshoe to Little Strawberry and Jack Islands—limestone shoals crowded with screeching gulls and terns—as well as the northern end of the Door Peninsula, hazy blue-grey in the distance.

The adjacent **Eagle Trail**, a 2-mile-long loop *(trailhead located at Eagle Terrace)* traces a steep and rocky traverse between the bluff and the water below. At the park's northernmost point, the 1868 Eagle Bluff lighthouse stands sentinel over the shoaly waters. The lighthouse is accessible by vehicle on Shore Road, by bicycle on Sunset Trail, and by foot on **Trail Tramper's Delight.**

Across the peninsula, **Whitefish Dunes State Park** *(920-823-2400)* preserves ancient dunes that rise some 90 feet above Lake Michigan. Grasses and spreading juniper act like snow fences in the sand, taking hold and stabilizing the dunes. The 2.8-mile **Red Trail** *(trailhead N of park nature center)* skirts the sand ridges, passing poison ivy and the spiky white blooms of false Solomon's seal,

View along trail in The Ridges Sanctuary

and ends at an observation deck on 93-foot-tall "Old Baldy," the tallest dune in this 867-acre park.

The **White Trail** heads north of the park office toward **Cave Point County Park.** Here, sand gives way to limestone bluffs sculpted into tunnels and caves. On calm days, Lake Michigan's endless blue swell nudges the steep faces; when the east winds blow, huge waves heave against the rock with a roar, shattering into a dramatic spray of white foam.

Continuing north on the lake side, the Lake Michigan shoreline changes again along the northern rim of Baileys Harbor. At **The Ridges Sanctuary,** boreal conifers rise up from a series of ancient sand dune ridges, the former shoreline of a once-larger Lake Michigan. This 1,000-acre preserve is home to an outstanding variety of wildflowers, including 25 kinds of native orchids. The delicate dwarf lake iris, found only in the northern Great Lakes region, sprouts amid a brown carpet of fallen needles and pinecones.

Farther north at Rowleys Bay, the **Mink River** oozes through clattering cattails and wild-rice paddies before flowing serenely into Lake Michigan. This estuary—an area where river water mixes with a large lake or ocean—is one of the most pristine in the region, if not the country. These unique wetlands provide a vital spawning ground for numerous fish and a migratory hideaway for a variety of birds, including marsh hawks, herons, bitterns, sandhill cranes, and the threatened Cooper's hawk. A short **hiking trail** *(off Newport Rd.)* leads to the river from the east, traversing the drier portion of the tract, which is thick with red-osier dogwood, willow, white cedar, and the threatened dune thistle.

Newport State Park *(920-854-2500)* occupies the promontory of land at the north end of Rowleys Bay. Managed as a wilderness area, the 2,400-acre park includes 11 miles of undeveloped Lake Michigan shore. Its 30 miles of hiking trails wind along rocky ledges, smiling arcs of sand beach, and through meadows filled with wild daisies and the whir of grasshoppers.

The 3-mile-long **Hotz Loop** *(access via Europe Bay Rd.)* wends north to Europe Lake, once a bay of Lake Michigan until wave action isolated it by depositing a sand and gravel ridge. The 4-mile-long **Europe Bay Trail** parallels a corduroy landscape of ancient sand ridges—their swales filled with tiny bog communities—before spilling out onto the rocky limestone shelves above Lake Michigan. The park includes a swimming beach and 16 hike-in campsites.

The Door Peninsula ends a few miles farther north at **Porte des Morts Passage** ("death's door")—the strait that separates mainland Door County from **Plum Island,** a mile and a half off its tip. The grisly name is in deference to the once treacherous passage, where Green Bay and Lake Michigan often tussle in an opposing swirl of currents and wind. From Plum, half a dozen islands string north, allowing boaters to hopscotch their way across the lake to the Upper Peninsula of Michigan. ■

Chipmunk in North Woods forest

Hiawatha National Forest

■ 894,599 acres ■ Central and eastern sections of Upper Peninsula of Michigan ■ Year-round ■ Camping, hiking, cross-country skiing, snowshoeing, wildlife viewing ■ Contact the forest supervisor's office, 2727 N. Lincoln Rd., Escanaba, MI 49829; phone 906-786-4062. www.fs.fed.us/r9/hiawatha

"BY THE SHORES OF GITCHE GUMEE, / By the shining Big Sea Water," Henry Wadsworth Longfellow wrote of Lake Superior in *Hiawatha*. Although it's doubtful Longfellow ever visited the Upper Peninsula of Michigan, his poem inspired the name for this national forest that preserves a large swath of it from Lake Superior across to Lake Michigan.

Like many national forests, the Hiawatha is a patchwork affair, divided into two main sections. These pages cover the large portion in the middle of the Upper Peninsula, managed by ranger districts in Rapid River, Manistique, and Munising, and by a forest headquarters in Escanaba. Another unit lies farther east near the Straits of Mackinac, with ranger districts in St. Ignace and Sault Ste. Marie.

What to See and Do

Stonington Peninsula

Tucked up in the northwestern corner of Lake Michigan in northern Green Bay, two large peninsulas—Stonington and Garden—dangle down from the Upper Peninsula, forming **Little Bay de Noc** and **Big Bay de Noc.** More than 200 miles of undulating, protected shoreline and relatively warm, shallow waters make this area a prime fishery. Northern pike, smallmouth bass, and especially walleye are found here in substantial numbers.

Tempered by the waters of Green Bay, the Stonington Peninsula is among the warmest spots in the Upper Peninsula. It receives just a quarter of the snowfall (about 50 inches annually) that smothers the rest of the Upper

Peninsula. Stonington is a quiet, peaceful place, with smooth slabs of limestone bedrock shoreline and sunny meadows sprouting wild daisies. On the western side, the 1.2-mile **Bayshore Trail** parallels the shoreline in the **Little Bay de Noc Recreation Area** between Twin Springs Loop and Hunters Point boat launch.

About halfway down the peninsula, the tea-colored waters of **Squaw Creek** course through the 65-acre **Squaw Creek Old Growth Area.** Loggers in the 19th century practiced selective cutting—a rarity in those days—and left behind several large hemlocks, hardwoods, and pines. The spared trees have since grown tall, broad, and gracefully noble.

Though marked trails are few, it's easy to walk among these giants; the high canopy precludes much growth in the shady understory, leaving little more than a broad forest floor, spongy with a century of fallen needles. The plumpest hemlocks lie south of the creek, while gnarled red oak and immense birch lie to the north of it. To find the tract, drive south on County Road 513 until you cross Squaw Creek, then walk in on the faint old logging roads to the east.

At the tip of the peninsula, the **Peninsula Point Lighthouse**—built during the last year of the Civil War—stands guard over the bays, once busy with ships hauling iron ore, lumber, and fish. In the 1930s, its light was extinguished, as the United States Coast Guard replaced the lighthouse with a more effective shoal light several miles offshore. Shortly thereafter, the U.S. Forest Service took over

Northern flicker in a rare restful moment

maintenance and restoration of the buildings.

Climb the lighthouse tower to the lantern room. From there, you'll get a view of the Garden Peninsula's bleached limestone shore, the deep blue waters of Lake Michigan, and Wisconsin's Door County, 17 miles to the south.

The tip of the peninsula is a natural stopping point for songbirds and monarch butterflies as they embark on—or complete—a tiring journey across Lake Michigan.

Fayette Historic State Park

The Garden Peninsula rises higher and higher above the waters of Lake Michigan as it extends south, climbing to 100-foot-high cliffs of limestone as dry and bright white as chalk. Above the high hook of land that forms tight Snail Shell Harbor lies Fayette Historic State Park *(906-644-2603),* a wonderfully restored 19th-century industrial town.

Once the site of a large smelting operation, Fayette's limestone furnaces converted raw iron ore into pig iron that was loaded

Big Spring raft crossing

A Fabulous Freshet

Palms Book State Park guards one of the Upper Peninsula's more remarkable natural attractions. *Kitch-Iti-Kipi*, or "big spring," looks like a deep, dark pool tucked away in a grove of cedars—until you get up close. Then you discover that it's an enormous spring, where crystal-clear water bubbles out of a limestone bowl at a staggering 10,000 to 16,000 gallons per minute, making it the largest fresh-water spring in Michigan.

The park maintains a raft with a hand-powered cable, enabling visitors to propel themselves across the 300-foot-wide spring. From above, peer 45 feet down into its eerie emerald waters and erupting sand bottom, where lunker brown trout glide among the skeletons of downed trees.

The spring—which covers an area of 1.2 acres—is a popular attraction, so come in early morning—or, better yet, in midwinter, when steam billows from the placid pool. For more information, contact the park *(Rte. 2, Box 2500, Manistique, MI 49854, 906-341-2355. www.dnr.state .mi.us; fee)*.

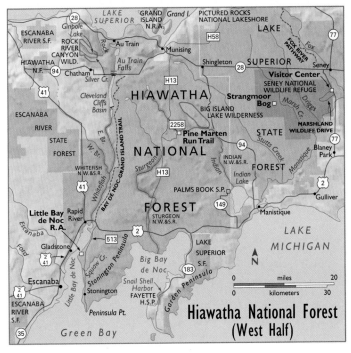

Hiawatha National Forest
(West Half)

onto barges bound for processing centers on the lower Great Lakes. Industrial Fayette boasted a population of about 500, and its loud, hot blast furnaces cranked away seven days a week. By 1891, nearby forests that had fueled the furnace were all but depleted, and more efficient methods of making steel had come into vogue. After more than two decades of operation, the furnaces were permanently shut down.

Nearly a century later, Fayette was reborn as an outstanding historic site and state park, with 20 surviving structures tucked along the sheer white bluffs and deep, clear waters of Snail Shell Harbor. The visitor center gives a good historical overview and features a helpful scale model of the village. You can wander in and out

of the hotel, opera house, homes, and other buildings (open mid-May–mid-Oct.), some intact, some more decayed. Visitors are welcome to explore the grounds anytime. Indeed, an early morning or off-season visit can add to the ghostly appeal of the place.

With the historic townsite acting like a magnet for visitors, the rest of the 711-acre park is often overlooked. It includes a campground and 5 miles of hiking trails, swinging north along the bluffs above Snail Shell Harbor and down to the sand beaches along Big Bay de Noc.

North of Rapid River and Manistique

North of the Stonington Peninsula, the **Bay de Noc-Grand Island Trail** (trailheads 2 miles E of Rapid

Black-eyed Susan, Sand Point

River off City Rd. 509, 10 miles SW of Munising on Mich. 94) follows an old Ojibwa portage route used to carry canoes and supplies between Lakes Michigan and Superior. It hopscotches over a few streams and passes a number of lakes, gradually climbing up the eastern bluff of the Whitefish River and giving hikers high, sweeping views of the forested river valley. Primitive camping is permitted along the entire 40-mile route.

The Whitefish River is a designated national wild and scenic river and a productive trout stream. The Whitefish, Sturgeon, and Indian Wild and Scenic Rivers are all navigable, flowing north-south through this region. They offer paddlers a chance to delve deep into the Hiawatha's peaceful interior, drifting serenely past towering mixed conifers and grassy lowlands.

Where the Indian River crosses Forest Road 2258, the **Pine Marten Run trail network** invites you to sample 26 miles of hiking and horseback trails. Five interconnecting loops wind through huge hemlocks and white pines, as well as bogs and wildlife clearings.

The trail network is named for the small fur-bearing mammal that dens in the hollows or fallen roots of northern conifers. It feeds mainly on small rodents and birds and their eggs, and is an exceptional climber. Related to the sable, the pine marten was once heavily trapped for its fur; as a result, it came close to disappearing from much of the Great Lakes region. Declining interest in (and prices for) furs has helped it rebound.

Rock River Canyon Wilderness

One of six wilderness areas in Hiawatha National Forest, the 5,285-acre Rock River Canyon Wilderness *(4 miles NW of Mich. 94 at Chatham)* protects an area were the Rock River and Silver Creek have carved deep crevices in the soft sandstone, forming dark, narrow canyons 150 feet deep in places.

The moist canyon floors are thick with brush and moisture-loving species such as ferns and fungi. Fat hemlocks cling to ledges, their roots suggesting big, gnarled fingers grasping at the rock. From the late 1800s until the 1930s, nearly all of this area was cut over. Northern hardwoods now cover much of it, with swamp conifers found in wetlands and along streams.

Along the edge of the canyons, sandstone undercuts delve into a 10-foot-deep amphitheater, with water trickling down from above. In winter, it transforms into a magnificent ice cave, with a 50-foot-long curtain of icicles in aqua and polar blue.

In spring, the **Rock River** pours 15 feet over Rock River Falls and continues on to **Ginpole Lake,** a placid, 13-acre wetland hemmed in by canyon walls. Rainbow, brown, and brook trout cruise the shallow waters of the lake. Area wildlife includes muskrat, red squirrel, pileated woodpecker, and ruffed grouse. There are no trails here, but the remnants of old logging roads, two abandoned railroad grades, and a number of ski trails crisscross the area. The only means of access is by bushwhacking. ∎

Lake Superior, Pictured Rocks National Lakeshore

Pictured Rocks
National Lakeshore

■ 73,000 acres ■ Upper Peninsula of Michigan, between Munising and Grand Marais ■ Best months May-Oct. ■ Camping, hiking, boating, kayaking, swimming, fishing, beachcombing, cross-country skiing, snowshoeing, bird-watching, wildlife viewing ■ Adm. fee ■ Contact the national lakeshore, P.O. Box 40, Munising, MI 49862-0040; phone 906-387-3700. www.nps.gov/piro

COLORED SANDSTONE CLIFFS are the marquee attraction at Pictured Rocks National Lakeshore, which stretches 40 miles along the southern edge of Lake Superior. Rising 200 feet straight up from the lake's inky blue waters, the sheer rock faces are bathed in bands of red, yellow, orange, blue, and green. These colorful "pictured rocks" are caused by the water—rich with minerals such as iron, copper, and manganese—that seeps from the rock much like chocolate sauce oozing down a sundae.

The multihued cliffs of Pictured Rocks extend more than 15 miles, sculpted into crazy castle-like turrets, arches, and caves by centuries of pounding waves and pushing ice. The national lakeshore also features a lesser-known but equally spectacular stretch of shoreline called the **Grand Sable Banks,** where 200-foot-high sand dunes climb up from a 5-mile ribbon of sand and pebble beach. Just inland lie kettle lakes, hardwood forests, and clear streams pouring over waterfalls on their hurried path to Lake Superior.

The cliffs are a sandwich of three different rock formations. Mottled red sandstone—Precambrian rock nearly a billion years old—forms the base layer near the lake's surface. Cambrian sandstone, a softer rock some 500 million years old, lies above that; it has eroded into picturesque lakeshore formations such as **Miners Castle** and **Grand Portal Point.** Capping it all is 400-million-year-old Ordovician sandstone, a harder, limy sandstone that protects the underlying sandstone from more rapid erosion.

What to See and Do

Pictured Rocks is a long but narrow reserve, just 3 miles wide in places. County Road H-58 winds roughly along its southern boundary, with short spur roads providing access to overlooks, trailheads, and other park attractions. This road, a large stretch of it unpaved and often deteriorated to washboard, follows an inland route through the trees. It will indeed get you from one end of the lakeshore to the other, but the trip can be slow and somewhat monotonous; plan on a 90-minute trip from one end of the park to the other. You'll want to get out of the car—either on foot or in a boat—to properly explore this spectacular area.

Munising Falls & Sand Point

Just inside the park's western boundary, a 0.7-mile **trail** leads to 50-foot Munising Falls, which spills into a narrow gorge before emptying into Lake Superior's Munising Bay. The falls marks the west trailhead for the **Lakeshore Trail,** a 43-mile segment of the North Country National Scenic Trail, the trail that spans seven states from New York to North Dakota. The Lakeshore Trail runs the length of the Pictured Rocks National Lakeshore—predictably, never far from the water's edge.

Past Munising Falls, Sand Point was home to a Coast Guard Station from the 1930s to the 1960s. Today it serves as the National Lakeshore Headquarters, and also features some interesting Coast Guard and shipwreck artifacts on its grounds. Just across a narrow bay lies the tombolo of Grand Island (see pp. 127-130) and its distinctive (but sadly decaying) wooden lighthouse.

Nearby, the **Sand Point Marsh Trail** (*wheelchair accessible*) spans

Pictured Rocks National Lakeshore

a spruce and cedar wetland created by ancient sand ridges. A half-mile boardwalk, it features 19 interpretive wayside exhibits describing the marsh plants and marsh-loving animals that inhabit the area—including beavers, which have built channels and lodges here.

Miners Castle

This nine-story-high rock formation (*access via end of Miners Castle Rd.*) spotlights the artistry of erosion. At its base, waves have burrowed deep chasms into the sandstone. Boardwalks and steps lead to two viewing platforms out on the rock, where you can peer down into the gloriously clear waters of Lake Superior. If that entices you to do a little beachcombing and wading, a 1-mile-long trail from Miners Castle leads down some steps through the pines to inviting Miners Beach and the mouth of the Miners River. Farther upstream, the river tumbles 40 feet over a rocky escarpment; to see it, follow the signs for Miners Falls.

Chapel Basin

Chapel Falls is the key attraction of the Chapel Basin area, the next auto-accessible spot along the national lakeshore. Amid a pale birch forest, frothing water drops like a horsetail some 60 feet into a deep gorge and **Chapel Lake** below. Continue past the falls for another 1.75 miles to reach **Chapel Beach,** where river otters sometimes frolic along the water's edge and the hoofprints of white-tailed deer stitch the sand.

At Chapel Beach, turn right (east) on the Lakeshore Trail and follow it 1.5 miles to **Spray Falls.** In one of the park's loveliest and least visited waterfalls, **Spray Creek** drops over the sandstone cliffs 70 feet into Lake Superior.

If you turn left (west) instead of right at Chapel Beach, you can make a 10-mile loop around the ravine-like Chapel Basin. Along the way, you'll pass **Grand Portal Point**—another significant Pictured Rocks landmark—before returning to the parking area.

The Chapel Basin area also includes another sublime falls west of Grand Portal Point: The **Mosquito River** spills over a series of ledges, creating an accessible waterfall calm enough for wading and soaking fatigued hiking feet. A new trail (*access end of Chapel Rd.*) leads to various sections of the falls and links up with the Lakeshore Trail.

Beaver Lake

Located near the park's center, 800-acre Beaver Lake is the largest inland lake in Pictured Rocks. It's a classic kettle lake, formed when the outwash of receding glaciers buried an enormous block of ice. The block made a huge depression in the land, which subsequently filled with the meltwater.

Anglers are drawn to Beaver Lake and the tributaries that feed it, especially for the trout that cruise its depths and the bass that favor the grassy beds near shore. Boats on Beaver Lake and **Little Beaver Lake** (connected by a small channel) are limited to 10 horsepower or less, making this a pleasant waterway for paddlers. Little Beaver has one of the park's three auto-accessible campgrounds, with eight sites available on a first-come, first-served basis. (Wetlands cover much of the land between Beaver Lake and Lake Superior, so bugs can be a problem, especially in June and early July.)

Two good hiking trails leave from the Little Beaver Lake Campground. The short and pleasant 0.7-mile **White Pine Trail** is a self-guided nature path circling through a 300-year-old pine forest that took hold on an old glacial riverbed. The 5-mile **Beaver Basin Loop Trail** makes a lap around Little Beaver and Big Beaver Lakes, then along the Lake Superior shore past sea caves cut by the lake's pounding waves. Boardwalks skirt the wetlands before returning you to the trailhead.

Twelvemile Beach and Au Sable Point

The Beaver Basin marks the west end of Twelvemile Beach, a pristine ribbon of sand. This is the kind of spot that makes Lake Superior so special: You can walk the beach and watch curling waves for hours, with nothing for company but peregrine falcons, bald eagles, and perhaps even the occasional black bear trundling through the sand.

Au Sable Point thrusts northward into Lake Superior at the east end of Twelvemile Beach. The Au Sable Light Station, built in 1874, guided ships around the point for decades; today, the restored light and keeper's home is open for tours in July and August.

Unfortunately, Au Sable Point was just the proverbial tip of the iceberg when it came to the area's navigational hazards: Sandstone shoals extend out from Au Sable Point for nearly a mile, leaving waters as shallow as six feet.

At least 10 ships have wrecked here. As you walk the North Country National Scenic Trail from the Hurricane River Campground *(off Cty. Rd. H-58 along Hurricane River),* you may still encounter partial skeletons of these century-old ships, sometimes strewn on the beach, sometimes poking through the sand in Superior's shallows.

Just east of Au Sable Point and one mile north of County Road H-58, the **Log Slide Overlook** marks the site of a once-busy logging operation. In the late 1800s, loggers used this high point—some 300 feet above Lake Superior—to send freshly cut logs down to the

Following pages: Grand Sable Dunes, Pictured Rocks National Lakeshore

Chapel Rock, near Grand Portal Point

Grand Sable Banks and Dunes

Slanting up from Lake Superior at a rakish 30-degree angle, the imposing Grand Sable (French for "big sands") Banks and Dunes stretch nearly five miles. The banks refer to the high gravel bar beneath the dunes, formed when retreating glaciers dumped loads of gravel and debris in a deep rift. Today the gravelly banks rise more than 250 feet high.

Atop the banks lie Lake Superior's largest dunes, adding another 50 or 75 feet in height. These are perched dunes; formed by winds carrying sand up from beaches, they are the centerpiece in an ever-shifting landscape that changes with the wind and the water levels. Near the Grand Sable Visitor Center, a quarter-mile **trail** *(access from Sable Falls parking lot)* winds into the dunes, where marram grass, beach pea, and sand cherry cling to the sand for dear life.

water's edge. After being rafted to Grand Marais, the logs were loaded on Great Lakes schooners. Today, you can stand on a platform and marvel at the view—the lighthouse to your left, the Grand Sable dunes to your right, the brilliant blue of the big lake filling the horizon.

Just south of the dunes, on County Road H-58, **Grand Sable**

Lake glitters in the afternoon sun. A kettle lake created by glaciers, it has sandy shores and often-warm waters that make it an inviting spot for a swim or a picnic. Sable Creek spills from the north end of the lake, then drops in tiers through a narrow canyon and out to a rocky Lake Superior beach. The **Sable Falls Trail** (*access from Sable Falls parking lot*), essentially a series of steps, offers several vantage points of this lovely falls.

From the Water

The best view of Pictured Rocks National Lakeshore comes from the water, where you can properly appreciate the colored cliff faces that give the park its name. Pictured Rocks Cruises (*906-387-2379. Mid-May–mid-Oct.*) in Munising offers trips up and down the lakeshore.

For an even more dramatic view, consider slithering along the corrugated rock in a sea kayak. Local outfitters offer day-long trips even for rank beginners. Weather permitting, guides will draw you in close enough to touch the multihued sandstone, which looks much brighter up close. You can poke in and out of sea caves, nooks, and crannies, perhaps feeling the splash of a waterfall as it pitches over the cliffs into Lake Superior. ■

Grand Island National Recreation Area

■ 13,500 acres ■ Near south-central shore of Lake Superior ■ Best months May-Oct. Ferries run Mem. Day–early Oct. ■ Camping, hiking, backpacking, kayaking, fishing, mountain biking, cross-country skiing, snowshoeing, bird-watching, wildflower viewing, van tours ■ Adm. fee. ■ No drinking water available on Grand Island; bring water or water-purifier ■ Contact Munising Ranger District, Hiawatha National Forest, Rte. 2, Box 400, Munising, MI 49862; phone 906-387-2512. www.fs.fed.us/r9/hiawatha/grand.htm

TUCKED UP TIGHT AGAINST THE UPPER PENINSULA mainland, Grand Island practically looms over Munising—less than half a mile away, the island looks as if you could almost hurl a rock to its shores. And though reachable by ferry in just 15 minutes, Grand Island is effectively isolated by the surrounding waters of Lake Superior, giving it a distinctly off-the-beaten-path feel.

The largest island along Lake Superior's southern shore—8 miles long and 3 miles wide—Grand Island lives up to its name in more than just size. Beautiful burnt-red cliffs of Jacobsville sandstone line its western shore, rising nearly 200 feet from the lake and rivaling the nearby Pictured Rocks. With the exception of a 40-acre patch of private property, the island is owned and managed by Hiawatha National Forest as a relatively undeveloped forest area the size of Manhattan. Here black bears, coyotes, foxes, and wolves wander undisturbed through woodlands; loons

Wooden lighthouse, Grand Island

bob in sand-ringed bays; and the occasional peregrine falcon or eagle wheels overhead.

Like neighboring Pictured Rocks National Lakeshore, Grand Island is composed of various types of sandstone, shaped by ice sheets that advanced and retreated ice sheets during the last ice age some 10,000 years ago. The bluffs, terraces, and beaches are more recent, largely the work of Lake Superior's cutting waves. Most of the island has only a thin layer of soil atop the sandstone, supporting mostly beech, maple, and jack pine forest, mixed with shrubby ground cover such as wintergreen or blueberries. A few large hemlocks remain, too, though most were logged or lost to windstorms. Some wetlands exist inland, especially around 228-acre **Echo Lake,** the island's largest.

Humans have occupied Grand Island for more than 3,000 years. There is much evidence of the Ojibwa, who summered on the island

Kayakers, Trout Bay, Grand Island

from the mid-1600s to the mid-1800s. They would arrive here in spring for maple sugaring; after clearing fields, planting corn and squash, and fishing the bays, they left in the fall for hunting grounds on the mainland.

By the 1840s, white settlers had arrived. In the early 1900s, the Cleveland Cliffs Iron Company used the island as a private hunting preserve for the firm's executives and stockholders. Caribou, moose, elk, pronghorn, and game birds were all introduced to the island, while various non-native trees and shrubs were planted to accommodate their dietary needs. In 1990, the federal government purchased Grand Island and turned it over to Hiawatha National Forest.

What to See and Do

Exploring the Island

Grand Island is served by passenger ferry from Munising, Michigan. *(For ferry information and reservations, contact ALTRAN, 906-387-3503.)* The island is not open to public auto traffic.

About 50 miles of trails crisscross Grand Island, mostly old roadbeds. A mountain bike is the best way to make a 23-mile trip around the island. Nearly all the trails are wide, relatively flat, and suitable for most skill levels.

From the ferry dock at Williams Landing, it's about a 2-mile trip to a **day-use area** on **Murray Bay,** where a blanket of pine needles and a sandy curve of beach make a fine picnic spot. One of the island's two designated campgrounds—primitive sites with pit toilets and fire rings—is here; the other is at **Trout Bay.** Backcountry camping is permitted elsewhere on the island.

The gravel road that traces the island's eastern shore narrows and rises as it continues north. A split-rail fence marks the Trout Bay overlook, with Lake Superior now glimmering far below. Across the water, Pictured Rocks National Lakeshore stretches off to the northeast. Following the shoreline roads, it's about another 7 miles to the island's remote northern point, characterized by high cliffs, creeks, and untouched beaches. In recent years, peregrine falcons have nested nearby.

If you desire a shorter adventure, head northwest from the ferry dock across the island. After four miles on the trail, you'll skirt the lower end of mile-long Echo Lake, which is largely surrounded by marshlands buzzing with insects and bullfrogs. Though somewhat difficult to access, the shallow lake is an excellent smallmouth bass fishery.

After another half-mile, the woods suddenly give way to the wide blue landscape of Lake Superior at **Mather Beach.** Gnarled limbs of driftwood, worn smooth by sand and waves, scatter along a soft sand beach. From here, it's a 4-mile trip (mostly downhill) along a grassy shoreline trail and through a grove of red pines back to the ferry landing.

Van Tour

Vans operating under special permit offer 2.5-hour tours of the island *(906-387-4845 for reservations and ticket information).* As you bump along dirt roads and stop at several overlooks, guides discuss the island's history.

Kayaking

Grand Island offers superb kayaking, especially near the bluffs and caves around Trout Bay. Local outfitters offer trips for all experience levels. However, only accomplished paddlers should attempt even the short crossing to Grand Island without a guide, or venture farther around the island. The waters of Lake Superior are quick-changing and very cold; waves can be six feet or more, while currents in the bays and along the rock cliffs are treacherous. Experienced paddlers should budget two or three days to circumnavigate the island. ■

Williams Landing, Grand Island

Sunken ship's female figurehead

Graveyards of the Great Lakes

For centuries, the Great Lakes were like today's interstates—the fastest and most efficient way to get around. Schooners and freighters hauled commodities such as lumber and iron ore from the forests and mines to Great Lakes ports. Steamships transported passengers from southern Great Lakes urban areas to imbibe the fresh, cool air of northern resorts.

Unfortunately, the Great Lakes are also known for shallow reefs, clocking winds, and violently exploding storms. An estimated 6,000 vessels have been wrecked there. Unlike oceans, the fresh, cold, barnacle-free waters of the Great Lakes keep wrecks exceptionally well preserved, even after decades under water. Many of them remain where they went down, undisturbed and almost unchanged, like submerged museums.

About one-third of the shipwrecks lie in Michigan's waters. In areas where wrecks are particularly prevalent, the state has established underwater preserves, protecting the shipwrecks for their historic significance, and mapping and marking them for divers. Together, they cover 1,900 square miles of Great Lakes bottomland—an area about the size of Delaware.

Underwater preserves are located off the Keweenaw Peninsula, Marquette, Munising, and Whitefish Point on Lake Superior; around the Straits of Mackinac, off Thunder Bay, the tip of the Thumb, and the Sanilac Shores on Lake Huron; and along the Manitou Passage on Lake Michigan. Dive charters serve all the preserves. For more information, contact the Michigan Underwater Preserve Council *(560 N. State St., St. Ignace, MI 49781. 800-338-6660).*

Nondivers can inspect the century-old shipwrecks between Grand Island and the Upper Peninsula mainland from the comfort of a glass-bottom boat. Here, in **Lake Superior's Alger Underwater Preserve,** you can peer down at three different shipwrecks, one in as little as 10 feet of water. They fill the viewing windows in the hull like historic paintings, perfectly visible in the clear water and looking close enough to touch. For information and reservations, contact Shipwreck Tours, Inc. *(1204 Commercial St., Munising, MI 49862. 906-387-4477. www.shipwrecktours.com; operates June-Sept.).*

Swans, Seney NWR

Seney National Wildlife Refuge

■ 95,238 acres ■ Michigan's Upper Peninsula, 35 miles east of Munising ■ Best months May–mid-Oct. Visitor center and Marshland Wildlife Drive open mid-May–mid-Oct. ■ Hiking, walking, canoeing, fishing, biking, mountain biking, snowshoeing, bird-watching, wildlife viewing, wildflower viewing, auto tour ■ Contact the refuge, HCR 2, Box 1, Seney, MI 49883; phone 906-586-9851. midwest.fws.gov/seney/index.htm

"HELLTOWN IN THE PINE!" That's what loggers once called the small settlement of Seney, now little more than a crossroads in the central Upper Peninsula. For in the 1880s, Seney—situated along a railroad siding and the Fox River—was the rollicking center of a logging trade that had crept northward after depleting the lucrative stands of red and white pine farther south and west.

Unfortunately, the Seney area, with its sandy soils and mats of wetlands, never boasted the valuable timber found elsewhere in the northern Great Lakes. The pines that did grow here were leveled quickly. Loggers took the smaller conifers next, burning the scrub as they went, and deeply scarring the fragile soils of the denuded land. Optimistic farmers came in after that, burning brush and draining the wetlands with mile after mile of 20-foot ditches.

Finally, in the 1930s, humans began helping instead of hurting the beleaguered land. Seney National Wildlife Refuge was established in 1935, and the Civilian Conservation Corps began building a series of dikes and control ponds to restore the wetlands. Today these dikes form part of an intricate control system that raises and lowers the water levels in 21 pools, thus simulating a natural wetlands cycle. Along with more than 7,000 acres in these pools, thousands of acres of wetlands and uplands extend beyond, all of it providing a sanctuary and nesting area for a rich variety of wildlife.

Large, boisterous Canada geese serve as the local hosts at the Seney Visitor Center, where you'll find displays and handouts to help you make the most of your visit. The **Pine Ridge Nature Trail** departs from the visitor center, looping 1.5 miles through a wetland habitat. Hikers and cyclists are also welcome to traverse the hundred miles of dikes in the refuge, which offer an even better chance of spotting birds. Feathered visitors to Seney include a wide variety of ducks, songbirds, sandpipers, terns, and scores of others. Trumpeter swans were released here between 1991 and 1993 and are now seen regularly. Tundra swans also migrate through in spring and fall.

Many birds of prey also frequent the refuge. Among them are the merlin, American kestrel, northern harrier, peregrine falcon, bald eagle, and osprey, as well as a variety of owls (great horned, snowy, barred, long-eared, short-eared, and the northern saw-whet) and a number of nesting hawk species, including sharp-shinned, Cooper's, rough-legged, and broad-winged.

Just as notable are the mammals that ply the refuge. Though few visitors ever catch a glimpse of them, moose, wolves, fishers, and pine marten are all present here in growing numbers. The dense jack pine forests in Seney—regenerated from logging days—also provide ideal habitat for snowshoe hare.

The **Marshland Wildlife Drive** forms a 7-mile loop among the refuge pools, with several interpretive signs along the way. The route includes three observation decks equipped with spotting scopes. It

Water lilies, Seney NWR

also passes an eagle's nest and pools favored by sandhill cranes, loons, and swans.

Paddling is an excellent way to explore Seney National Wildlife Refuge. The easily navigable Manistique River scribbles through Seney's western end. Rent canoes or arrange a trip for yourself through North-land Outfitters *(906-585-9801)* or put-in at the roadside pull-off on Mich. 77 *(1 mile S of Germfask).*

One of the refuge's most unusual features, **Strangmoor Bog,** lies deep in the wetlands near its western boundary. Strangmoors, or string bogs, are fingerlike bogs alternating with sand ridges that are relics of ancient beaches. They are typically found only in Arctic and subarctic regions, making Seney's bog one of the southernmost examples of them in North America. Because the bog lies within the refuge's designated 25,000-acre wilderness area, it is not easily accessible. ■

Lake Superior State Forest

■ 1.1 million acres ■ Eastern end of Michigan's Upper Peninsula ■ Camping, hiking, kayaking, canoeing, fishing, swimming, biking, bird-watching, wildlife viewing ■ Year-round. Best bird-watching April-May, Sept.-Oct. ■ Contact the state forest, 5100 State Hwy. 123, Newberry, MI 49868; phone 906-293-5131

STRETCHING FROM THE EASTERN END of Pictured Rocks National Lakeshore to the St. Marys River and Drummond Island in Lake Huron, and from the south shore of Lake Superior to the north shore of Lake Michigan, this swath of land remains one of the most inaccessible and lightly traveled in the entire Great Lakes region—a long-ago pine forest reduced to sandy or marshy cutover land by turn-of-the-20th-century loggers.

Far more rivers than roads twist through the north-central part of the state forest. Clear, spring-fed waters, such as the Fox and the Tahquamenon, are prized by anglers and paddlers who know that the extra effort required to reach their banks will be well rewarded.

A far less dramatic landscape than the nearby Pictured Rocks area, the land here flattens out but has its own quiet charms—from secluded lakes to blue-ribbon trout streams to wetlands rich with the twill of birds.

In 1919, Ernest Hemingway stepped off a train in Seney, asked for a good trout stream, and was directed up an old railroad grade to the east branch of the Fox River. That experience yielded "Big Two-Hearted River," a Nick Adams short story. (Though Hemingway fished the Fox, he chose the more lyrical name of the Two Hearted, which flows 25 miles to the northeast.) As a result, the Fox has always carried a special cachet in the Upper Peninsula and among trout fishermen. The allure has a lot to do with the Fox's reputation for enormous brook trout, 15 inches and longer, lurking beneath its smooth-flowing surface.

What to See and Do

Open to nonmotorized use only, the **Fox River Pathway** stretches 27 miles from Seney to just shy of Pictured Rocks National Lakeshore. At its southern end, the trail parallels the Fox's main channel for 10 miles, then follows the Little Fox and the west branch. Heading north, the path traverses the Kingston Plains, one of the Upper Peninsula's most productive logging areas, where loggers left behind vast stump prairies. Markers along the route provide informa-

tion about the logging.

At the pathway's terminus at **Kingston Lake Campground,** a lovely hiking trail winds through cool pines and sunny blueberry patches. This is part of the **Pictured Rocks Buffer Zone,** a section of Lake Superior State Forest that offers additional protection for the national lakeshore's ecosystems. The trail spills out onto a particularly deserted and delightful stretch of **Twelve-mile Beach** on Lake Superior, a segment

Sunset near mouth of Two Hearted River, Lake Superior State Forest

belonging to Pictured Rocks National Lakeshore.

South of Muskallonge Lake State Park, the state forest's **Pretty Lakes Quiet Area** *(27 miles NW of Newberry via Mich. 123 and Cty. Rds. 407 and 416)* encompasses five small, clear lakes. Some are ringed with sand beach; all are linked by short portages. Motors are banned in this out-of-the-way spot, so you can relax to the whistle of loons rather than the whine of powerboats and passing cars.

West of Newberry, the headwaters of the **Tahquamenon River** bubble up from beneath the ground and begin a gentle roll through stands of pine and vast wetlands. Rambling and twisting northeast through Luce County, the river grows wide and majestic by the time it enters its namesake state park and thunders over the state's largest waterfall.

With the notable exception of Tahquamenon Falls (see p. 194), nearly all 94 miles of the Tahquamenon are excellent for paddling. Beyond Newberry, the river meanders far from roads, rolling through rich woodlands where bear, deer, and otter occasionally wander down to its banks. Canoes can be rented from Marks Rod and Reel Repair in Newberry (906-293-5608) or from Northland Outfitters in Germfask (906-586-9801).

Northeast of Newberry, the shoreline sharpens to a sliver at **Whitefish Point.** Because most birds avoid crossing large bodies of water unless necessary, this northward-jutting point forms a natural corridor for migrating birds, funneling them to the tip.

Finches and hawks lead the migration in April. Toward the end of the month, loons wing through by the thousands, along with common shorebirds and unusual species such as arctic loons and arctic terns. Songbirds follow in May. The entire migration can be more spectacular still in fall.

Even without the staggering number of migrating birds, this wave-washed point is a fine spot for beachcombing or watching gulls and plovers skitter along the surf line. Small dunes anchored by jack pines rise behind the beach. Trails wind up the dunes and to the end of the point. ■

Whitefish Point

Edmund Fitzgerald

The Mystery of the *Edmund Fitzgerald*

At dusk on November 10, 1975, the 729-foot lake carrier *Edmund Fitzgerald* was rounding the Keweenaw Peninsula on her way from Superior, Wisconsin, to the port of Detroit, when one of the worst storms in 30 years screamed across Lake Superior.

The *Fitzgerald* was prepared for bad weather. Superior is notorious for its November gales, and like the captain of the *Arthur M. Anderson* traveling nearby, the *Fitzgerald's* captain had chosen a more protected route across the lake, some 20 to 40 miles farther north than usual. Ominously, however, the 90-mph winds began to shift from northeast to northwest, leaving the ships exposed to the brunt of the storm. At 7:10 p.m., the *Fitzgerald's* captain reported, "We are holding our own." Five minutes later—without a single distress call—the *Fitzgerald* disappeared from the *Anderson's* radar screen.

When the storm cleared, the wreck of the *Fitzgerald* was found in 530 feet of water, just 17 miles from the shelter of Whitefish Bay. She lay at the bottom in two pieces, 170 feet apart. Debris was scattered over three acres—evidence of the force with which the massive hull hit bottom.

But even after an exhaustive Coast Guard investigation and several dives to the site, no one really knows what happened. The Coast Guard's best deduction is that the ship, which had taken on water through leaking hatches and developed a list, was tossed forward by enormous waves and torpedoed bow first. Others believe that she scraped bottom on uncharted shoals or snapped in two when caught between two particularly large waves. Whatever the cause, it happened quickly: Divers confirmed that no attempt had been made by the crew to detach the lifeboats on the laker's deck.

The *Edmund Fitzgerald* remains at the bottom of Superior, along with her 29 crewmen. It ranks among the worst modern-day disasters on the Great Lakes—a constant reminder of the power of these inland seas.

Tahquamenon Falls State Park

■ 36,000 acres ■ East end of Michigan's Upper Peninsula ■ Year-round
■ Camping, hiking, walking, canoeing, fishing, cross-country skiing, bird-watching
■ Adm. fee ■ Contact the park, 41382 West M-123, Paradise, MI 49768; phone
906-492-3415. www.dnr.state.mi.us

IN A LAND RICH WITH WATERFALLS, the grand Tahquamenon trumps them all. With the roar of a freight train and the power of a fire hose, the Tahquamenon River plunges over a 50-foot sandstone ledge, creating a golden fountain 200 feet wide. As much as 50,000 gallons of water per second gush over Upper Tahquamenon Falls, making it the second largest falls (by volume) east of the Mississippi, outdone only by Niagara.

Tahquamenon is made even more majestic by its color—streaks of bronze and amber from the tannic acid of cedar and hemlock swamps drained by the river. Voyageurs' diaries from the 1700s refer to the unusual color of the falls. The Tahquamenon was also chronicled by Henry Wadsworth Longfellow: In his epic poem about the Ojibwa, *Hiawatha,* he describes how Hiawatha built his canoe along the banks "of the rushing Tahquamenaw."

What to See and Do

Accessing Tahquamenon Falls is easy. Both the Upper Falls and the Lower Falls are located within a state park that has provided short, well-marked paths to prime viewing sites. At the **Upper Falls,** a **trail** leads from the parking lot down a long series of steps to an observation deck. The path hovers close enough to the cascade that you can feel the thundering power of the falls and its cool mist on your face.

Four miles downstream, the Tahquamenon plunges again, this time over a series of cascades known as the **Lower Falls.** The best vantage point is from a small island mid-river, where a short trail leads you right to the base of the mist-shrouded falls (which are particularly spectacular in winter). Canoes and rowboats are available to rent for the short river crossing.

Focused on the dramatic centerpiece of Tahquamenon Falls, many visitors understandably overlook the rest of this park, Michigan's second largest. In sharp contrast to the often frenzied crowds at the falls, most of the park remains almost untouched— free of roads, buildings, or power lines, but etched with 25 miles of little-used hiking trails.

A 12-mile segment of the **North Country National Scenic Trail** (*access at Upper or Lower Falls*) roughly parallels the river, though rarely close enough for water views. At the east end of the park the North Country NST meets up with the **Rivermouth Campground,** where the Tahquamenon flows into Superior's **Whitefish Bay.** ■

Upper Falls, Tahquamenon Falls State Park

Fisherman, north side of Drummond Island

Drummond Island

■ 87,000 acres ■ Off east end of Michigan's Upper Peninsula in Lake Huron
■ Year-round ■ Hiking, fishing, kayaking, canoeing, mountain biking, cross-country skiing, snowshoeing, bird-watching, wildlife viewing ■ Contact Drummond
Island Tourism Association, Box 200, Drummond Island, MI 49726; phone 906-
493-5245 or 800-737-8666. www.drummond-island.com. For auto ferry information, contact Drummond Island Ferry, 906-235-3170.

THOUGH IT STANDS OUT as the largest U.S. island in the Great Lakes,
Drummond Island is a subtle place. Tourist trappings are few, and coves
and beaches lie hidden behind a tangle of trees. Black bears, white-tailed
deer, bobcats, and even a few moose inhabit the island. More than half
the island is state-owned, managed by Lake Superior State Forest.

Most of Drummond's attractions are along its shores. Some 150 miles
of lakeshore, ragged with coves and harbors, ring the island. Along its
eastern shore, the land rises into 175-foot-high bluffs at **Marble Head.**
Potagannissing Bay takes a bite out of the island's northwest corner, with
more than 40 named islands scattered through its deep blue waters. They
range from **Harbor Island,** the largest, with a long and narrow cove, to
tiny **Propellor,** probably named for the number of boat props it has
destroyed.

Inland, though well-marked hiking trails are few, miles of old truck
trails and snowmobile routes snake across the island. (Drive where you
dare, but be aware that many roads disintegrate into rough washboard or
deep sand.) In spring, roadsides brighten with the pale yellow of pussy
willows, and warblers migrate through in force in May.

Morel mushrooms hide among leaf litter and decaying tree trunks. In
late spring, the island erupts in a riot of wildflowers, from marsh mari-
golds in low-lying areas around the **Potagannissing River** to trillium and
two dozen species of orchids in the woods. ■

The Straits of Mackinac

■ Where Upper and Lower Peninsulas of Michigan meet; surrounding islands and shoreline ■ Best months May-Oct. Ferry service to Mackinac Island and Bois Blanc Island seasonal; ice road to Mackinac makes passage possible in winter by ski or snowmobile. Other islands accessible only by private boat ■ Hiking, boating, biking, cross-country skiing, snowshoeing, bird-watching, wildflower viewing ■ Adm. fee for state parks ■ Contact Mackinac Island Chamber of Commerce, Box 451, Mackinac Island, MI 49757; phone 800-454-5227 or 906-847-3783. www.mackinacisland.org

"THE STRAITS" IS MICHIGAN SHORTHAND for the Straits of Mackinac (pronounced MAK-i-naw), the 5-mile-wide passage that links Lakes Huron and Michigan—and cuts the state of Michigan in two.

In many ways, the break between the two parts of the state is emotional as well as geographical. Until the Mackinac Bridge was completed in 1957, the only way across the straits was by ferry or private boat. This effectively stymied development of the Upper Peninsula and contributed to a longstanding rivalry between Lower Peninsula residents, who sometimes view the Upper Peninsula as a bug-infested backwater, and the "Yoopers" who relish their outdoor lifestyle and feel little affinity with their neighbors to the south.

The Straits of Mackinac have been a crossroads for hundreds of years, navigated by Native Americans, French-Canadian voyageurs, European explorers, feuding French and British soldiers, commercial fishermen, passenger steamships, and a wide range of commercial shipping traffic. They remain a point of convergence for the state today—a place where quiet, wooded isles lie just a stone's throw from the gilded Victorian retreat of Mackinac Island, and where the two disparate halves of Michigan are forced to meet, if only by the tenuous tether of a man-made bridge.

What to See and Do

Mackinac Island

The native Ojibwa and Ottawa Indians called Mackinac Island *Michilimackinac*, "the great turtle," which pretty accurately describes the hump of limestone that is the 3.5-square-mile island.

Mackinac, its neighboring islands, and **Waugoshance Point** in **Wilderness State Park** are all part of the same limestone escarpment formed by a prehistoric tropical sea. The Indians summered here and on nearby Bois Blanc Island, hunting in the island's forests, fishing its productive waters, and traveling through the straits to trade some of their harvest for grains and vegetables with tribes farther south.

In 1817, Mackinac became the headquarters of the American Fur Company. The company bartered with the Native Americans for the area's beaver pelts and stored them in warehouses on

Mackinac Island

Mackinac, until overhunting devastated the fur industry and commercial fishing became the island's mainstay.

By the second half of the 19th century, Mackinac had evolved into a gracious getaway, promoted by railroads and steamship lines for its clear, cool, pollen-free air. Mackinac has freeze-framed this era: Today it is renowned as a Victorian-era fairy-tale resort, free of cars and filled with grand gingerbread mansions and the clip-clop of horse-drawn carriages.

Few visitors realize that 78 percent of the island is state park. **Mackinac Island State Park** comprises a restored 18th-century fort and largely undeveloped woodlands, crisscrossed with hiking and biking trails and sprinkled with rare wildflowers and sculpted limestone outcroppings.

The natural history of Mackinac Island has attracted scientific observation for nearly 200 years. In the early 19th century, botanist Thomas Nuttall listed some 60 plant species growing on the

island, more than a third of them previously unknown. Some of the flowers first recorded on Mackinac Island include the salmonberry, northern orchid, bird's-eye primrose, pitcher's thistle, calypso orchid, northern wild comfrey, pink pyrola, and the dwarf lake iris.

Early scientists also marveled at the island's distinctive geology, which is mostly brecciated limestone that has been sculpted and massaged by eons of wind and waves. The result is some dramatic rock formations: the giant inland slab of limestone called **Sugar Loaf Rock,** the lakeside caves of **Devil's Kitchen,** and impressive **Arch Rock,** which rises nearly 150 feet above the eastern shore and spans some 50 feet.

A paved 8-mile **path** (*Mich. 185*) circles the island. Never straying far from the shoreline, it passes some well-marked trails—such as the one from Fort Mackinac to Arch Rock—that lead inland to many of the island's natural features. Beach pea, wrinkled rose,

Fort Mackinac, Mackinac Island

and silverweed bloom along the limestone gravel shoreline, and swallows often swoop down from their nests in the crooks of limestone cliffs. All six species of eastern swallows—bank, cliff, barn, tree, rough-winged, and purple martin—inhabit the island.

Even a casual walk inland is a treat, where fuchsia gaywing and colonies of snow-white trillium brighten woodlands of red oak and beech. Because the island was never farmed to any significant extent, the old trees extend their canopy high above, giving the woods an airy feel. If you intend to hike inland, be prepared for steep hills as you scale the back of "the great turtle." Contact Mackinac Island State Park *(P.O. Box 370, Mackinac Island, MI 49757. 231-436-4100. www.mackinac.com/his toricparks)* for more information.

Bois Blanc Island

Overshadowing Mackinac in size but certainly not stature, Bois Blanc is a simple, somnolent place, home to a handful of summer houses, a general store, and towering stands of century-old red and white pine in its interior. Pronounced "Bob-Lo" by locals, Bois Blanc takes its name ("white wood" in French) from the birch forests that once covered much of the outer island.

More than half of the 12-mile-long island belongs to Mackinaw State Forest. A gravel road rings the island, and several other routes—ranging from gravel to nearly impassable sand—wind inland. Well-marked trails here are few, but you can easily find your way to the island's interior lakes or a secluded and sandy swimming beach. On rockier stretches of beach, look for fossils in the limestone—evidence of an ancient Silurian sea.

Bois Blanc is served by ferry from Cheboygan. Overnight visitors can stay at rental cottages or at a primitive state forest campground on the island's northwest shore. *(For ferry services, contact Plaunt Transportation 888-752-8687 or 231-627-2354.)*

Wilderness State Park

Across the Mackinac Bridge in the Lower Peninsula, Waugoshance

Point stretches west into Lake Michigan and dribbles off into a series of islands. This is the fine setting for 8,286-acre Wilderness State Park. Twelve miles of trails trace sandy beaches and limestone ledges, dipping into forested dunes where pine trees have taken hold. Three of the most popular paths are **East Ridge** (1 mile one-way), **Red Pine** (1.25 miles one-way), and **Sturgeon Bay** (2.25 miles one-way), all of which can be combined to make for a longer hike.

The endangered Great Lakes piping plover is among the many avian residents that appreciate the solitude of Wilderness State Park. These small shorebirds nest here in spring and early summer, keeping company with terns, ducks, and other waterbirds. Cormorants dry their wings on weathered gray driftwood stumps, while great blue herons stand frozen in the grassy beds along the point's southern shore. Contact Wilderness State Park *(898 Wilderness Park Dr., Carp Lake, MI 49718. 231-436-5381)* for more information.

Grass Bay Preserve

On the east side of the Mackinac Bridge, the Nature Conservancy's Grass Bay Preserve protects one of the Great Lakes' finest examples of interdunal wetland habitat, with beach pools, marshes, flats, and wetlands all separated by low dunes. This delicate ecosystem supports a great diversity of plants, including 11 types of conifers.

The Nature Conservancy considers Grass Bay one of its most significant properties. The preserve's original 80 acres have grown to more than 700, including a 1-mile stretch of Lake Huron shore. From May to September, Grass Bay is noted for its carpet of wildflowers, including lady's slipper, blue harebell, and sundew. Access is only by field trips led by The Nature Conservancy *(2840 E. Grand River Ave., East Lansing, MI 48823. 517-332-1741).* ■

Mackinac Island

Sleeping Bear Dunes National Lakeshore

■ 71,000 acres ■ Northwestern shore of Lower Peninsula of Michigan
■ Best seasons spring-fall. Ferry service to South Manitou Island May-Oct., to North Manitou May-Nov. ■ Camping, hiking, backpacking, boating, kayaking, canoeing, swimming, scuba diving, beachcombing, fishing, biking, cross-country skiing, snowshoeing, bird-watching, wildlife viewing, wildflower viewing, auto tour, historic sites ■ Adm. fee ■ Contact the national lakeshore, 9922 Front St., Hwy. M-72, Empire, MI 49630; phone 231-326-5134. www.nps.gov/slbe

Empire Bluffs and the view north across the Lake Michigan shore

GLACIERS AND MILLENNIA OF WIND AND WATER have sculpted Sleeping Bear Dunes National Lakeshore, a 35-mile-long wonder of forests and immense mounds of sand that rise up in pyramids along the shoreline of Lake Michigan.

The glaciers that scrubbed across this region during the last ice age 10,000 years ago left behind heaps of rubble and ground much of the shoreline into fine-grained sand. That, along with the prevailing western winds that blow across Lake Michigan, proved to be the perfect recipe for building dunes. Beach dunes—dunes created by wind blowing beach sand onto low-lying shores—line the southern part of this national seashore. Perched dunes, built by wind-blown sand accumulating atop piles of glacial debris, sit high on the bluffs.

It is these perched dunes for which the national lakeshore is known.

Great buff-colored mountains of sand, they climb from Lake Michigan to the sky at an impossible angle. At their highest, the lakeshore's perched dunes once measured 600 feet high. Today they top out at approximately 460 feet.

The Ojibwa named the Sleeping Bear Dunes. According to legend, a mother bear and her two cubs were driven from a raging forest fire in what is now Wisconsin, and in desperation they were forced to swim across Lake Michigan. The mother reached the far shore and climbed to the top of a bluff to await her cubs, who had grown tired and lagged behind. The lakeshore's largest dune, Sleeping Bear, is the mother bear lying in wait. The Manitou Islands that lie offshore are the cubs, which tragically drowned.

In all, Sleeping Bear Dunes National Lakeshore encompasses 35 miles of scalloped Lake Michigan shoreline, both North and South Manitou Islands, lakes, rivers, beech and maple forest, waving dune grasses, clattering beach peas...and always those unforgettable dunes.

What to See and Do

Southern Lakeshore

Start your visit to Sleeping Bear Dunes National Lakeshore in Empire, where the visitor center offers an orientation slide program and various displays, as well as maps and information.

South of Empire, the 0.75-mile **Empire Bluff Trail** furnishes one of the park's best overviews of Sleeping Bear and the other perched dunes. The trail climbs through old farm fields and orchards, then crests above a forest of maple, poplar, and sumac before erupting into a clearing. From the boardwalk at the edge of a high bluff, the dunes rise to the north, so large and out of scale they look like a mirage. Lake Michigan sparkles in bands of brilliant tropical green far below, clear enough to reveal schools of big lake trout cruising by.

Farther south still, the shoreline curves inland to form **Platte Bay,** ringed by the **Aral Dunes.** These classic beach dunes front older dunes, now well inland and anchored by pines (and, in the wetter low-lying areas between the ridges, white cedar). Because most lakeshore visitors head for the showpiece perched dunes, you are likely to have this glorious stretch of beach to yourself.

The **Platte Plains Trail system** *(trailheads south of Empire)* and the **Old Indian Trail** *(access off Mich. 22, S of Empire)* loop through the wooded dunes and lead to the beach. (These are cross-country ski trails in winter.) The Platte Plains system includes more than 14 miles of trails, including a 4.6-mile **loop** that circles small **Otter Lake** and follows **Otter Creek** to its outlet at Lake Michigan. A pair of 2.5-mile loops make up the **Old Indian Trail,** named for the Ojibwa who used this route to travel from their camps to their favored fishing grounds.

Pierce Stocking Scenic Drive

North of Empire, the 7.4-mile

paved Pierce Stocking Scenic Drive *(access off Mich. 109)* winds through hardwood forest and snakes through the sand up to the crest of the dunes, 1,082 feet above sea level. Along the way, it passes many of the lakeshore's most scenic spots and some interesting interpretive trails. About 2 miles into the drive, a platform at the **Dune Overlook** caps a 200-foot dune and offers 360-degree views of the lunar-like perched dunes landscape, the Manitou Islands offshore, and the vivid cobalt waters of **Glen Lake.**

About half a mile farther along the drive, stop for a self-guided hike on the 1.5-mile **Cottonwood Trail.** (Stay on designated trails to protect this fragile environment.) Though the dunes look desert-like, they receive about 30 inches of rainfall per year. Still, this is a harsh environment for plants, racked with strong sunlight, incessant winds, and a lack of humus-rich soil that would hold moisture. The cottonwood, adapted to this challenging environment, is the only common tree of the dunes. Its fast rate of growth allows it to avoid being buried by the shifting sands, and it reproduces by sprouting new trunks from its roots. Cottonwoods stabilize the dune in two ways: The strong root system holds the sand in place, and the trees serve as windbreaks, trapping more sand and slowing wind erosion atop the dunes.

Continuing along the scenic drive to about mile 6, you'll find another observation platform jutting out over the dunes at the **Lake Michigan Overlook.** From here, you can peer across the big lake to

Descending the Dune Climb

Wisconsin's Door Peninsula, 54 miles away on the hazy horizon, or down a precipitous sand slope 450 feet into the waters of Lake Michigan. Though the barren dune looks inviting to slide down, it's deceptively steep. Head instead for the **Dune Climb** *(access via Mich. 109, N of scenic drive entrance),* a barren 130-foot dune a few miles away on the lee side of the plateau. Free of vegetation, there's nothing to harm here, so the Park Service invites you to scamper in the sand to your heart's content.

Glen Haven and North
As you drive north on Mich. 109 from the Dune Climb, Lake Michigan fills the horizon as the road drops down to Glen Haven. Between Memorial Day and Labor Day, the **Sleeping Bear Point Coast Guard Station Maritime Museum** depicts the work of the U.S. Lifesaving Service, the forerunner of the U.S. Coast Guard. Exhibits include lifesaving boats

Tubing on the Platte River

and the cannon used to shoot lifelines out to sinking vessels, while videos illustrate the drill and the rigorous life the crews led. They got more than an occasional workout: Some 80 ships wrecked along this passage between the mainland and the nearby Manitou Islands.

North of Glen Haven, along Mich. 22 to Point Oneida Road, **Pyramid Point** crowns the northernmost mainland part of the national lakeshore. A 2.7-mile **trail** leads to the high bluff, passing through distinctly different environments of shady beech-maple forest and open meadow. East of the point, coastal dunes follow the

curve of **Good Harbor Bay,** an inviting spot for a beach walk or a swim on a calm day. A 2.8-mile **trail** circles back inland through intermittent wetlands and pine-oak forest.

Manitou Islands

North and South Manitou Islands lie about 17 miles off the mainland, part of a chain of islands extending north to the Straits of Mackinac. Together, 15,000-acre North Manitou and 5,260-acre South Manitou represent once-developed land that has largely been reclaimed by nature and is now managed as wilderness. Both islands are served by a 90-minute ferry ride *(Manitou Island Transit 231-256-9061. www.leelanau.com/manitou)* from Leland, a town north of the national lakeshore.

South Manitou Island was first settled in the 1830s, even earlier than the nearby mainland. Islanders made a living by farming and logging, and by supplying food and fuel to the wood-burning steamers that traveled through the busy **Manitou Passage.** Because the island marked the only natural harbor for 200 miles, many ships also weathered squalls here. The **South Manitou Light,** built in 1871, still stands guard over the passage. Visitors can climb the lighthouse's 100-foot-high tower in summer months for a grand panorama of Lake Michigan.

On the south end of the island, the battered skeletal remains of the *Francisco Morazan* offer ample evidence of the trickiness of the Manitou Passage. This Liberian freighter ran aground in 1960 and now sits largely above the water's surface just a few hundred yards offshore. A draw for kayakers, it also provides a convenient resting spot for cormorants, which congregate on its hull to dry their outstretched wings.

By the 1960s, South Manitou had become mostly a summer cottage getaway. A decade later, the National Park Service began buying up the land for national lakeshore. A 3.5-mile **trail** leads from the village to **Valley of the Giants,** a grove of virgin white cedars—some more than 500 years old—that hides on the southwestern shore of the island. Deemed too isolated to log, the slow-growing trees are the largest white cedars left in North America. They create a damp and dim primeval forest, where orchids and ferns ring trunks more than 15 feet around and nearly 90 feet tall.

Like South Manitou, **North Manitou Island** was once a farming and lumbering community, then a summer getaway. Acquired by the National Park Service in 1984, this large island still harbors small patches of private property, but it is even less developed than its southern neighbor. Those who come here do so to camp, hike, hunt, and fish. The island's topography ranges from rugged bluffs on its northwest end to low dunes in the southeast. Bass thrive in the island's single large inland body of water, **Lake Manitou.**

North Manitou receives far fewer visitors than South Manitou—until fall hunting season, anyway. Nine deer were introduced here in the 1920s in the hopes of developing a herd large enough to hunt. By 1981, more than 2,000 deer roamed the island, devouring the forests so thoroughly that, according to the Park Service, the island took on an "open park-like appearance." Today, Sleeping Bear Dunes National Lakeshore manages the herd—which currently numbers about 200—by allowing hunting *(permit required).*

Both islands include rustic campgrounds but limited water supplies. Even day-hikers should bring water and food. Backcountry camping is permitted only on North Manitou. Although old roads are usable as trails, no bikes are allowed on either island. ■

Old Mission Light, Old Mission Peninsula

Grand Traverse Bay Region

■ Northwest Lower Peninsula of Michigan, from about Traverse City to Charlevoix ■ Year-round ■ Camping, hiking, kayaking, canoeing, swimming, fishing, biking, cross-country skiing, snowshoeing, bird-watching, wildlife viewing, scenic drive ■ Adm. fee for state parks ■ Contact Traverse City Convention and Visitors Bureau, 101 W. Grandview Parkway, Traverse City, MI 49684; phone 800-872-8377. www.mytraversecity.com

SOMEONE LONG AGO DUBBED the Lower Peninsula "the Mitten"—not a bad description of this landmass shaped by the surrounding Great Lakes. But its northwest corner looks more like a glove, its fingers splayed wide and every crack and crevice filled with bays and long, leggy lakes.

The largest is Grand Traverse Bay, which burrows inland 30 miles to Traverse City. The Leelanau Peninsula forms its western shore, a ragged region of hills, lakes, and rivers north of Sleeping Bear Dunes National Lakeshore (see pp. 146-151). A much thinner peninsula, Old Mission, needles up from Traverse City and nearly carves the bay in two.

Grand Traverse Bay glitters with remarkable color and clarity over a

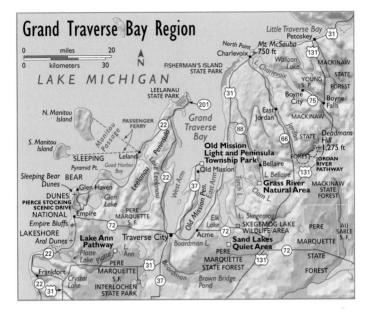

Grand Traverse Bay Region

lake bed of fine white sand. From teal to turquoise to aquamarine, its shades of Caribbean color shift like a chameleon warming in the sun. An undeniably popular vacation area, Grand Traverse Bay also preserves a number of natural areas, none of them far from its brilliant bay waters.

The Old Mission Peninsula extends north from Traverse City, splitting the bay into its West and East Arms. This whaleback ridge stretches 18 miles, a quiet agrarian landscape crosshatched with cherry orchards and striped with vineyards. Nowhere else grows more cherries per acre than the peninsula, which produces three-quarters of the world's tart cherry crop. Veer onto a country road off Mich. 37 and you're likely to spot row after row of reddish bark—some trees young and spindly, others gnarled and sturdy, all drooping under the weight of luminescent fruit.

What to See and Do

The ridgetop roads of the Old Mission Peninsula abound with incredible views, often taking in both arms of Grand Traverse Bay. Follow Mich. 37 to its north end, where the **Old Mission Light** stands sentinel over the point. The surrounding **Peninsula Township Park** includes some 400 acres of forest and abandoned orchards laced with hiking and mountain-

biking trails, as well as a curve of sandy beach where the shallow waters warm quickly in the sun, making it one of the area's best swimming beaches.

South of Traverse City, the **Boardman River** twists gently through Grand Traverse County before melting into the bay's West Arm. Two miles south of the city, the **Grand Traverse Natural**

Education Reserve *(231-941-0960)* protects 370 acres along the Boardman River and two small flowages, **Sabin Pond** and **Boardman Pond.** This surprisingly peaceful area includes 7 miles of self-guided nature trails that wind along the river and cross through marshes and grasslands. The Traverse Bay region attracts a particularly large population of mute swans; one pair frequently nests here, gliding gracefully across the glassy ponds.

Farther upstream on the Boardman, large stands of oak crown a steep bluff climbing up from the river and another small flowage, **Brown Bridge Pond.** Trails of 0.25 to 6 miles *(access from Ranch Rudolf Rd.)* lead out to observation platforms and down to the water's edge.

Motorized vehicles are banned from the **Sand Lakes Quiet Area,** a 2,500-acre preserve east of Traverse City off Mich. 72. More than 12 miles of interconnecting trails loop through this serene little area of small fishing lakes and woods,

Historic Fishtown, Leeland, Leelanau Peninsula

where the harp of a blue jay may be the only sound that interrupts a peaceful hike. Fishing and back-country camping are permitted throughout the preserve.

The marshes and swamps at the southern end of **Lake Skegemog,** northeast of Traverse City, were sufficiently forbidding to keep this area free of cultivation and development for decades. Today it is officially protected as the **Skegemog Lake Wildlife Area** *(access via Mich. 72, E of Acme),* 2,700 acres of high-quality wetlands. Follow an abandoned railroad grade to a swamp boardwalk, where you can peer over a rich mix of quaking bogs, sedges, cattails, cedar swamps, and streams. The marshy landscape is home to the massasauga rattlesnake, while bobcat, badger, and black bear inhabit its drier areas.

The **Grass River Natural Area** *(231-533-8576; on Alden Hwy. N of Mich. 72)* has the perfect moniker; here a mellow river leaches through bending grasses, sedge meadow, and bog on its casual route from **Lake Bellaire** to **Clam Lake.** Boardwalks let you traipse through the 1,100-acre preserve, where northern goshawks swoop from the treetops and orange wood lilies, yellow lady's slipper, and carnivorous pitcher plants grow amid lacy larch trees and young aspens.

The **Jordan River** cuts a wide swath through the landscape south of **Lake Charlevoix.** Nowhere is the view more dramatic than from **Deadmans Hill,** off US 131 south of **Boyne Falls:** More than 1,000 feet below, the Jordan straggles through a woodland of pines

Michigan Wineries
The Grand Traverse Bay region provides a surprisingly fruitful climate for growing cherries, apples, peaches, and, increasingly, wine grapes. Locals like to note that the Old Mission Peninsula sits at the same latitude as the Bordeaux region of France, but they really should thank Lake Michigan. Slowly changing lake temperatures keep things nice and cool during the growing season; come winter, they insulate the delicate grapevines and fruit trees from fatal deep freezes.

Most wineries here offer tours and tastings. Visiting them often brings benefit as well: The ridgetop roads of the region afford incredible views that often take in both arms of Grand Traverse Bay.

interspersed with beech and maple reaching out across the lowlands like the silk threads in a spiderweb. (The hill's morbid name memorializes Stanley Graczyk, a 21-year-old logger who, in 1910, mistakenly drove his team of horses up the hill and right over the edge.)

Deadmans Hill is also the trailhead for the **Jordan River Pathway,** which loops over the valley floor for 18 miles, part of a 27,000-acre tract of state forest. From here the Jordan rolls silently northward, its pale brown color framed by weeping willows sprouting from grassy banks. Flowing clear and cold over its gravelly bed, the Jordan is among the finest trout streams in the state.

Polished Petoskey stones

Petoskey Stones

Michigan's official state stone isn't really a stone at all—it's a chunk of fossilized coral more than 300 million years old. They are remnants of the reefs that once grew throughout the warm-water seas that covered much of northern Michigan. Petoskey stones are characterized by a small, distinct ring-like pattern. They are common enough that they don't have much real value, but rockhounds and anyone looking for a truly local souvenir prize them nonetheless.

When dry, Petoskey stones often look like, well, stones. Usually a dusty gray-brown color, their pattern becomes more apparent when wet (and especially when polished). The stones are quite soft; locals recommend polishing them by hand with fine-grained wet sandpaper— but not with rock tumblers.

Found along public beaches almost anywhere in the Traverse Bay region, the stones are particularly bountiful at Fisherman's Island State Park, southwest of Charlevoix, and Magnus Park in Petoskey.

Just minutes to the west of bustling Charlevoix on Bells Day Road, **Fisherman's Island State Park** *(231-547-6641; fee)* feels like a much more remote stretch of lakeshore. It curves along the water for seven miles, a mix of limestone ledges, stretches of soft sand beach, wooded dunes, and tamarack and cedar swamps. The park is nearly divided in two by a parcel of private property. The northern portion is the more popular of the two; it has five miles of hiking trails, a pretty day-use area, and 90 rustic campsites, including several right on the beach.

To reach the day-use area from the park entrance, hike the marked trail along the dune ridge past the campgrounds until you hit a trail leading across bubbling **Inwood Creek** to the beach. On a clear day, you can see the tip of the Leelanau Peninsula from this fine stretch of sandy beach.

High dunes roll down to Lake Michigan at **Mount McSauba Recreation Area** *(Mt. McSauba Rd., N of Charlevoix off US 31)*. Along with a soft sand beach, this 52-acre tract includes some pretty hiking and cross-country ski trails that wind through the woods behind the dunes. Hike to the top of the dunes for a view stretching all the way to Little Traverse Bay.

At its north end, Mount McSauba shares a boundary with **North Point Nature Preserve** *(access off Mt. Mcsauba Rd.)*. In the late 1980s, the Little Traverse Conservancy purchased this 28-acre parcel of woods and beach, which was being eyed for a condo development. North Point includes some steep nature trails through beefy old birches and cedars—a dappled forest with a thick, leafy understory of ferns, vines, trillium, and other wildflowers. Out on the rugged beach, tongues of rock stretch into the lake and shatter the incoming waves. ■

Pigeon River Country

■ 105,000 acres ■ Northern Lower Peninsula of Michigan, 13 miles east of Vanderbilt ■ Year-round; elk mating season late Sept.–mid-Oct. ■ Camping, hiking, fishing, horseback riding, wildlife viewing ■ Contact the Gaylord Operations Service Center, Michigan DNR, P.O. Box 667, Gaylord, MI 49734; phone 989-732-3541

ELK ARE RARE EAST OF THE MISSISSIPPI, but about 900 of them populate the northern Lower Peninsula of Michigan. The Pigeon River Country is in the heart of their roughly 800-square-mile range. Once a common sight in Michigan, the eastern woodland elk disappeared in the late 1800s. Seven Rocky Mountain elk—the ancestors of today's herd—were released in 1918. Now about a third of the elk live in the Pigeon River Country, where planted fields of rye, alfalfa, clover, and buckwheat provide easy grazing. (The herd's size and range are managed by limited hunting.)

Though hiking trails, one horse trail, and pristine rivers cross the meadows and woodlands of the Pigeon River Country, the main attraction is the prospect of glimpsing an elk herd. Promising viewing sites include **Inspiration Point,** near the intersection of Osmun Road and Clark Bridge Road; 6 miles northeast of Vanderbilt along Fontinalis Road; 8 miles east of Vanderbilt along Sturgeon Valley Road; and 18 miles east of Gaylord along County Road 622. (The latter, unnamed sites are marked by designated parking areas and elk viewing signs.)

Dawn or dusk is the best time of day to spot elk. The most magnificent time of year is during the fall rutting season, when the bulls compete for a harem of 3 to 15 females and stage impressive displays to attract mates. Using their great racks, they may spar with other bulls. If you're really lucky, you'll witness a bull elk throw back his head and fill the forest with his bugling—an eerie, high-pitched whistle that is the elk's distinctive mating call.

The Pigeon River Country was logged between 1860 and 1910. The Civilian Conservation Corps worked here in 1933, replanting trees and building campgrounds, roads, and bridges. Today, the forest is a mix of northern hardwood; aspen; red, white, and jack pine; swamp conifers; and grassy openings—all managed with the forest's stated objectives in mind: To protect the area from overuse and overdevelopment, including providing favorable habitat for elk, and food, cover, and seclusion for other wildlife.

What to See and Do

The **High Country Pathway** is an 80-mile loop that snakes east through state land in four counties. It passes through rolling hills and crosses several creeks and rivers, traversing the Pigeon River Country and linking up with the 13-mile **Shingle Mill Pathway.**

Beginning at the Pigeon Bridge Campground, the Shingle Mill Pathway follows the mellow **Pigeon River** and delves through deep woods. You can create loops of 1 to 6 miles. Keep an eye out for the forest's wildlife, which includes white-tailed deer (very common), ruffed grouse, turkey, coyote, black bear, mountain lion, snowshoe hare, osprey, and bald eagle. Pine marten, a small mammal trapped to near extinction for its fur, was reintroduced to the forest in the mid-1980s and is doing well.

The Pigeon, Black, and Sturgeon Rivers all pass through the Pigeon River Country and harbor healthy populations of brook and brown trout. The Pigeon and Sturgeon also host seasonal runs of rainbow. A fishing license is required and may be purchased over the Internet via the Michigan Department of Natural Resource's website *(www.mdnr-elicense.com /welcome.asp).* ■

Elk grazing in Pigeon River Country

Civilian Conservation Corps Museum

■ North Higgins Lake State Park ■ South of Grayling, Michigan ■ Open Mem. Day-Labor Day ■ Adm. fee for park ■ Camping, hiking, swimming, fishing, cross-country skiing, snowshoeing in surrounding park ■ Contact North Higgins Lake State Park, 11252 N. Higgins Lake Dr., Roscommon, MI 48653; phone 517-373-3559. www.sos.state.mi.us/history/museum/museccc/index.html

IN MARCH 1933, IN THE DEPTHS OF THE GREAT DEPRESSION, President Franklin D. Roosevelt asked Congress for the power to create the Civilian Conservation Corps (CCC). A New Deal program, the proposed corps would recruit 250,000 unemployed young men to work on federal and state-owned land for "the prevention of forest fires, floods, and soil erosion, plant, pest, and disease control."

Through artifacts and photographs, the Civilian Conservation Corps Museum in **North Higgins State Park** tells the story of Michigan's CCC crews, among the most active in the nation. The museum comprises several buildings, including a replica barracks and an original cone barn, where workers extracted seeds from pinecones for reforestation. The replanting of land cutover by loggers was a key project for CCC crews; in Michigan alone, they planted 484 million trees in less than a decade.

Other CCC projects included fire prevention, developing state parks, and building dams, bridges, and roads—all for a monthly stipend of $30, of which the young workers had to send home $25. In addition to field work, education was a hallmark of the CCC. Camps helped members obtain their high school diplomas and provided supplemental training in at least 30 different vocations.

Roosevelt's CCC idea was not without controversy. Some criticized the cost of the program; others balked at the idea of military control over labor, comparing it to fascism. Still others contended that young men belonged with their families—or, as Michigan Congressman Fred Crawford suggested, that they should work in farm fields rather than in "some camp in the woods to participate in a face-lifting operation of Mother Earth."

But Roosevelt saw it differently. Not only was the nation's economy in ruins, its environment was as well. Whereas virgin forests had once covered 800 million acres of the United States, old growth had dwindled to just 100 million acres. Erosion had laid waste another 100 million acres of the nation's tillable land, and more was eroding at an alarming rate. Through the CCC, Roosevelt believed, two invaluable and impoverished resources—the nation's young men and the nation's land—could be brought together in an attempt to save both.

The measure was easily passed, and so was Roosevelt's goal of 250,000 workers. On April 17, 1933, the nation's first CCC camp opened in George Washington National Forest in Virginia. By the beginning of July, 250,000 men were at work in more than 1,300 camps—the fastest large-scale mobilization of men (including World War I) in U.S. history. And by 1935, "Roosevelt's Tree Army" had ballooned to more than 500,000 workers.

Evidence of the CCC's work remains apparent throughout the Great Lakes region. CCC workers eradicated white pine blister rust in Minnesota, built fire towers and fire roads in Wisconsin, and improved hundreds of miles of game-fish streams in Michigan. They built park shelters in Ohio, campgrounds in Indiana, trails in Illinois. They planted thousands of acres of trees and fought countless wildfires. They even moved moose from Isle Royale to the Upper Peninsula for wildlife studies.

By 1936, the CCC was above reproach, supported by more than 80 percent of Americans and endorsed even by Roosevelt's political opponents. With the bombing of Pearl Harbor in 1941, however, the nation soon found a more pressing duty for its young men. The U.S. entry into World War II, along with an improving economy, spelled the end of the CCC. But its legacy, like the trees it planted, continues to grow in our nation's parks and forests. ■

Hartwick Pines State Park

■ 9,672 acres ■ Northern tier of Lower Peninsula of Michigan, near Grayling ■ Year-round ■ Camping, hiking, mountain biking, cross-country skiing, snowshoeing ■ Adm. fee ■ Contact the park, 4216 Ranger Rd., Grayling, MI 49738; phone 989-348-7068. www.dnr.state.mi.us

A 49-ACRE FOREST OF IMMENSE OLD-GROWTH white and red pines—one of Michigan's largest remaining stands—is this park's centerpiece. With wide boughs scraping at the sky several stories above, the forest feels almost primordial—an out-of-scale, fantasy landscape. In a 1.25-mile loop, the **Old Growth Forest Trail** starts behind the Michigan Forest Visitor Center (*follow signs from main entrance*) and weaves among the regal giants, some of which predate the Revolutionary War.

At 155 feet, the "Monarch" was the tract's largest specimen until a windstorm destroyed the top 40 feet of the now diseased and dying tree. Part of nature's cycle, several other contenders tower nearby, ready to take the Monarch's place in the record books.

These impressive stands of pine blanketed nearly half of Michigan until the last century. Throughout the 1800s, axes thunked and saws hummed across the state as lumbermen working in remote camps harvested more than a billion logs.

Somewhat ironically, the history and heritage of the logging industry are told within the park at the visitor center. The center is loaded with interactive exhibits, where you can hear the stories of logging camp workers, examine pinecones and pollen through a microscope, and learn to manage your own forest through a computer game. Outdoor displays

Logging wheels, Hartwick Pines State Park

include a re-created logging camp that shows how the loggers lived, and pieces of the actual equipment (such as a log jammer and a sprinkler sled) that were used to drag the harvest to the sawmills.

While many park visitors rarely venture beyond the pine grove and logging exhibits, Hartwick Pines also encompasses four small lakes, glacial moraines, and the East Branch of the Au Sable River spreading across a wide valley. The 3-mile **Au Sable River Trail** *(access via park picnic area)* threads through young stands of jack pine and paper birch, crosses the river, passes through a remnant of old-growth eastern hemlock forest, and then climbs to an overlook of the valley. From here, this well-known trout stream spills east across the state and empties into Lake Huron. ■

Huron National Forest

■ 500,000 acres ■ Northeastern Lower Peninsula of Michigan, between Grayling and Oscoda ■ Best seasons spring-fall ■ Camping, hiking, boating, canoeing, swimming, fishing, mountain biking, horse-back riding, cross-country skiing, snowshoeing, bird-watching, wildlife viewing, wildflower viewing, scenic drive ■ Vehicle passes required for some locations ■ Contact Huron Shores Ranger Station, 5761 N. Skeels Rd., Oscoda, MI 48750; phone 989-739-0728. www.fs.fed.us/r9/hmnf/index.shtml

THE AU SABLE RIVER begins as a small twisting creek northwest of Grayling, then swings east and widens as it flows clear and quick over a clean gravel bottom. Designated a wild and scenic river, this is the Au Sable renowned among anglers, one of the best brown trout streams in the nation.

Continuing east, the Au Sable broadens into a graceful river valley, coursing between lofty banks and over a bed of sand whose French word gives the river its name. Along the river's lower reaches, a series of dams creates four long impoundments, linked by marshlands and the serpentine Au Sable, before the river finally debouches into Lake Huron near the town of Oscoda.

Though other rivers flow through Huron National Forest, the Au Sable River Valley is its main attraction to nature lovers. It includes a surprisingly diverse array of habitats, from jack pine woods that are home to the exceedingly rare Kirtland's warbler, to marshes and wetlands filled with amphibians and migrating waterfowl, to high banks surveyed by bald eagles and ospreys.

Great blue herons, Tuttle Marsh, Huron National Forest

What to See and Do

River Road Scenic Byway

This 22-mile route follows a portion of the southern shore of the Au Sable and stitches together some of the forest's most scenic spots. It begins on Mich. 65, just above the Loud Dam Pond. The West Gate Welcome Center here has maps and other forest information, along with two viewing decks overlooking the pond.

Iargo Springs (*about 4 miles E of welcome center*) is one of the first stops along the scenic byway. Several springs gush forth from the side of a high bluff, forming small creeks that flow into the Au Sable. Boardwalks and decks wander through the pretty spring area, which lies at the bottom of a long flight of steps. Legend has it that the Ojibwa named the springs and believed they had mystical powers. At the top of the stairway, an observation platform offers a sweeping view of the river valley and Cooke Pond.

Iargo Springs also marks the western trailhead of the **Highbanks Trail**, a 7-mile linear route that traces a 70-foot bluff on the south side of the Au Sable River. The sandy path weaves through fragrant pine forests and gnarled oaks that hide twittering songbirds. It's also the perfect habitat for nesting bald eagles, which prefer lofty perches with views of water. Watch for the raptors circling high above the river valley.

At about the midpoint of the drive, the **Lumberman's Monument** pays homage to Michigan lumbermen. When the area's logging operations ended in the early 1900s, forest fires swept through much of what is now Huron National Forest, scorching the soil and blackening acre after acre of pine stumps. In some cases, the fires were so hot they destroyed the seedlings of the dominant white pine and prevented regeneration. Today's forest is a mix of hard-woods such as oaks and maples, as well as a red and jack pine planta-tion established by the Civilian Conservation Corps in the 1930s.

Continuing along the scenic byway, the bluffs dip toward the river. The Whirlpool Fishing Area, 3 miles west of Oscoda, provides river access for paddlers, who can enjoy a mellow float down to the river's mouth. Anglers can enjoy a test of their skills against salmon and steelhead—"big water" fishes that frequent Lake Huron and the Au Sable's lower reaches.

Tuttle Marsh

About 7 miles southwest of Oscoda, Tuttle Marsh sprawls across 5,000 acres. Once just a mix of shrub land, grass, and sedge, the marsh became a collaborative project of the Forest Service, the Michigan DNR, and Ducks Unlimited in 1990, when the three joined forces to build a water control system and impoundment.

The resulting wetlands and 35 nesting islands now attract an enormous variety of birds. Herons, Virginia rails, cranes, American bitterns, and egrets stalk through the marshlands. Tuttle Marsh Road *(6 miles W of Oscoda, off old US 23)* borders the impoundment; climb atop the low dike for a perfect bird-watching vantage point.

Au Sable River rental canoes

Kirtland's Warbler

To call the Kirtland's warbler endangered is an understatement. Fourteen Michigan counties, especially the area around the Au Sable River between Grayling and Mio, are the only places in the world where the bird is known to breed today. The world population is estimated at fewer than 800 pairs.

A tiny blue-gray bird with a yellow breast, the Kirtland's warbler winters in the Bahamas, then returns to the Au Sable River area, where it finds the proper habitat to suit its highly particular nesting requirements: young stands of jack pine with small, grassy clearings.

The bird's precarious plight is a classic case of habitat loss. When forest fires occur naturally, jack pines are one of the first trees to regenerate in the burned areas. But decades of logging and fire suppression translated to fewer forest fires, which in turn led to fewer young jack pines.

To help the warbler, the forest service and other government agencies now do nature's job, cultivating, harvesting, and replanting 2,500 acres of jack pines to keep an ample supply of young trees suitable for the warbler's nesting needs.

Corsair Trail System

West of Tawas City, the folds of the Silver Valley hide 26 miles of hiking trails, the most extensive trail network in the national forest. The 12-mile **Corsair Trail** (*trailhead NW of Tawas City*) is quite popular. Routes circle small marsh potholes and skip over **Gordon Creek** and **Silver Creek,** where brook and rainbow trout hover in the riffles (*fishing license required*). In spring, wild calla lily, spotted touch-me-not, marsh marigold, water plantain, and other wildflowers burst forth in lowlands and along the streams. The well-marked trails are groomed and tracked for cross-country skiers in winter.

Hoist Lakes Foot Travel Area

West of Harrisville, 24 miles of trails (*trailhead on Mich. 65, N of Glennie*) weave through the Hoist Lakes Foot Travel Area, dipping and climbing over unexpectedly rugged hills and through aspen and pine forest. Routes wind past pothole lakes formed by glaciers and floodings created by beavers. This backcountry area provides excellent habitat for turkey, ruffed grouse, woodcock, and other upland game birds.

Canoeing

Canoeists flock to the Au Sable, especially the stretch just downstream from Grayling, which can get frenetic on summer weekends. Better to begin farther downstream, beyond Mio, where the river flows through undeveloped banks that dip and rise above the river. In some spots, willows arc gracefully over low-lying shores; in others, jack pines sprout from high banks. Patches of old growth hemlock, cedar, and pine extend above the surrounding forest, reminding the passing paddler what this region looked like before it was extensively logged a century ago. ■

Great Lakes Plains

Horicon National Wildlife Refuge, southeast Wisconsin

HEAD SOUTH FROM THE THICK FORESTS that define the
Northern Highlands and you may be tempted to dismiss
the vast plain of glacial drift that stretches across southern Wisconsin and Michigan. From the interstate, at least,
the land smooths out flat and wide; dominated by cropland rather than woods, it is a seemingly uniform tableau
of dry prairies in a broad, sandy basin.

Get off that highway, however, and you will discover
the most varied region of the Great Lakes states. Here you

will find sinewy sandstone river valleys that narrow into deep canyons; a zigzag of ridges, mounds, and other odd topographical formations; vast rivers of grass; and a shoreline of dunes and sugar-sand beaches that unfurls for hundreds of miles along Lake Michigan's eastern shore.

It's all the work of eons of glaciers, which shaped and sculpted this part of the continent. In the Great Lakes Plains—the level or slightly rolling lowlands that border the southern Great Lakes—evidence of gla-

ciers is everywhere. Four ice ages left their signature on the upper Great Lakes, and in each one the primary instrument of inscription was mile-thick ice sheets that marched across the Earth's crust. As these tongues of ice inched forward in an irregular pattern, they flattened the land in their path and plowed up piles of glacial drift at their farthest advances.

Kettle Moraine State Forest, in southeast Wisconsin, is a textbook example of this topography: It showcases conical kames, snaking eskers,

Scaling sandstone ledges outside Grand Ledge on Michigan's Lower Peninsula

kettle lakes, and a wide sampling of other ice age sculptures. The perimeter of all this glacial activity, called a terminal moraine, is traced by the Ice Age National Scenic Trail, which ripples 1,000 miles across Wisconsin.

In other areas, vast glacial lakes invaded the terrain, laying down thick beds of sand and sediment. When glacial Lake Wisconsin dried up, for instance, its sandy lake bed remained. Today this central-Wisconsin area is known as the Sand Counties; in them dry savanna commingles with low-lying wetlands such as Necedah, a remnant peat bog, and Horicon, the largest freshwater cattail marsh in the country. These are just two examples of the vital nesting grounds and migratory bird routes that are woven through the Great Lakes Plains.

It's not hyperbole to suggest that Wisconsin's Sand Counties helped shape the conservation ethic of the United States. Two of our nation's great naturalists—John Muir and Aldo Leopold—spent their formative years in the fields and woods of the Sand Counties, and the simple land left an indelible mark on both men. Muir, whose family homesteaded on a farm in Marquette County, grew up to become one of America's preeminent advocates for the wilderness, the "father" of our national parks system and the founder of the Sierra Club. Leopold, who found solace in an abandoned farmstead between Portage and Baraboo, did pioneering work in wildlife ecology and authored a masterpiece of conservation literature, *A Sand County Almanac.*

On the other side of Lake Michigan, glaciers pushed the topsoil south, leaving a high, sandy plain across much of Michigan's interior. Sand virtually outlines southern Michigan as well: Flat, sometimes marshy Lake Huron beaches frame its eastern shore, while its western boundary contains the longest stretch of freshwater dunes in the world.

In the sparse, sandy soil of the Great Lakes Plains, coniferous forests took hold and flourished. Although white pines once blanketed much of central Wisconsin and Michigan, nearly all of them were felled during

Great blue heron, Horicon National Wildlife Refuge, Wisconsin

logging's heyday in the second half of the 19th century. Once the trees were gone, farmers figured out the handful of crops that could thrive in their wake. Today, Wisconsin's seven Sand Counties are one of the nation's leading producers of cranberries, while Michigan dominates the blueberry harvest. Southern Michigan's sandy, well-drained soils and moderating lake-effect temperatures also create a microclimate ideal for growing a variety of fruit trees and wine grapes.

South of the sandy plains stretch fertile soils and rolling hills that make up some of the richest agricultural land in the Midwest. Southern Wisconsin—home to fields of waving alfalfa and contented Holsteins switching their tails along fencerows—is picture-book dairy country.

Yet the southern Great Lakes Plains also embrace the region's most urbanized area: A string of industrial cities, including Chicago, Detroit, and Cleveland, lies at the foot of the Great Lakes. These key ports on the busy Great Lakes commercial waterway bring in raw materials such as iron ore and ship out finished goods such as steel and automobiles. They also constitute a gritty industrial core that has spawned many of the Great Lakes' environmental woes and sullied their reputation. Lake Erie, beleaguered and abused with industrial effluents for decades, is the infamous poster child. It took a watery conflagration—the Cuyahoga River, which flows into Lake Erie at Cleveland, literally caught on fire in 1972—before anyone began responding to the environmental alarms.

Thankfully, some of these industrial injustices are finally being corrected, and we can turn the proverbial tide: Lake Erie flushes itself completely in less than three years. If we continue to mend our mistakes, the lakes will continue to heal.

We certainly have the role models, as we walk in the footsteps of Muir and Leopold. And we certainly have the inspiration, in the raucous bird-filled wetlands, the glacier-sculpted hills, and the grand windswept dunes of the Great Lakes Plains. ■

White-tailed deer, Necedah National Wildlife Refuge

Necedah National Wildlife Refuge

■ 43,696 acres ■ Central Wisconsin, 4 miles west of Necedah on Wis. 21
■ Year-round (bird migration peaks mid-Oct.) ■ Hiking, bird-watching, auto tour, berry-picking ■ Contact the refuge, W7996 20th St. West, Necedah, WI 54646; phone 608-565-2551. midwest.fws.gov/necedah

EPITOMIZING WISCONSIN'S Sand Counties—a low-lying glacial lake bed that stretches across seven counties in the central part of the state—is Necedah National Wildlife Refuge. The Yellow River drains the refuge, its namesake hue the result of iron and other minerals. "Necedah" is derived from the Ojibwa term for "land of yellow waters."

The pine trees that blanketed this region were logged off in the 1800s, leaving nothing but a barren landscape. Farmers moved in during the early 20th century. Aided by steam-powered ditchdiggers and hoping to create

Wasp nest, Necedah NWR

fertile cropland out of the "useless" marsh, they built extensive drainage ditches. The strategy was successful in drying out the land, but the sand and peat soil proved too acidic and lacking in nutrients. By the Great Depression of the 1930s, poor soils and poor economic conditions had forced even the most tenacious farmers off the land.

With the establishment of Necedah National Wildlife Refuge in 1939, work began to restore the land. Early refuge managers sought to re-create a marsh environment that would attract waterfowl, so they dammed drainage ditches to restore wetlands and used controlled burns to maintain nesting habitats. Modern ecologists understand that this savanna—a mix of grasses, wildflowers, oaks, and pines subject to fires fanned by prevailing northwest winds—forms a natural part of Necedah's ecosystem: Pines need open areas to regenerate, while oaks are one of the few deciduous trees with bark thick enough to withstand the fires' intense heat.

This savanna once covered more than four million acres of Wisconsin; today fewer than 10,000 acres remain. A priority project at Necedah is the restoration of nearly 3,000 acres of savanna, which support more than 100 species of nesting birds and an assortment of rare species, including the Blanding's turtle and the eastern massasauga rattlesnake.

Necedah is also home to the world's largest population of the Karner blue butterfly, a purplish-blue insect with a 1-inch wingspan. The larvae of Karner butterflies feed only on lupine, a beautiful blue wildflower that grows in abundance in the dry soil of the oak barrens. The adult insects feast on lupine nectar, as well as on other wildflowers in the refuge, and can be viewed from mid-May to early July. Contact the refuge for up-to-date information and prime viewing locations.

Birds thrive in both the savanna and the marshlands of Necedah. An avian ruse helped wildlife biologists reintroduce trumpeter swans here in 1994: They acclimated the cygnets (immature swans) by donning mature swan costumes and drifting about the ponds in waders. Today the birds are most evident in **Rynearson Pool #1** (*observation deck and spotting scopes*), and their buglelike call rings across the wetlands.

Some 2,500 sandhill cranes—the greatest concentration of any national wildlife refuge—gather here in spring and fall. This impressive bird stands 4 feet tall, with a bright scarlet band atop its head. Its long neck and legs protrude stiffly in flight, while its wings stretch 7 feet across. That profile, combined with the bird's raucous and guttural call, makes the sandhill seem positively prehistoric.

To witness the courtship ritual of the sandhill crane is an unusual treat: The male crouches, bows, arches up, and circles about in an

The Scoop on Cranberries

The Sand Counties' granular, acidic soil is tailor-made for growing cranberries. You'll spot the crop throughout the area—especially around Warrens, the center of Wisconsin's cranberry industry, where the shrubby plants grow in low-lying rectangular bogs.

Visit in fall and you can observe an unusual but efficient harvesting technique: Workers cut the cranberries from the stems, then flood the bogs and scoop up the berries with rakes as they bob to the surface.

The harvest usually peaks in late September, but you can learn about the process from April to October at the Cranberry Expo visitor center and museum (*608-378-4878; www.cranberryexpo.com*) on County Road EW in Warrens.

Green teal feathers on white-oak leaf

exotic-looking dance, punctuating the show with flapping wings, shriek-ing cries, and leaps of 6 feet into the air.

Because the refuge road often runs between dikes, the numbered stops along it *(detailed in brochure available from refuge headquarters on Wis. 21)* are the best places to view Necedah's natural beauty. These pull-outs also allow you to access a handful of short, level nature trails that pass through savanna characteristic of the wildlife refuge and lead to pools and observation towers. Bicycles and cross-country skis are permitted on refuge roads. ■

Operation Migration

Necedah National Wildlife Refuge played a role in a unique reintro-duction program in October 2000: Dressed in a crane costume, an ul-tralight pilot led 11 immature sand-hill cranes from Necedah more than 1,200 miles to wintering grounds at St. Martins Marsh Aqua-tic Refuge in Florida. Because the cranes had been bred in captivity, the goal was to teach them safe migratory routes; in subsequent seasons, biologists hope, the birds will follow these on their own.

The 39-day mission was con-ducted under the auspices of Oper-ation Migration, a nonprofit enterprise that made headlines in 1994—and became the subject of a feature film, *Fly Away Home*—by leading 18 Canada geese from Ontario to Virginia.

If the sandhill crane project succeeds and the birds return to Necedah, Operation Migration plans to use the same migratory route to reintroduce a flock of whooping cranes in 2001. Fewer than 200 migratory whooping cranes exist in the wild, traveling from Canada's Northwest Territo-ries to Texas. The Operation Migration project aims to lead hand-raised chicks on a permanent eastern migration route; with luck, the birds will return to spend their future summers at Necedah.

Sandhill Wildlife Area

■ 9,460 acres ■ Central Wisconsin, 17 miles west of Wisconsin Rapids ■
Year-round; bird-watching best in autumn ■ Camping, hiking, bird-watching,
wildlife viewing, auto tour ■ Contact the wildlife area, P.O. Box 156, Babcock,
WI 54413; phone 715-884-2437

THIS CONSERVATION AREA LIES WITHIN the Sand Counties, the lake bed of
glacial Lake Wisconsin. Supervised by the state of Wisconsin, the Sandhill Wildlife Area rubs elbows with three other preserves: Meadow Valley
Wildlife Area and Wood County Wildlife Area, both managed largely for
hunting and other recreation, and the Necedah National Wildlife Refuge.
Together this Wisconsin quartet occupies more than 200 square miles of
undeveloped public lands.

Sandhill is characterized by a series of low, undulating sand ridges,
marshy areas, and increasingly rare upland oak savanna (often called oak
barrens). Also visible are large mounds known as outliers, which predate
the glacial lake bed; these are the remnants of a sandstone plateau laid
down by an ancient Paleozoic sea. North Bluff, which rises 200 feet above
the surrounding plain, is a chunk of even more ancient Precambrian
quartzite sealed in sandstone.

Farmers tried to scratch a living out of the poor soils here, building
a series of dikes and ditches to drain the marshes and convert them to
cropland. When the farms failed during the Depression, a local biologist
and businessman named Wallace Grange bought the abandoned, tax-
delinquent lands and set up a game farm. He erected a fence around the
property, then began raising deer, grouse, ducks, and even buffalo.

Today, Sandhill is managed as a demonstration area and living laboratory. Biologists use it to study fire management, timber extraction, game
harvests, and the effects these practices have on animals and their habitats. A variety of mammals live within Sandhill's borders, including
beaver, otter, badger, bear, and deer. Researchers use the deer herd, enclosed by 17 miles of fencing, to study the effects of deer hunting and the
accuracy of deer-census techniques. The wildlife area permits hunting in
the fall to control the population.

Whether by foot, bicycle, or car, the best way to explore the area is on
the 14-mile **Trumpeter Trail.** With 17 stops along the way, it provides
lots of information on Sandhill's management practices. The Trumpeter
Trail also passes the area's bison herd, descendants of Wallace Grange's
original game-farm herd. Though normally associated with the western
plains, bison likely roamed the Sand Counties up until the late 1700s,
when they fell to overhunting.

Three trailside observation towers overlook marshlands and pools.
More than 100 species of birds pass through area marshes, including
some 6,000 sandhill cranes in fall—one of the largest staging areas east of
the Mississippi. At stop 4, the 7-mile (round-trip) **Swamp Buck Hiking
Trail** begins by passing through marshes en route to North Bluff. ■

The Shack that incubated a philosophy

Leopold's Land Ethic

In the simple, subtle beauty of the Sand Counties, forester Aldo Leopold (1887-1948) found the insights that made him a conservation pioneer. Leopold became enamored of, and eventually purchased, an abandoned farmstead south of the Wisconsin River near Portage. There he renovated a tumbledown chicken coop dubbed the Shack and spent endless hours reflecting on the land.

The sandy soils of the counties around his farm helped Leopold see the true riches of the land. Most people viewed the region as worthless—that is, unsuitable for crops, pasture, or timber. Introducing the concept of a land ethic, Leopold suggested that land has an intrinsic value that transcends mere economics. "We abuse the land because we regard it as a commodity belonging to us," he wrote. "When we see land as a community to which we belong, we may begin to use it with love and respect."

Eventually, Leopold's musings evolved into the essays that make up the remarkably poetic *Sand County Almanac.* Often cited as the 20th century's preeminent piece of conservation literature, it laid the groundwork for modern-day land management, imploring us to recognize our responsibility for the natural landscape and to reevaluate the "plethora of material blessings" that we blithely call progress.

Today, Aldo Leopold's beloved Shack is on the National Register of Historic Places. His original 80 acres of land, along with 1,500 more, now form the Aldo Leopold Memorial Reserve *(608-355-0279; visits by appt. only),* dedicated to advancing ecological awareness.

The U.S. Fish and Wildlife Service, private landowners, and the Aldo Leopold Foundation are working to protect even more land—an 8,120-acre site between Portage and Baraboo that would restore a drained wetland basin containing wooded swamps, wet prairies, and associated uplands. In addition to re-establishing a cold-water fishery, the rejuvenated land would provide important breeding habitat for waterfowl, shorebirds, and sandhill cranes.

Wisconsin Dells

Wisconsin Dells

■ 10 miles long ■ South-central Wisconsin, 50 miles northwest of Madison via I-90/94 ■ Year-round; commercial boat tours available May-Oct. ■ Camping, hiking, boating, fishing, bird-watching ■ Adm. fee for state parks and boat launches ■ Contact Wisconsin Dells Visitor and Convention Bureau, 701 Superior St., Wisconsin Dells, WI 53965, phone 800-223-3557, www.wisdells.com; or Rocky Arbor and Mirror Lake State Parks, E10320 Fern Dell Rd., Baraboo, WI 53913, phone 608-254-2333

KITSCHY TOURIST ATTRACTIONS—water parks, go-cart tracks, miniature golf—have become synonymous with the Wisconsin Dells. Look beyond the neon, however, and you'll find the real Dells: 100-foot-high bluffs of honey-hued limestone that rise from the banks of the Wisconsin River.

Ancient seas helped create the Dells. They carried metamorphic rocks from as far away as Canada, crumbling them and mixing them with sand, quartz, iron oxide, and organic matter. That formed the area's 510-million-year-old Cambrian sandstone—ancient rock found only in a handful of spots on Earth. Much later, ice sheets surrounded but never flattened the sandstone. When they receded, glacial meltwater tore through the area, carving gorges and creating rivers. Erosion added the final touch, buffing the sandstone into curvaceous sculptures.

The sandstone canyons support a number of unique plant species, including cliff cudweed, a type of aster found only in Wisconsin. The Dells of the Wisconsin River State Natural Area protect a 5-mile stretch of the river corridor from encroaching commercialism.

The historic Kilbourn hydroelectric dam straddles the Wisconsin River and divides the Dells into the Upper Dells, where the river squeezes past towering cliffs and gradually widens into a broad lake, and the Lower Dells, a deep, narrow valley that snakes between grand sandstone formations. A variety of commercial boat tours (including amphibious vehicles called "Ducks," one of the first Dells attractions) offer a look at the Dells and the river valley. Boat launches, especially in the Lower Dells, mean you also can navigate the waters in your own motorboat or canoe.

Off the river, two nearby parks merit a visit. **Rocky Arbor State Park** *(608-254-2333, Mem. Day–Labor Day only)* on Wis. 12 preserves a narrow gorge carved by the Wisconsin River, which later shifted to its present course a mile northeast. The 1-mile (round-trip) **Nature Trail** starts near the park office and needles through the gorge, then climbs to the top of the bluff before returning through towering white pines.

Just 2.5 miles south of the hustle and bustle of the Dells, **Mirror Lake State Park** *(608-254-2333, year-round)* showcases a placid sliver of water bounded by 50-foot sandstone bluffs. This is a lovely lake for paddling, especially the stretch called the Narrows, where the high bluffs squeeze together *(boat and bike rentals May-Oct. at boat landing, 608-254-8702)*. Twenty miles of trails wind through the park, passing through pine communities, patches of prairie, and wetlands. Great blue herons often stalk fish in the shallows. ■

Fishing the Lower Dells of the Wisconsin River

Balanced Rock Trail, Devils Lake State Park

Baraboo Range

■ 25 miles wide ■ South-central Wisconsin, 30 miles northwest of Madison; central access via US 12, eastern access via I-90/94 ■ Year-round ■ Camping, hiking, rock climbing, scuba diving, bird-watching, scenic drive ■ Adm. fee for state parks ■ Contact Devils Lake and Natural Bridge State Parks, S5975 Park Rd., Baraboo, WI 53913, phone 608-356-8301 (campsite reservations 800-947-2757); or The Nature Conservancy, 107 Walnut St., Baraboo, WI 53913; phone 608-356-5300

AS YOU HEAD NORTHWEST FROM MADISON, the gently rolling landscape suddenly thrusts upward as soon as you cross the Wisconsin River. This is the Baraboo Range, a 500-foot-high quartzite bluff that is one of Earth's oldest visible physical features: The range is the eroded remains of a mountain chain at least 1.5 billion years old.

Extending 25 miles across Sauk County and part of Columbia County, the Baraboo Range (also called the Baraboo Hills) constitutes a treasure trove of significant plant and animal communities, geologic formations, and archaeological sites. The range hosts microclimates ranging from warm and sunny hilltops and rocky cliffs to cool, moist gorges and stream valleys. Each microclimate fosters a different array of plant and animal species.

The Nature Conservancy has named the Baraboo Range a Last Great Place, a recognition it gives only to the most significant ecosystems in the country. Within the Baraboo Range are several Nature Conservancy preserves, state and federal natural landmarks, and some of Wisconsin's most notable state parks.

What to See and Do

Devils Lake State Park

The most dramatic spot in the Baraboo Range and a headliner in Wisconsin's excellent state-park system is this 9,117-acre site, 3 miles south of Baraboo off Wis. 123. Ragged bluffs 500 feet high ring a clear glacial lake, often placid enough to reflect the changing light and lavender hues of the surrounding sheer rock walls.

An ancient river carved the valley now occupied by Devils Lake. When the last of the glaciers licked at the region, the terminal moraine (the farthest extent of the ice sheet) plugged both ends of the valley with rocks and other debris, rerouting the river and leaving behind a basin of meltwater that became spring-fed Devils Lake.

The bluffs often create an inversion: cooler air below the bluffs, warmer air on top. That's why northern species such as white pine, cranesbill, and trillium sprout among lichen-covered boulders at the base of the rock, while prairie remnants and pygmy forests of gnarled oak and hickory scratch out a place on blufftops.

Picture-postcard views await hikers who scale the talus slopes to the crest of the bluffs. The 0.8-mile **CCC Trail,** the 0.3-mile **Potholes Trail,** and the 0.4-mile **Balanced Rock Trail** all switchback up the steep, rock-strewn southeastern face; all three trails can be accessed near the visitor information station on the lake's southern shore. Squeezing beneath a shattered rock slab, through a rock arch, then past a 5-ton quartzite boulder perched on end, the trails showcase many of the geologic oddities left behind by the glaciers. This face is also popular with rock climbers, who rate the routes at Devils Lake among the finest in the Midwest.

Once you've reached the top, the short (0.1-mile) **Devil's Doorway Trail** parallels the edge of the bluff (hang on tight to small children), with higher-than-hawk views of the valley. Continue west to pick up the 1.1-mile **East Bluff Trail,** which continues to hug the bluff as it traces the shore of Devils Lake. Rock outcrops make sublime picnic spots or photo ops—unless you have active children.

For the elevation-averse, other fine hiking options stand out among the park's 23 miles of trails. The 1.4-mile **West Bluff Trail** offers high views of the lake without the steep precipices. The **East Bluff Woods Trail** wanders for 1.3 miles through maples and birches along the back of the bluff. The longer **Ice Age Trail** (4.7 miles) and the **Johnson Moraine Trail** (2.8 miles) traverse a glacial lake bed and pass some kettle ponds.

Despite its chilly, spring-fed waters, Devils Lake is popular with swimmers, who fill the sandy north-end beach. Just northeast of the beach is a collection of well-preserved effigy mounds (see sidebar, p. 238). Canoes, fishing boats, and small sailboats all take to the waters *(only electric motors allowed; rowboat and canoe rentals available at park),* but the winds can be fluky. Devils Lake is a favorite

Following pages: Hiking trail through Parfrey's Glen State Natural Area

Rock climbing on the Devil's Doorway

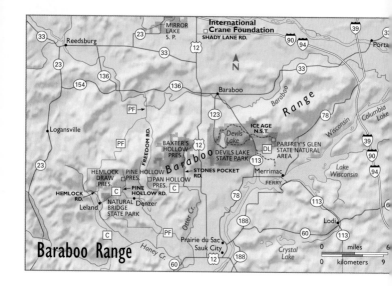

Baraboo Range

among divers, who love to plumb its clear depths (*Three Little Devils Dive Shop 608-358-5866*).

Parfrey's Glen State Natural Area

Just 4 miles east of Devils Lake but still within the state park, a tiny creek trickles through a narrow gorge hemmed in by 100-foot sandstone walls. (Studded with purplish pebbles of quartzite, the walls are known locally as plum pudding.) This cool, dank spot is the state's oldest natural area, a fragile glen of mountain maple, ostrich ferns, mountain club moss, and quartzite boulders dragged here by glacial ice. The gorge receives only minimal sunlight, so plants in the glen are more typical of northern Wisconsin than they are of this part of the state.

The 2-mile *(round-trip)* **Parfrey's Glen Trail** leads from the parking area on County Road DL to the gorge's upper end. Scouring rush—a fern relative named for

the silica in its stem, which pioneers used to scrub pots—forms a low thicket along the creek.

Baxter's Hollow Preserve

This 4,000-acre tract west of Devils Lake represents one of the most significant properties owned and managed by the Wisconsin Nature Conservancy. Otter Creek is central to the preserve; running clear and fast over quartzite boulders, it forms one of southern Wisconsin's last undeveloped watersheds. The creek is home to the rare pickerel frog and 75 types of caddis flies, a vital food source for the trout that flash through the waters.

Baxter's Hollow helps protect the state's largest intact southern deciduous forest. Leading into the preserve, a faint (and faintly blazed) **foot trail** *(2 miles round-trip; access from main entrance)* passes under stands of stately oak, hickory, maple, and ash. Alder thickets sprout near the creek, providing key nesting habitat for more than 60 bird species, including hooded, cerulean, and worm-eating warblers. Baxter's Hollow also encompasses bedrock glades and many forest types normally found farther north, such as sugar maple and yellow birch forests.

To reach the preserve, take US 12 south from Baraboo to County Road C. Turn west on County Road C, then go north on Stones Pocket Road 2 miles to a gate and sign marking the entrance.

Scenic Drive

A 35-mile loop through the Baraboo Range links several more Nature Conservancy preserves and Natural Bridge State Park. From Baraboo, follow Wis. 136 west 4 miles to County Road PF, which winds southwest through crumpled foothills of ancient quartzite.

Just before Leland, turn left (east) on Hemlock Road to reach **Hemlock Draw Preserve,** another prime Nature Conservancy site. The glaciers stopped 10 to 15 miles east of here, leaving a rich geologic legacy. A 20-foot-tall sea stack—a narrow pillar of rock deposits—showcases the region's billion-year-old quartzite. The sandstone cliffs, much newer, prove that 500 million years ago this area belonged to a chain of islands in a tropical sea.

Lacy hemlocks grow dense along the bluffs surrounding a narrow gorge. Wood anemone, wild geranium, and toothwort carpet the ground. Trees typical of southern Wisconsin—red oak, American elm, and ironwood—thrive on former grazing land along the preserve's northern boundary. Because several different plant communities coexist in one site, the University of Wisconsin Botany Department uses the 730-acre preserve as a study area.

From the preserve, continue south to County Road C, then follow it east to **Natural Bridge State Park.** Also spared the grinding effects of the last ice age, this 530-acre park features a natural sandstone bridge with an opening that measures 25 feet high and 35 feet wide. In the cave below the bridge, archaeologists found evidence of hunter-gatherers living here more than 10,000 years ago, when glacial ice covered the land just 12 miles to the north.

Continue east on County Road C to US 12. The industrial site before you is a former munitions plant; conservationists would like to see the 7,000-acre site returned to its original habitat of prairie and savanna. Follow US 12 about 8 miles north back to Baraboo. ∎

Caring for Cranes

Eight miles north of Baraboo (on Shady Lane Rd.) stands the International Crane Foundation (608-356-9462. www.savingcranes.org), a group world-renowned for protecting the planet's largest flying birds. Here visitors can see more than a dozen species of cranes, all of them endangered or threatened; they include the rare whooping crane, slowly rebounding from its 1940 nadir of 15 birds.

Tour the facility to take in the open-air bird pens, a center with exhibits and videos, and some restored Wisconsin prairie.

Great egret at Horicon Marsh

Horicon Marsh

■ 32,000 acres ■ East central Wisconsin, 50 miles northeast of Madison and 50 miles northwest of Milwaukee ■ Geese migration March-April and mid-Sept.–mid-Dec., peaking late Oct.–early Nov. ■ Hiking, canoeing, biking, bird-watching ■ Contact Horicon National Wildlife Refuge, W4279 Headquarters Rd., Mayville, WI 53050, phone 920-387-2658, midwest.fws.gov/Horicon/index.html; or Horicon Marsh State Wildlife Area, Department of Natural Resources, N7725 Hwy. 28, Horicon, WI 53032, phone 920-387-7860

DARKENING THE SKIES in long, precise V formations, as many as 250,000 Canada geese per day make this large cattail marsh the midpoint of their twice-yearly migration between summer nesting grounds in northern Hudson Bay and wintering grounds in southern Illinois. The birds descend upon the refuge every spring and fall, blanketing its open fields and seeking out the soft shoots and leaves of meadow plants, grasses, and wild rice in its vast, reedy pools.

The autumn edition of this migration begins around mid-September, peaks in late October or early November, and continues until the refuge waters ice up (usually in mid-December) and snow covers the food supply. The return migration occurs in spring, though in smaller numbers. The best time to view the geese is at sunrise, when they leave the marsh to feed on waste corn in surrounding farm fields, and at sunset, when they return.

Covering more than 60 square miles, Horicon Marsh is an extinct postglacial meltwater lake that slowly evolved into a wet meadow and peat marsh rich in wildlife. A few naturally dry spots—the tops of glacial drumlins, now stranded in the marsh as islands—remain.

Though dominated by geese, this "Everglades of the North" is home to more than 265 species of birds. About 100,000 ducks pass through, including buffleheads, northern shovelers, blue-winged teals, and redheads. Great egrets, black-crowned night-herons, tundra swans, Forster's and black terns, yellowlegs, and even some cattle egrets are among the shorebirds seen here, many of them nesting. The refuge safeguards one of the largest great blue heron rookeries in the Midwest, with an estimated 500 pairs.

Nomadic hunters knew the riches of Horicon Marsh more than 10,000 years ago. For generations this vast wetland served as the headwaters of the Rock River; the wetland teemed with fish and small mammals, grew thick with wild rice, and welcomed thousands of migrating birds.

In 1846, locals hoping to harness the river's power built an earthen dam at the foot of the marsh. The dam raised the marsh level 9 feet, creating a huge man-made lake and prompting much of the wildlife to move on. Land disputes led to the dam's removal a couple of decades later, whereupon the marsh slowly subsided to its original level.

State and federal agencies began buying up Horicon's marshland in the 1930s and '40s. The state of Wisconsin now manages the southern tier of the marsh—roughly 11,000 acres—as the Horicon Marsh State Wildlife Area, while the U.S. Fish and Wildlife Service manages the northern two thirds (21,000 acres) as Horicon National Wildlife Refuge.

What to See and Do

The visitor center on County Road Z (3.5 miles S of Wis. 49) has good displays on the site's natural history. The center also provides entrée to nearby nature trails and an observation tower.

The best overview of the marsh is from the Wisconsin Department of Natural Resources Field Office, 2 miles northeast of Horicon on Wis. 28. Its observation deck (with spotting scopes) occupies a high vantage point on the south side of the marsh, offering a panoramic view that includes the **Fourmile Island** heron rookeries.

Surprisingly good views of the bird life can also be had from the roads that skirt the marsh. The marked 36-mile **Horicon Marsh Parkway** begins in Horicon and circles the marsh clockwise on a series of state and county roads. If you lack the time required to follow the entire route—a trip of about two hours—drive the 4-mile segment of Wis. 49; it traverses the northern tip of the marsh and offers wide shoulders where you can pull over and break out the binoculars. Be prepared for bumper-to-bumper traffic during the height of the fall migration.

In the northwest corner of the refuge off Wis. 49, you can take the 3.2-mile **Horicon TernPike** auto tour from mid-April to mid-September *(open to hikers and bikers rest of year)*. Interpretive signs and pull-offs punctuate this loop route.

Three short hiking trails branch off the TernPike. About halfway along, try the half-mile (round-trip) **Egret Trail,** a must-see for its floating boardwalk and viewing platform. The dike roads also welcome pedestrian and bicycle traffic.

The **Wild Goose State Trail** *(access off Cty. Rd. 26),* a 34-mile multiuse path, abuts the marsh's west edge. Though the trail is pleasant, its marsh views are often veiled by woods. Mountain bikers will probably prefer the dike roads.

Boats are permitted in the southern third of the marsh only; nesting areas are sometimes closed in spring. Paddlers should avoid fall hunting season (ask the DNR for season dates). The best canoe routes wind along the east branch of the **Rock River** from the Greenhead Landing northeast of Horicon; this is the closest launch for viewing (though from a distance only) the rookeries on Fourmile Island.

Burnett Ditch provides a launch on the marsh's southwest side. Blue Heron Landing *(920-485-4663)* in Horicon offers canoe rentals and narrated boat tours. ■

Kettle Moraine State Forest

■ 51,000 acres (30,000 acres in Northern Unit, 21,000 acres in Southern Unit)
■ Southeastern Wisconsin, north and west of Milwaukee ■ Year-round. Fall colors best Sept.-Oct. ■ Camping, hiking, mountain biking, horseback riding, cross-country skiing, snowshoeing, bird-watching, scenic drives ■ Adm. fee
■ Contact the state forest, N1765 Hwy. G, Campbellsport, WI 53010, phone 262-626-2116 (northern unit); or S91 W39091 Hwy. 59, Eagle, WI 53119, phone 262-594-6200 (southern unit)

IF THE CONCEPT OF GLACIERS SCULPTING the Great Lakes landscape strikes you as a bit abstract, take a trip to Kettle Moraine State Forest. This swath of forest, stretching 125 miles across southeast Wisconsin, is a life-size geology lesson in one tidy package. Two finger-like lobes of the Wisconsinan Glacier converged here, leaving behind ample evidence of the last ice age more than 10,000 years ago.

Hike a few trails—or even drive a couple of back roads—and you will see clear examples of kettles (small pothole lakes formed by ice blocks), moraines (large hills of glacial debris that mark the farthest reaches of the ice sheet), kames (cone-shaped hills created by debris as meltwater cascaded through holes in the glacier), drumlins (wedge-shaped hills of glacial debris), eskers (serpentine gravel ridges deposited by rivers in the glacier), and erratics (random boulders left behind by the moving ice sheets). Because much of the landscape was deemed too rugged to farm, wildflowers and other native plants still thrive within the now-protected forest.

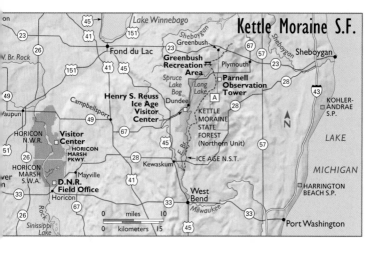

What to See and Do

Kettle Moraine State Forest is divided into two main units (a third and smaller unit lacks the scenery to draw large numbers of visitors). The Northern Unit forms a 31-mile-long corridor between Fond du Lac and West Bend; the Southern Unit doglegs south from I-94 midway between Madison and Milwaukee. Both offer an extensive network of trails, all of which are open to hiking, and some of which cater to mountain biking, cross-country skiing, or horseback riding as well. Each unit features a scenic drive, well marked with acorn-shaped road signs.

If it's possible, begin your visit at the **Henry S. Reuss Ice Age Visitor Center** *(920-533-8322)*, west of Dundee in the Northern Unit. Located on the crest of a high moraine, this fine facility helps make sense of the glacial and natural history of the forest with exhibits, films, and the short, self-guided **Moraine Trail.**

Northern Unit

The lumpy landscape of Kettle Moraine makes it an appealing hiking destination. Of 133 miles of trails weaving through the forest, the granddaddy is the **Ice Age National Scenic Trail** (see sidebar, p. 190). A 31-mile segment runs the length of the Northern Unit. You can backpack the whole thing, camping at one of the segment's five overnight shelters, or combine it with other trails to create loop hikes. Near the **Greenbush Recreation Area** at the segment's north end, the trail gives you a good look at the large **Greenbush Kettle.**

To scope out a kame, head for the **Summit Trail** south of **Long Lake.** It winds nearly a mile up **Dundee Mountain**—actually a 270-foot-high kame. Signs along the way explain the glacial geology.

The best views are those from the Parnell Observation Tower. From the parking lot on County Road U, the 3.5-mile **Parnell Trail** winds through lowlands, hardwoods, and a pine-tree plantation to reach the tower. The lumpy landscape below is cloaked in oaks and maples that stage a fiery fall show.

Two miles northwest of Dundee, a quarter-mile **boardwalk** *(access off Airport Rd.)* leads to **Spruce Lake Bog,** a national natural landmark. Tamarack and black spruce shadow this shallow, undisturbed, lowland, home to a trio of carnivorous plants: sundew, bladderwort, and pitcher plant. All three ingest insects to get the nutrients they need; as a result, they thrive in soils that would not support many plants.

Southern Unit

More than 110 miles of trails stitch across the glacial hills of Kettle Moraine's Southern Unit. North of La Grange, the **Nordic Trail**

Walk, don't ride, the Ice Age Trail

Ice Age National Scenic Trail

Arcing across Wisconsin from the St. Croix Riverway to Lake Michigan, the Ice Age Trail traces the path of glaciers that bulldozed one-third of North America thousands of years ago. Hike even a portion of the trail and you'll see how these powerful ice sheets rearranged the land into glacial lakes, conical hills, and high ridges of gravel and sand.

The completed Ice Age Trail will wind more than 1,000 miles across Wisconsin. For now it's a stop-and-start affair, yet it offers plenty of scenic stretches ideal for one or several days of hiking. Many of the longer segments cross public lands such as state parks, county recreation areas, and national forests.

In **Chequamegon National Forest** northwest of Wausau, the trail twists 40 miles along the crests of eskers, threading tall hemlocks and pines. You can access the trail at several points; one is west of Wis. 13 and Rib Lake. Follow signs to the parking area and trailhead off Forest Road 101. From here, the trail leads west into the forest toward Mondeaux Flowage, popular for swimming, fishing, and camping. After skirting the north end of the flowage and passing a CCC cabin, you'll enter a lightly traveled area of streams, small lakes, and bogs, all formed by the meltwater of retreating glaciers.

Other inviting trail segments lie within Hartmans Creek State Park, Devils Lake State Park, and Kettle Moraine State Forest. Because other trails branch off the Ice Age Trail, keep an eye out for the yellow markers and tree blazes delineating the route. For more information, contact the Ice Age Park & Trail Foundation *(800-227-0046 or 412-278-8518, www.iceagetrail.org).*

system (groomed for cross-country skiing in winter) offers a good mix of terrain, with 22 miles of loop trails winding past kettles and climbing over kames and moraines.

Just across County Road H, the **John Muir Trail system** is a favorite of fat-tire fanatics far and wide. This 27-mile network of loop trails passes through a mix of open fields, pine plantation, old-growth hardwoods, and leatherleaf bogs. (The 9.2-mile **Blue Loop** offers the best technical single track.) The challenging 5-mile **Connector Trail** links the John Muir system with the **Emma Carlin Trail network** (another 8.4 miles of challenging mountain-bike terrain) to the north. One loop of the Emma Carlin Trail climbs a steep razorback ridge with a good view of a glacial sand plain; another loop passes through an old farm, its fields still dotted with apple and walnut trees.

East of the state forest, **Lulu Lake State Natural Area** preserves one of the state's best examples of an oak savanna—an airy, upland community of grasses, mature oaks, and hickories. More than 5.5 million acres of oak savanna once covered Wisconsin; today, less than 0.01 percent of the original remains. This habitat supports the Cooper's hawk, a threatened species. Below the oaks, **Lulu Lake,** a pristine example of a kettle lake, is home to such rare fishes as the long-eared sunfish and the star-head topminnow, as well as a healthy population of bluegills and bass. The marshy upper reaches of the Mukwonago River—a mix of bog, fen, and sedge meadow—border the lake. The endangered cricket frog lives here, and sandhill cranes frequently hide among the taller grasses. ■

Aerial view of esker on border of Kettle Moraine State Forest

Indiana Dunes National Lakeshore

■ 15,012 acres ■ Northwest Indiana, on Lake Michigan shore off US 12
■ Year-round. Fall color best Sept.-Oct. ■ Camping, hiking, swimming, beach-combing, horseback riding, cross-country skiing, bird-watching, historic sites
■ Adm. fee for West Beach ■ Contact the lakeshore, 1100 N. Mineral Springs
Rd., Porter, IN 46304; phone 219-926-7561. www.nps.gov/indu

AN OASIS IN THE MOST INDUSTRIAL POCKET of the Midwest, high hills of wild, windswept sand rise up from the water along the southern shore of Lake Michigan. This is Indiana Dunes National Lakeshore, a sharp contrast to the gray backdrop of power plants and steel mills. The lakeshore stretches east from Gary, preserving a fragile dune environment that holds one of the National Park System's most diverse plant collections.

After the last glaciers retreated from the Great Lakes region about 10,000 years ago, a drastically altered landscape emerged from beneath the ice. The Lake Border moraine—ridges of mud, silt, gravel, and sand —marked the edges of glacial Lake Michigan and formed the base of the Indiana dunes. The winds that blow across Lake Michigan then took over, transporting sand to the southern shore and onto the rolling ridgelines, where beach vegetation anchored it.

Due to the vagaries of dune formation, plant communities often change drastically as you move inland. Closest to the water are the newest and most active dunes. **Mount Baldy,** 123 feet high, is under siege from northwest winds, which pick up sand grains and blow them inland. As a result, Baldy is creeping away from the lake at 4 to 5 feet per year.

Moving inland, vegetation such as marram grass takes hold and begins to stabilize the dunes. A single marram-grass plant can establish a tenuous root system 20 feet in diameter, laying the foundation for other dune plants such as sand cherry, wild grape, and cottonwood. Farther inland, middle dunes have established larger plant communities that include arctic bearberry, jack pine, white pine, and common juniper. Still farther back from the water, older dunes host black oak and a variety of shrubs. Between the dunes, hummocky low areas hold wetlands.

A surprising array of more than 1,400 plant species thrives in this ever evolving dune community. In **Cowles Bog,** these include white cedar, rare yellow birch, and water-loving plants such as skunk cabbage and marsh marigold. In **Pinhook Bog** (tour access only), 12 miles southeast of Mount Baldy, they include leatherleaf, highbush blueberry, yellow fringed orchid, pink lady slipper, and the insect-eating pitcher plant and sundew.

All this botanical diversity puzzled and fascinated Professor Henry Cowles of the University of Chicago, who began studying the Indiana Dunes as a living laboratory in the early 1900s. Using research he conducted here, Cowles formulated the concept of plant succession—the

Paraglider above Mount Baldy dune, Indiana Dunes National Lakeshore

Local resident, Indiana Dunes NL

way in which the plants growing on a site change it, paving the way for other plants.

To experience dune succession yourself, walk the 1-mile loop that is **West Beach Trail** *(access near West Beach parking area off US 12)*; it leads from bare foredunes back to dunes sheathed in shrubs and grasses. The **Cowles Bog Trail** *(trailhead parking on Mineral Springs Rd. off US 12)* explores low-lying interdunal communities in a series of connected paths that allow loops of 2.5 to 4.6 miles. Eventually, as part of dune succession, these bogs will fill in and become meadow, then forest.

To protect the dunes' fragile plant communities, most trails follow boardwalks. An exception is the dune climb on Mount Baldy. Because no plants are yet established on this young dune, visitors are welcome to scale the mountain of sand, then skip and slide their way back down— a simple pleasure that brings out the kid in everyone.

Naturally, beach activities are the park's other main draw. **West Beach** is the most popular, with lifeguards, a bathhouse, and concessions. But if it's solitude you seek, just head for the eastern reaches of the national lakeshore; before long you'll find miles and miles of sand for everyone. ■

Claw- and pawprints in the sand, Indiana Dunes National Lakeshore

Cardinal flower   Great lobelia

Warren Woods Natural Area

■ 311 acres ■ Southwest Michigan, 5 miles east of I-94 and Union Pier ■ Open April-Oct. ■ Hiking, cross-country skiing, snowshoeing, bird-watching ■ Vehicle fee ■ Contact the area's administrator: Warren Dunes State Park, 12032 Red Arrow Hwy., Sawyer, MI 49125; phone 616-426-4013. www.dnr.state.mi.us

LOCALS RIDICULED MERCHANT EDWARD K. WARREN in 1878 when he bought a large patch of forestland five miles due east of Lake Michigan with plans to do nothing more than preserve it. But the foresighted Warren clearly understood its value as one of the last stands of virgin beech-maple forest in the state of Michigan.

Today this wooded oasis surrounded by farmland is a national natural landmark and a living specimen of what southern Michigan once looked like: Pale green beeches and sturdy maples leaf out high overhead, creating a cool and shady glen. The grand old trees have grown so big that two people cannot link arms around one. Morel mushrooms sprout among decaying trunks on the forest floor in spring (picking is prohibited). Come autumn, the maples brighten to a vivid orange that joins the yellow birches and russet oaks in an Impressionist blur.

An unnamed 3.5-mile **loop trail** *(access via Warren Woods Rd. and then Three Oaks Rd. off 1-94)* circles through the woods and along the banks of the meandering Galien River. Thanks to the natural area's abundant nesting areas and its proximity to the Lake Michigan shore, the leafy canopy is often atwitter with birds. Particularly likely here are sightings of warblers and pileated woodpeckers. ■

Lake Michigan's Eastern Shore

■ 200 miles of shoreline, from Sawyer north to Manistee ■ Western shore of Michigan's Lower Peninsula ■ Year-round ■ Camping, hiking, swimming, beach-combing, cross-country skiing, snowshoeing, bird-watching ■ Vehicle fee for state parks ■ Contact **Grand Mere State Park,** 12032 Red Arrow Hwy., Sawyer, MI 49125; phone 616-426-4013. **Ross Coastal Plains Marsh Preserve,** phone 810-324-2626. **Saugatuck Dunes State Park,** 2215 Ottawa Beach Rd., Holland, MI 49424; phone 616-637-2788. **P. J. Hoffmaster State Park,** 6585 Lake Harbor Rd., Muskegon, MI 49441; phone 231-798-3711. **Ludington State Park,** P.O. Box 709, Ludington, MI 49431; phone 231-843-2423. (For Michigan state park camping reservations, call 800-447-2757.) **Nordhouse Dunes Wilderness Area,** Manistee Ranger Station, 412 Red Apple Rd., Manistee, MI 49660; phone 231-723-2211

LIKE SALT ON A MARGARITA GLASS, sand rims the eastern shore of Lake Michigan for nearly its entire length. From broad beaches to gentle ridges of forested sand to immense windblown mounds, together they represent the world's largest collection of freshwater dunes.

We have the glaciers to thank for building these beaches and dunes.

Beach grasses at sunset, Nordhouse Dunes Wilderness Area

During the last ice age, continental glaciers spread south from Canada, repeatedly burying this area under sheets of ice. When the ice sheets retreated for the last time about 10,000 years ago, they ground bedrock into powder and deposited huge piles of sand and rock debris. Prevailing westerly winds blowing across the lake took over from there, piling up sand on the lake's leeward shore.

Visitors will find two distinct varieties of dunes here. Beach dunes—those classic, low-lying hillocks of wind-sculpted sand—make up much of the shoreline. Perched dunes—huge deposits of glacial debris—are larger and more dramatic, sitting high above the shore. Nature continues this process today, eroding the great dunes with waves and building them up again with westerly winds.

To the delight of outdoors enthusiasts, much of Michigan's beachfront is protected, undeveloped, and accessible to the public in a string of state parks, national forests, and other preserves. You can explore the hiking trails for the lesson they offer in dune ecology, or simply enjoy a classic day at the beach: The same winds that create the dunes push Lake Michigan's surface water toward its eastern shore. While temperatures on the Wisconsin side may be in the chilly 50s, the sun-warmed surface waters licking at the Michigan beaches can be almost 20 degrees higher.

What to See and Do

Grand Mere State Park

While urbanites flock to the convenient beach at Warren Dunes park, locals head for its shy neighbor just a few miles farther north: Grand Mere State Park (616-426-4013). The park's 1,000 acres preserve wooded swamps, remnant bogs, and three interdunal lakes that were scooped out by glaciers.

Unusual vegetation abounds in this diverse community. Bluebead lilies sprout in the lowlands, as does musclewood—a tough hardwood named for the sinewy ridges on its thick trunk. The slow-growing (and short-lived) witch hazel tree grows here, too. It stands out in fall, when it begins to flower just as the other trees are losing their leaves. The park's vegetation also attracts a wide variety of birds, notably mockingbirds, Bell's vireos, and yellow-throated warblers.

Grand Mere State Park, just west of I-94, is largely undeveloped. Four miles of hiking trails wind among its open dunes. A half-mile walk from the parking lot off Thornton Road delivers you to the park's mile-long Lake Michigan shoreline.

Ross Coastal Plains Marsh Preserve

Managed by the Michigan Chapter of The Nature Conservancy (517-332-1741), this 1,440-acre preserve contains some sterling stretches of coastal plain marsh, a habitat more commonly associated with the Atlantic seaboard. Several warbler species—including the hooded and Blackburnian—make themselves at home in the preserve's varied habitats of marsh, wooded inland dunes, wetlands, small lakes, and northern hardwood forests. The site also harbors the globe-fruited seedbox (a rare sedge) and some century-old white pines. Ross Preserve is near Watervliet, north of I-94 (turn W on 44th Ave. off Mich. 140).

Saugatuck Dunes State Park

In the heyday of lumbering, the city of Saugatuck was accustomed to the sight of logs floating through town on the Kalamazoo River. Although the timber is long gone, the town has been reborn as a popular resort filled with shops and galleries. Those enterprises must keep most visitors busy, because very few venture north of town to Saugatuck Dunes State Park (616-637-2788) off I-96 and Blue Star Hwy. The park attracts fewer than 75,000 people a year; by comparison, 1.25 million descend on nearby Holland State Park.

Much of the 889-acre park is dunes forested with scrub pine and oak—ideal habitat for birds seeking woodlots not yet interrupted by farmland. Scarlet tanagers, bluebirds, indigo buntings, and even the rare prairie warbler nest in the black pines.

Fourteen miles of surprisingly empty trails (stay on them to curtail erosion) spiral through these fragile mountains of sand to a lengthy expanse of Lake Michigan shoreline. Here you'll find barren, 200-foot-high lakefront dunes standing sentinel over the empty beach and the limitless blue waters of Lake Michigan. Because reach-

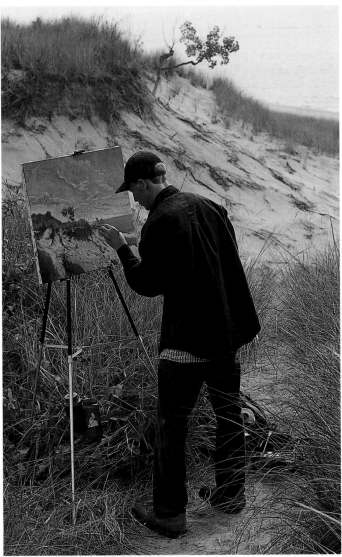
Dauber in the dunes, Saugatuck Dunes State Park

ing the shore requires a mile-long
trudge through sand on the **Beach
Trail** *(accessed from parking lot)*,
you're likely to share it only with
sandpipers and sanderlings, skittering along the water's edge.

P. J. Hoffmaster State Park

South of Muskegon off US 31 on
Pontaluna Road, P. J. Hoffmaster
State Park *(231-798-3711)* features

a thin, 2-mile ribbon of sand that
lies between water's edge and a
high wall of dunes. Twelve miles of
trails wind through forested dunes
and interdunal swales; tackle the
Dune Climb Stairway for panoramic views. Beach grasses rattle
in the breeze, their tenacious roots
stabilizing the volatile sand.

The park's **Gillette Nature Center** *(Tues.-Sun.)*, tucked among the

high golden dunes, gives a good introduction to dune ecology. Slide shows, dioramas, and other displays demonstrate the natural forces that shaped (and continue to shape) these mountains of sand.

Ludington State Park

Near the visitor center to this 5,200-acre park, wood stairs climb a steep dune to a boardwalk offering a fine overview of the park's variety: In just a few steps you can see open Lake Michigan, barren sand hills, scrub pines growing in a dune forest behind the main dunes, and the **Big Sable River** sluicing through the maples.

Ludington State Park stretches nearly six miles along Lake Michigan, including an elbow of sand around Hamlin Lake known as Big Sable Point. The 1867 Big Sable Point Light Station, painted in tiers of black and white, stands guard here—one of the western-most points on the lake's eastern shore. It also serves as a beacon for hikers, who can make the 3.5-mile round-trip trek from the beach to climb the lighthouse (*fee*).

A 1,600-acre wilderness area—undeveloped beach cloaked in forested dunes—stretches from the lighthouse to the park's northern boundary. Watch for endangered piping plovers, which can often be seen darting along the waterline.

A canoe pathway traces the shore of Hamlin Lake, weaving through marshes and ponds (*canoe rentals available at concession at lake's edge*). White cedars rise above the reeds and cattails, while turtles sun on muddy banks.

Nordhouse Dunes Wilderness Area

Beachcombers seeking solitude need only walk south from Manistee National Forest's Lake Michigan Recreation Area (*N of Ludington on*

Michigan's Fruit Belt

Well-drained soil, combined with the moderating effects that Lake Michigan and the prevailing western winds have on local temperatures, have given rise to a flourishing fruit industry just inland from the Lake Michigan shore. This fertile fruit belt dates to the 1850s, when farmers from St. Joseph and Benton Harbor noticed that their peaches survived the severe winters that killed off the crop in other parts of the state. By the 1860s, with bustling Chicago crying out for fresh fruit, peaches were being shipped across Lake Michigan almost as fast as they could be picked.

Eventually, fruit farming and fruit-related industries spread throughout much of Van Buren and Berrien Counties. By 1906, the latter was blanketed by approximately 1.3 million peach trees.

In the early 1900s, hard freezes and higher competition (in the form of the new refrigerated railroad car) led many farmers to abandon peaches in favor of heartier apples. Blueberries regained popularity later in the century, with the town of South Haven proclaiming itself the "Blueberry Capital of the World." Indeed, in 2000 Michigan grew and sold 62 million pounds of high-bush blueberries.

Lake Michigan's Eastern Shore

MANITEE N.W.&S.R.
PERE MARQUETTE S.F.
Manistee
31
MANISTEE
PINE N.W.&S.R.
PERE
131
Nordhouse Dunes Wilderness Area
LUDINGTON S.P.
Big Sable
FERRY
Manitowoc
151
Hamlin Lake
Big Sable Point Light Station
Ludington
PERE MARQUETTE N.W. & S.R.
MARQUETTE
Baldwin
10
WIS.
Pere Marquette
STATE
Sheboygan
23
43
CHARLES MEARS S.P.
NATIONAL
SILVER LAKE S.P.
B15
FOREST
LAKE
FLAT N.W.&S.R.
Port Washington
DUCK LAKE S.P.
31
Muskegon
Muskegon
ROGUE N.W.&S.R.
MICHIGAN
43
P.J. HOFFMASTER S.P.
Gillette Nature Center
Grand Haven
MILWAUKEE
Grand
96
31   Wyoming
Grand Rapids
Kentwood
96
HOLLAND S.P.
196
131
94
Racine
Holland
SAUGATUCK DUNES S.P.
Saugatuck
Kalamazoo
Kenosha
196
MICHIGAN
KALAMAZOO N.W. & S.R.
N
South Haven
Kalamazoo
94
Waukegan
Ross Coastal Plains Marsh Preserve
Covert
ILL.
94
31   131
Benton Harbor
miles   40
294
St. Joseph
kilometers   60
Evanston
GRAND MERE S.P.
90
WARREN DUNES S.P.
94
CHICAGO
WARREN DUNES S.P.
290
Union Pier   Sawyer
31
Niles
55
INDIANA DUNES NATIONAL LAKESHORE
WARREN WOODS NATURAL AREA
St. Joseph
294   57
Michigan City
80   90
Hammond   Gary   Porter
South Bend
INDIANA
90
31

Forest Trail Rd. off US 31) to reach the tranquillity of this wilderness area *(231-723-2211)*. Here a 3,450-acre swath of sand stretches unbroken for 3 miles, letting wind and waves play out their give and take.

Though fragile, the dunes have stood here for nearly 4,000 years. Beyond the barren foredunes, marram grass, sand cherry, and pasture rose take root, and the cheerful yellow-orange flowers of puccoon sprout among the sandy ridges. The rare pitcher's thistle also grows here, hiding among the dogwood and other shrubby plants. Juniper, jack pine, and hemlock form a coniferous fringe.

Ducks and geese congregate in the interdunal ponds, or raft up on the open lake in calm water. Watch mergansers, with their slender, saw-toothed bills, dive underwater for food or safety.

From the beach, 10 miles of sparsely signed trails spin inland. ■

Shiawassee National Wildlife Refuge

■ 9,200 acres ■ Southeast Michigan, 5 miles south of Saginaw off Mich. 13
■ Year-round; spring and fall best for viewing bird migration ■ Hiking, biking,
bird-watching ■ Contact the refuge, 6975 Mower Rd., Saginaw, MI 48601;
phone 989-777-5930. midwest.fws.gov/shiawassee

FOR A STATE THAT AFFECTIONATELY REFERS to its Lower Peninsula as the Mitten, it seems only logical that the large hump of land in the southeastern corner would come to be known as the Thumb. Two bodies of water—Saginaw Bay to the west and Lake Huron to the east—outline the Thumb and wrap much of it in rural isolation.

A glacial lake covered the region more than 10,000 years ago. The lake eventually receded, leaving behind a table-flat landscape threaded with rivers and blanketed with pines, marshes, and paddies of wild rice. In the late 1800s, the Thumb proved an easy mark for loggers. They clear-cut the entire peninsula, floating logs by the millions down area rivers to waiting mills in Saginaw and Bay City. In their wake stretched a vast, barren "stump prairie."

Farmers took over the denuded land at the dawn of the 20th century, draining the lowlands and planting acre after acre of sugar beets and navy beans. Huron County, at the tip of the Thumb, is the world's top producer of navy beans per acre.

In 1953, the U.S. Fish and Wildlife Service stepped in to reestablish some of the area's wetlands for migrating waterfowl. It chose a site south of Saginaw that had always been a natural gathering spot for waterfowl, a place where four rivers—the Flint, the Cass, the Shiawassee, and the Tittabawassee—converge to form the Saginaw River.

Today Shiawassee National Wildlife Refuge is a carefully managed expanse of dikes, pools, floodplains, bottomland hardwoods, grasses, and crop fields; farmers who raise corn, soybeans, and other crops on the refuge agree to leave a portion of their produce standing as feed for wildlife.

Chippewa Nature Center

In Midland, just 25 miles from Shiawassee National Wildlife Refuge, stands Chippewa Nature Center (400 S. Badour Rd., 989-631-0830, www.chippewanaturecenter.com) deemed one of the finest facilities of its kind in the nation. The 1,032-acre complex includes exhibits, programs, and a 13-mile trail system that helps make sense of the area's natural history.

The main building was designed by Alden Dow, a celebrated architect who studied under Frank Lloyd Wright. Its centerpiece is a 60-foot-long room cantilevered over the Pine River—an inspiring spot to watch birds winging up and down the river valley.

Significant numbers of birds visit the refuge in spring and fall, among them hundreds of tundra swans and some 25,000 Canada geese. Duck sightings number in the tens of thousands; they include the common and hooded merganser, blue-winged teal, lesser scaup, and northern pintail. Bluebirds, thrushes, and warblers migrate through, and brilliant species such as the scarlet tanager and the indigo bunting are often in residence throughout the summer. Careful bird-watchers can spot barred, great horned, and eastern screech owls all year long.

The refuge has more than 10 miles of walking trails. The 4.5-mile **Ferguson Bayou Trail** *(trailhead at end of Curtis Rd.)* loops around swamps and pools atop a system of dikes, ultimately leading to an observation deck and blind with a spotting scope. The 4.5-mile **Woodland Trail** loop *(trailhead in parking area at intersection of Center and Stroebel Rds.)* passes through bottomland hardwoods and along the Tittabawassee River. ■

Point Pelee National Park

■ 3,840 acres ■ Southern Ontario, 6 miles southwest of Leamington off Hwy. 20 ■ Best seasons spring and fall (for viewing bird migration), Sept. (for viewing monarch butterfly migration) ■ Hiking, bird-watching, wildlife viewing ■ Adm. fee ■ Contact the park, 407 Robson St., Leamington, ON N8H 3V4; phone 519-322-2365. www.parkscanada.gc.ca/pelee

POINT PELEE FLOUTS THE POPULAR IMAGE of Canada as a frozen northern nation. Lying south of Detroit, Point Pelee is the southernmost extension of mainland Canada, a sandy spit extending like a shark's tooth 12 miles south into Lake Erie. The word *pelée* is French for "bald" or "denuded," a description given to the point in the late 17th century.

Point Pelee's quirky geography has endowed it with a diverse array of plants and animals, many found nowhere else in Canada. It is a key gathering spot for migratory birds—and, notably, for monarch butterflies.

Driftwood at the southern tip of Point Pelee National Park

Following pages: Marsh boardwalk through wetlands, east side of Point Pelee National Park

Purple paddler at Point Pelee

For these reasons the tip of the point has been preserved as a national park, albeit one of Canada's smallest.

A bar of sand and gravel only 10,000 years old, Point Pelee is a volatile landmass waging a constant war against water currents and wind. At times steep, narrow, and clear, the beach grows flat and wide after a storm sends waves crashing over it. The peninsula may be eroding as much as 2 feet per year on its eastern shore, but Mother Nature usually offsets that with sand and gravel brought in by waves on its wooded western shore.

Point Pelee lies within the Canadian Carolinian Zone: This habitat, normally associated with much more southerly areas, represents just one-quarter of one percent of Canada. The peninsula's southern location plays a role, but Lake Erie exerts an even more powerful force. Slow to warm up and slow to cool down, the lake moderates local temperatures, giving the park an especially long frost-free growing period for Canada.

Point Pelee encompasses one of the last large freshwater marshes on the Great Lakes, as well as a mix of beach, savanna grasslands, and jungle-like Carolinian forest. More than 700 species of flowering and nonflowering plants flourish in this diverse landscape. In dry forest areas, where the southern hackberry predominates, wild grape, Virginia creeper, and poison ivy vines dangle from the trees, creating an almost tropical canopy.

The open forest is made up of sycamore, with its easily recognizable patchwork bark, along with other trees associated with much warmer climates: sassafras, honey locust, shagbark hickory, and spicebush. In areas of red cedar savanna, wild potato vine and prickly pear cactus sprout in the openings amid grasses and herbs.

Canada's only wild hibiscus, the pink-flowered swamp rose mallow, appears among marsh ferns and water lilies. The beach habitat supports plants impervious to the harsh and changing environment, including the hop tree; a member of the citrus family, it grows as far south as Mexico.

What to See and Do

Birding

Two flyways—the Mississippi and the Atlantic—converge on Point Pelee. After flying hundreds of miles north, birds rain down on the welcome diversity of habitats they find at Point Pelee.

More than 370 species have been recorded in the Pelee area, and nearly a third of those remain to nest. Dead trees provide nesting sites for red-bellied woodpeckers, great horned owls, and eastern screech owls. The uplands host yellow-breasted chats, yellow-billed cuckoos, towhees, and vireos, while marsh areas provide habitat for the least bittern and a variety of herons.

More than 41 of the North American warbler species have been recorded in the area since the early 1900s. Birders also gather at Point Pelee to spot such rare species as the swallow-tailed kite, worm-eating warbler, black vulture, and lark sparrow.

Butterfly-watching

A remarkable migration kicks off in September, when thousands of monarch butterflies funnel through Point Pelee. They typically stay only briefly, gathering energy and waiting for the favorable winds that will help them fly across Lake Erie and south to their winter home in the mountains of central Mexico—an odyssey of nearly 2,000 miles.

Monarchs depend on milkweed, which grows abundantly in Ontario. The plant furnishes both sustenance and defense: Its cardiac glycosides are harmless to monarchs but poisonous to any bird that attempts to eat the insects. Scientists believe that birds avoid monarchs because they have come to associate sickness with the insect's bright wing patterns.

During the autumn butterfly migration, Point Pelee National Park offers guided hikes and encourages visitors to assist in counting butterflies. Accurate counts are vital in conservation efforts; Canada considers the monarch to be a species of special concern. ■

Rocky Landings

Habitat loss caused the early 1900s demise of the park's most interesting resident, the southern flying squirrel. The squirrel nests only in dead tree cavities. Past park-management practices did away with dead trees—and, consequently, with their squirrel occupants. Park officials reintroduced squirrels to the park in 1993-94, and their numbers are slowly rebounding.

The flying squirrel is held aloft by its gliding membrane, or patagium, a skin fold that extends from the wrist of the front leg to the ankle of the hind leg. When the legs are extended, the membrane forms a winglike gliding surface. The flattened tail serves as both rudder and stabilizer.

Most steering is done with the tail, or through variations in the tension on the membrane. After gliding for up to 50 yards, the squirrel lands hind-feet first on a tree trunk.

Marina and town of Put-In-Bay, South Bass Island

Lake Erie's Southwest Shore

■ 75-mile shoreline ■ Northwest Ohio; between Toledo and Sandusky ■ Year-round; ask at refuge for peak migration times of various birds. Island ferries run March-Sept. or Oct. ■ Camping, hiking, swimming, fishing, bird-watching ■ Contact Ottawa National Wildlife Refuge, 14000 W. State Rte. 2, Oak Harbor, OH 43449; phone 419-898-0014. midwest.fws.gov/ottawa/ottawa.html. Crane Creek State Park, 13531 W. State Rte. 2, Oak Harbor, OH 43449; phone 419-898-2495. Kelleys Island State Park, P.O. Box 851, 920 Division St., Kelleys Island, OH 43438; phone 419-746-2546. www.dnr.state.oh.us/parks/parks/lakeerie.htm

LAKE ERIE FORMS A GOOD TWO-THIRDS of Ohio's northern boundary. Its northwest corner is linked to Lake Huron by the St. Clair and Detroit Rivers and Lake St. Clair; 241 miles to the northeast, Erie empties into Lake Ontario via the Niagara River and its famous falls. Fourth largest of the Great Lakes, Erie is by far the shallowest: It averages just 62 feet deep. Its western end—a basin only 25 to 30 feet deep—is the shallowest of all.

Erie's vastly larger predecessor, glacial Lake Maumee, extended much farther south and drained into the Mississippi River. But glaciers punched a new outlet at the Niagara River, shrinking Lake Maumee to Erie's present size. It left behind a shallow, marshy shore between present-day Toledo and Sandusky Bay, reaching as far inland as Fort Wayne, Indiana. Settlers called this impenetrable lowland the Great Black Swamp, and they drained it with such a vengeance that only 5 percent of the original swamp remains.

Teeming with waterfowl and fishes, Lake Erie's southwest shore was a trove of astonishing biological richness and diversity. Bass and white bass clogged the mouths of rivers, while sturgeon were considered bony nuisances that cut up fish nets; steamships often burned them for fuel.

Lake Erie suffered some horrible insults over the last century, its waters flooded with agricultural runoff and a toxic stew of industrial waste (sulfuric acid from steel mills, calcium chloride from salt refineries). Miraculously, the fishery remained productive through it all, especially of perch, smallmouth bass, white bass, and channel catfish.

Today Erie's high nutrient levels and warm temperatures help its annual catch outrank that of any other Great Lake. Its water quality is improving, too, thanks to a 1992 water-quality agreement that imposed stricter standards, and the lake's ability to replenish itself: Erie flushes its water through in nearly 3 years, compared with 180 years for Superior.

What to See and Do

Ottawa National Wildlife Refuge

The 5,800-acre Ottawa National Wildlife Refuge preserves and restores Ohio's native wetland habitat. It also protects remnants of the Great Black Swamp in the form of stretches of beach and marsh. Shunting birds to both the Mississippi and Atlantic flyways, the refuge is the fork in the road for birds heading south. Tundra swans, pied-billed grebes, great egrets, American black ducks, and black-crowned night-herons are just a few of the 300 species that pass through the refuge. Shorebirds by the thousands fill the refuge in August; May is the peak month for viewing the songbird migration. Lake Erie's shoreline also provides one of the last strongholds of the bald eagle in Ohio, with several nesting pairs in the area.

Of 7 miles of trails, the 4.5-mile **Blue Trail** loop (*parking lot across from refuge headquarters off Ohio 2*) traverses the greatest array of habitats. It follows Crane Creek and passes through a vestige of the Great Black Swamp containing a patch of old-growth hardwoods.

Crane Creek State Park and Magee Marsh Wildlife Area

At the northeastern border of Ottawa National Wildlife Refuge, Crane Creek State Park and adjacent 2,600-acre Magee Marsh Wildlife Area protect more marshland habitat, along with a stretch of Lake Erie shoreline and a nice, sandy beach for swimming.

Even from the confines of your car, the bird-watching here is superb. Still, you'll want to get out and follow the 1-mile loop **Magee Marsh Bird Trail** (*trailhead at parking lot);* its boardwalk leads between a swamp forest and an open marsh, furnishing good chances of seeing songbirds and warblers. Crane Creek itself, which flows into Lake Erie just west of the park, is a bit of a misnomer. The creek is frequented by great blue herons and egrets, often misidentified as cranes.

The **Sportsmen's Migratory Bird Center** (*Mon.-Sat.*), located on Park Road 1 before you reach the state park, features displays of native wildlife species and tells the story of Lake Erie's marshlands. A four-story observation platform at the center offers a good overview of the environs.

Marblehead Peninsula

Split like a whale's tail, the 15-mile-long Marblehead Peninsula reaches east into Lake Erie from Port Clinton, forming Sandusky Bay and one of Ohio's most popular vacation areas. Fishing, boating, sightseeing, shopping, and lolling on the area's sand beaches are key summertime activities on the bustling shores of the bay. Things are a bit quieter inland, where the Lakeside daisy sprouts among limestone quarries. This delicate yellow wildflower grows only here and in a few spots in neighboring Ontario.

Lake Erie can be a sailor's nightmare. Storms whip across its waters with surprising speed and force, their effect amplified by the lake's meager depths. More than one ship's captain has relayed harrowing tales of waves cresting so high that they exposed Erie's sandy bottom. Thousands of shipwrecks litter the floor of the lake, which claims new victims every year.

All this makes Marblehead a particularly perilous spot on an already dangerous lake. Eastern gales sweep unobstructed across Erie's surface for more than 200 miles before hitting the peninsula, where they toss two-story waves onto the shallow shelf of its limestone shore. At the tip of the peninsula, the Marblehead Lighthouse warns off boaters as it has since 1821, making it the oldest active light tower on the Great Lakes.

Lake Erie Islands

Four islands—part of a tiny archipelago in western Lake Erie—scatter off the tip of the Marblehead Peninsula. South Bass, Middle Bass, and North Bass Islands march north from Catawba Island (really part of the mainland). Kelleys Island, largest of the four, lies a few miles east. Like the peninsula, the islands are limestone slabs shaped hundreds of millions of years ago by a warm, tropical sea.

As do the other Great Lakes, Lake Erie has a moderating effect on temperatures: It keeps things a bit cooler in summer and a bit warmer in winter. This lake effect, as it is known, gives the Erie quartet the longest growing season of any place in Ohio. As a result, grapevines thrive on all four islands. Middle Bass Island is largely given over to vineyards of catawba and Niagara grapes.

Kelleys Island State Park boasts some remarkable evidence of the glaciers that steamrollered the region. The advancing and retreating ice sheets left behind a series of glacial grooves resembling toboggan runs—troughs 15 feet deep and up to 400 feet long. Hard granite boulders embedded in the ice sheets probably etched these striae in the Earth's soft limestone surface. The grooves found on Kelleys Island may be the world's most impressive example of this glacial scouring. By analyzing the striations, geologists have determined that the glaciers advanced southwestward from present-day Quebec.

Six miles of hiking paths lead through the park. Both the **North Shore Loop Trail** *(parking lot at N end of Division St.)* and the **North Pond Trail** *(trailhead on Ward Rd., ½ mile E of Division St.)* wind up at nature preserves noted for their bird-watching. The park also offers a sandy swimming beach and 129 campsites. Kelleys Island is served by ferry from Marblehead. ∎

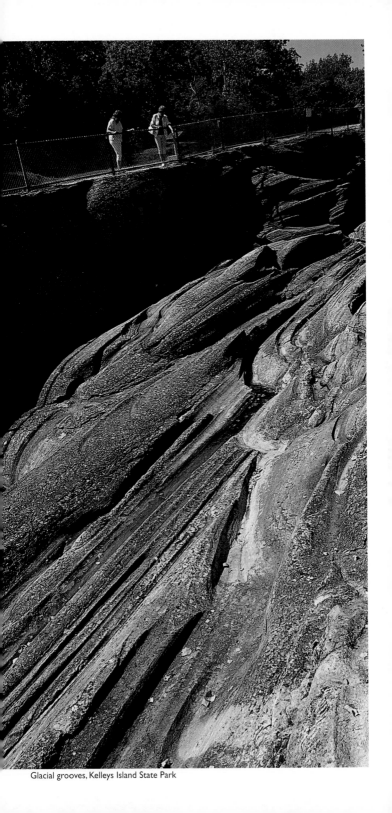

Glacial grooves, Kelleys Island State Park

Upper Mississippi River Valley

View of the Mississippi from Pikes Peak SP, Iowa

DEEP IN THE PINEY LAKE COUNTRY of northern Minnesota,
a small stream wanders north out of Lake Itasca. Pretty,
yet unremarkable, it gives little hint as to what it will
become: the Mighty Mississippi, the largest and second
longest river in North America, the third most voluminous on Earth.

From Lake Itasca, the fledgling Mississippi scribbles
along through pines and marshes, bleeding through wild
rice paddies and across large lakes. It arcs through

Minnesota like a giant question mark, fed by dozens of tributaries as it flows south to the Twin Cities. The river continues to broaden as it forms the Minnesota-Wisconsin border, where sandstone bluffs more than 500 feet high rise to frame it. Classic northern rivers such as the St. Croix and the Chippewa continue to add to its flow, draining hundreds of smaller white-water rivers and streams.

Dropping little in elevation, the Mississippi settles in across a yawning valley that ranges from 1 to 6 miles wide. Perhaps at its most majestic here, the river rolls smooth and strong between craggy bluffs that are rocky and barren on the westward-facing Wisconsin side and cloaked in hardwoods on the Minnesota-Iowa shore. As the Mississippi continues slaloming southward, it really begins picking up volume, absorbing the Illinois, the Missouri, and the Ohio. The Missouri, entering at St. Louis, doubles the Mississippi's size; the Ohio doubles it again. By the time it reaches the Gulf of Mexico, the Mississippi River has covered 2,350 miles and drained over 40 percent of the nation's water, from the foothills of the Rockies to the Appalachians. The Mighty Mississippi indeed.

More than 600 million years ago, a shallow sea covered what is now the Mississippi River Valley, depositing thick layers of mud, sand, and sediment. This eventually compressed into the sedimentary rock—the sandstone, shale, and limestone, or dolomite—that characterizes the region. While glaciers scoured many parts of the Great Lakes region relatively flat, the last ice age, about 10,000 years ago, never advanced through the upper Mississippi. Spared the leveling effects of glacial sediment or drift, this so-called driftless area is defined by chiseled rock faces, steep hills, and twisting ravines.

The glacier played a role in other ways, though. As the last ice sheets began melting away, torrents of meltwater filled with corrosive gravel poured forth, gouging out a great north-south trough along which the Mississippi now flows and sluicing out hundreds of other channels that eventually became its tributaries.

A diverse array of ecosystems evolved, including rivers, sloughs, braided channels, backwater lakes, prairies, and forests. Silver maple dominates the forest of the upper Mississippi River floodplain, accompanied by pin oak, American elm, and, moving south, sycamore and cottonwood. The river basin harbors 195 species of fish, almost one-third of the freshwater fish species in North America. For anglers, the Mississippi River system means everything from fly-fishing a pristine North Woods stream for trout, to poling a johnboat through southern-like sloughs in search of catfish.

With an abundance of natural cover and food sources such as pondweed and sedges, the river valley provides perfect habitat for waterfowl. The Mississippi flyway is one of the world's great migratory bird routes, an aerial highway followed by hundreds of species traveling between their summer nesting grounds in the north and warmer wintering spots. More than 40 percent of the nation's waterfowl and shorebirds migrate through the upper Mississippi River Valley each year. An estimated eight

Kayaker, St. Croix River

million ducks, geese, and swans winter in the lower part of the flyway, along with thousands of bald eagles and other raptors.

Man also has traveled up and down this river valley for thousands of years. Even before the last glaciers receded, Paleo-Indians hunted megafauna such as the woolly mammoth, mastodon, and giant beaver. Much later, about 2,000 years ago, a mound-building culture evolved, building tens of thousands of animal-shaped effigy mounds throughout the upper Mississippi River Valley. Several of these groupings of mounds, found nowhere else in the world, still exist in Iowa and Wisconsin.

The Ojibwa, who named the river the Missi Sipi, or "big river," traveled the region in birchbark canoes, as did other tribes, French explorers such as Marquette and Joliet, and the French-Canadian fur traders of the 17th and 18th centuries. But it was commerce of the early 1800s that would change the river forever. The Mississippi and its tributaries quickly became a key transportation network for the logging operations of the north, the lead mines of southwestern Wisconsin, and the Union Army during the Civil War. By the late 1800s, more than one thousand steamships plied the river.

The upper Mississippi's natural loopy course of winding channels and scattered sandbars confounded steamboat captains, so man began intervening. In the 1800s, workers dug a 9-foot-wide channel, which is still used and maintained today. In the 1930s, the U.S. Army Corps of Engineers joined in the effort to improve navigation, constructing a series of wing dams that narrow the river at low water times to increase its velocity, along with closing locks and dams that direct river flow to a main channel. Today 29 locks and dams span the Mississippi, controlling its depth to allow passage of massive barges as long as 295 feet, which haul coal, grain, iron, petroleum, chemicals, and other cargoes.

St. Croix National Scenic Riverway, Wisconsin

The diggings and dammings destroyed the natural ecology of the upper Mississippi, changing it from a free-flowing river to a series of highly controlled lakes, each 15 to 30 miles long. While birds seem to thrive in the open waters and endless backwater pools and marshes, increased silt and sediment threatens to choke out some aquatic life. By forcing the river away from one shore and against the other, the wing dams accelerated bank erosion, prompting the corps to armor hundreds of miles of shoreline with brush mats and stone.

We've impacted the river in countless other ways, too: widespread logging eroded the banks of northern rivers, adding more sediment; pesticides, fertilizers, and other agricultural runoff drain into tributaries; urban sewage seeps in; and industrial effluent, unchecked for too long, has added PCBs and other toxic substances to the mix.

But Mother Nature occasionally takes back the wheel, as the great flood of 1993 proved. After record-breaking rains soaked the Midwest in spring 1993, the swollen Mississippi overpowered all human attempts to control it. City after city along its banks drowned in muddy waters up to 50 feet deep—nearly 50,000 homes were destroyed and some 12,000 square miles of farmland rendered useless. More than 1,000 of the 1,300 levees designed to control floodwaters failed. Like the fires of Yellowstone, the event raised countless questions about what man could or could not, should or should not, do to prevent such a disaster from occurring again.

As the debates roll on, there's comfort in knowing that the Mississippi somehow manages to roll on, too. While we owe it to ourselves and future generations to address the river's complicated problems, we also can enjoy its charms. So slip a canoe into a quiet channel or hike up to a high point . . . and lose yourself among the beauty of the birds, the backwaters, and the bluffs. ■

St. Croix National Scenic Riverway

■ 252 miles ■ Northwestern Wisconsin, including a portion of Wisconsin-Minnesota border ■ Year-round. Boating generally April-Oct. Water levels typically highest in spring ■ Camping, hiking, boating, canoeing, fishing, wildlife viewing ■ Contact the riverway, P.O. Box 708, 401 Hamilton St., St. Croix Falls, WI 54024; phone 715-483-3284. www.nps.gov/sacn

WANDERING AIMLESSLY ACROSS northwest Wisconsin, the St. Croix River and its largest tributary, the Namekagon, flow clean and clear between largely undeveloped woodland shores. The St. Croix was one of the original eight river systems protected by the 1968 Wild and Scenic Rivers Act, ensuring that these waters retain their simple, unfettered beauty.

The St. Croix National Scenic Riverway protects nearly the entire length of both the St. Croix and the Namekagon Rivers. Characterized by ragged bluffs and deep valleys, the lower 50 miles of the St. Croix lie at the northern edge of the driftless area—an area untouched by the last glaciers that scrubbed across much of the upper Great Lakes region.

Boating is the best way to experience the rivers. The upper reaches of the St. Croix and Namekagon are canoe rivers, with narrow and twisting sections, and some rapids (but rarely any white water). Many paddlers plan multiday trips, spending the night at primitive canoe campsites that dot the shores. The lower St. Croix, below St. Croix Falls, is slower and wider, and frequented by motorboats.

A diverse and healthy population of fish attracts fishermen along the riverway. Anglers cast for trout in its upper reaches. In lower portions of the rivers muskie, walleye, northern pike, bass, and even the primitive-looking lake sturgeon may be the catch of the day.

What to See and Do

The Namekagon River

A lovely North Woods river, the Namekagon begins in the Chequamegon National Forest as a tea-colored trout stream. It flows through pine forest with sandy banks, occasionally widening into marshes and other lowlands frequented by great blue herons. Observant visitors may spy wood ducks, identified by their meticulous paint-by-numbers markings.

Intimate and narrow, the Namekagon is a snarl of tight corners and hairpin turns, perfectly suited for (and pretty much only for) a canoe. The 98-mile river can be roughly divided into three segments, each a two-day trip. The first segment, from the Namekagon Dam to Hayward, includes several rapids; these can swell to Class II in spring runoff or dry to a trickle in summer. (Check river levels with the Park Service.) The second segment, from Hayward to Trego, has more development along its banks, but offers a good water level and gradient for most of its run, with some Class I and II

Rock climbers, Interstate State Park, Wisconsin

rapids. The bottom third of the Namekagon is perhaps the most popular. It features steep sandy banks, little visible development, and lots of shoreline campsites.

The Upper St. Croix River

From its headwaters at Upper St. Croix Lake, the St. Croix River trickles out through boreal forest as a bony creek, navigable only during higher water levels in spring. The scenic riverway begins at the Gordan Dam on the St. Croix Flowage. After 20 miles, it meets up with the Namekagon, but remains unreliably shallow until mile 23.5 at Riverside Landing. Here the river deepens and begins an 86-mile journey through wide valleys with low banks to the dam at St. Croix Falls.

On the Minnesota side, **St. Croix State Park** *(320-384-6591)* lies north of the confluence of the pretty Kettle River and the St. Croix. At 34,000 acres, it's Minnesota's largest state park, offering camping, horseback riding, and an impressive 127 miles of hiking trails. Some of the prettiest paths wind along the forested banks of the Kettle.

The 20,000-acre **Governor Knowles State Forest** *(715-463-2898)* stretches along the Wisconsin shore, featuring 38 miles of hiking trails. Just east of the forest, near Nelsons Landing, trumpeter swans, sandhill cranes, and the rare yellow-headed blackbird hide among the prairie grasses and wetlands of the **Crex Meadows Wildlife Area**.

Farther south and on the Minnesota shore, **Wild River State Park** *(651-583-2125)* offers several

miles of hiking trails. Some climb high above the river, where you can spot hawks and bald eagles.

The Lower St. Croix River

The dam at St. Croix Falls marks the distinction between the upper and lower St. Croix. Added to the national scenic riverway in 1972, the lower St. Croix has a character completely different from that of its upper reaches—wider, deeper, and slower.

Just below the dam, the river squeezes through a narrow 200-foot-high gorge riven by glacial meltwater. Twin state parks in Minnesota and Wisconsin—each named Interstate—encompass the gorge, called the Dalles of the St. Croix. During the 19th century, the St. Croix was often choked with logs floating downstream to sawmills. Predictably, logjams often formed at the Dalles, including a 3-mile-long mess that occurred in 1883. Even with the help of dynamite, that blockage took eight weeks to untangle.

Below the Apple River, the St. Croix widens and becomes more appropriate for powerboats than canoes. Park rangers here are waging a war against the zebra mussel. Boat hulls must be powerwashed to remove the mussel if they have been in infected waters within two weeks. This invasive species kills native mussels and eats plankton, destroying the food chain for native fish and insects.

At its southernmost reaches, the river is known as Lake St. Croix, a playground whose sandy shores are filled with sailboats, houseboats, water-skiers, and sunbathers. ∎

Fall cyclists, Great River State Trail, Wisconsin

Upper Mississippi Bluffs

■ 261 miles ■ Wabasha, Minn. to Rock Island, Ill. ■ Year-round ■ Camping, hiking, boating, fishing, biking, cross-country skiing, snowshoeing, bird-watching, scenic drives ■ Adm. fee for Wisconsin state parks and Great River State Trail ■ Contact Upper Mississippi River National Wildlife and Fish Refuge, 51 East Fourth St., Winona, MN 55987, phone 507-452-4232. www.umesc.usgs.gov/umr_refuge.html; Trempealeau National Wildlife Refuge, W28488 Refuge Rd., Trempealeau, WI 54661, phone 608-539-2311. www.umesc.usgs.gov/umr_refuge/umrtre/umrtre.html; Perrot State Park, W26247 Sullivan Rd., Trempealeau, WI 54661, phone 608-534-6409

MORE THAN A BROAD RIBBON of water, the upper Mississippi bluffs region of the river valley is a lush and diverse mix of ecosystems, including rivers, marshes, sandbars, sloughs, backwater lakes, wooded islands, bottomland forests, and largely undeveloped hillsides of forest and prairie. Southeast of Minneapolis-St. Paul, below the confluence with the St. Croix, the Mississippi River broadens to fill a 2- to 5-mile-wide valley

hemmed in by high bluffs of limestone and sandstone as far south as Savanna, Illinois.

Much of the valley is protected as the Upper Mississippi River National Wildlife and Fish Refuge, a conservation area that extends 261 miles from Wabasha, Minnesota, to Rock Island, Illinois, and encompasses more than 200,000 acres. A patchwork of public lands on the Wisconsin side of the river—including Trempealeau National Wildlife Refuge, Merrick State Park, and Perrot State Park—offer additional protection and public access.

This is a dynamic environment. During years of heavy rain or snowfall, the Mississippi River rises, flooding islands, flushing marshes, and creating new backwaters. The high water also deposits tons of nutrient-rich silt across the Mississippi River Valley.

Humans have played a role, too. In an effort to improve navigation, the U.S. Army Corps of Engineers began constructing a series of locks and dams in the 1930s; 11 of them now span the Mississippi within the stretch protected by the refuge. The dams disrupt the river's natural cycle, creating a pool behind each dam. (The corps, in fact, describes the river in terms of numbered pools: Pool 10, for example, is the stretch of river between Lock and Dam No. 9 and No. 10.)

As the navigation pools have aged, the natural habitat has deterio-

Fishing on the Mississippi near Prairie du Chien, Wisconsin

rated. Backwaters are slowly silting up and river vegetation is disappearing as well.

Despite man's fiddling—and in some cases, because of it—the river valley supports an enormous variety of wildlife. The Mississippi River Valley is a major migratory route, so bird-watching is spectacular in spring and fall. Eagles and other raptors winter here, often fishing in the open waters below the dams. Herons, egrets, and warblers nest in the wooded bottomlands. Thousands of tundra swans migrate through, as do all kinds of ducks: The brilliantly marked wood duck frequents protected backwaters and sloughs, and as much as three-quarters of the lower 48's population of canvasbacks stop over in fall, especially on Pools 7 and 8 near La Crosse and Pool 9 near Ferryville, Wisconsin. In all, nearly 300 species of birds have been sighted here.

Around 1920, agricultural interests threatened the region with plans to dike the river just south of De Soto, Wisconsin, and drain the backwaters for farming. Concerned about the destruction of critical spawning grounds for smallmouth bass, Will Dilg, one of the founders of the Isaac Walton League, successfully lobbied Congress in 1924 to establish the Upper Mississippi River National Wildlife and Fish Refuge. The legislation marked two firsts: the first major conservation victory of the venerable Isaac Walton League and the nation's first wildlife and fish refuge.

What to See and Do

Great River Road

Wis. 35 slaloms between the Mississippi and towering bluffs stringing together dozens of sleepy river towns. It is part of the Great River Road, an amalgamation of byways that stretch from the river's headwaters to the Gulf of Mexico. The idea of a scenic byway running the length of the Mississippi started in Wisconsin, and the first stretch of the Mississippi River Parkway, as it was then named, was built near Trempealeau in 1953. If so inclined, you can create a loop drive between Red Wing and Winona, Minnesota, by following Wis. 35 down the river's east side, then crossing over to Minnesota and traveling the opposite direction on US 61.

Turnoffs at towns along the route offer peaceful spots to soak in the forested bluffs, scour the skies for birds, and watch the barges and other water traffic churn their way up and down the mighty river. Most of the locks and dams have viewing platforms open to the public, too.

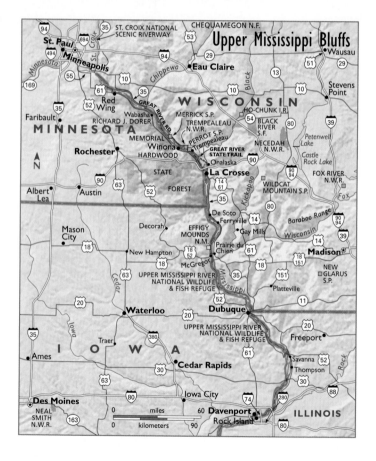

Great River State Trail

Wisconsin is a national leader in converting abandoned railroad right-of-ways into hiking and biking trails. The **Great River State Trail** *(Center for Tourism & Commerce 800-873-1901)* is arguably the state's finest. It roughly parallels the Mississippi for 24 miles from Marshland to Onalaska, passing Trempealeau National Wildlife Refuge and Perrot State Park before terminating at the La Crosse River.

Riverside ferns

Walking or cycling along the crushed limestone path, you'll pass through a mix of dry prairie and river bottomlands and cross several bridges spanning wetlands and tributaries. In spring, the woods bloom with violets, hepaticas, Dutchman's-breeches, wood geraniums, bellworts, and phlox. The river corridor is still an active commercial transportation network: Freight trains clatter up and down adjacent railroad tracks with surprising frequency.

Upper Mississippi River Nat. Wildlife and Fish Refuge

Because of the vastness of the refuge, it's best to start with a visit to the nearest district refuge office for suggestions on walks, observation points, canoe launches, and so on. Offices are located in Winona, Minnesota; Onalaska, Wisconsin *(608-783-8403)*; McGregor, Iowa *(319-873-3423)*; and Thomson, Illinois *(815-273-2732)*. If you plan to do any boating, ask for the pool maps; they offer a good interpretation of the confusion of endless bays and channels.

Boating, especially in a canoe or kayak, which can access the

shallow backwaters where birds and other animals congregate, is probably the best way to experience the refuge. Boat launches are numerous throughout the refuge. Because the maze of islands and channels can be befuddling, you may want to start with one of the area's marked canoe trails. At **Merrick State Park** *(608-687-4936. Adm. fee)* north of Trempealeau, Wisconsin, a 2-mile loop leads through a scatter of islands.

As its name implies, the Upper Mississippi River National Wildlife and Fish Refuge boasts a healthy and diverse fish population. At least 118 species have been recorded, from sport fish (walleye, smallmouth bass, and northern pike) to strange prehistoric species (paddlefish and lake sturgeon) to traditional shallow-water river fish (catfish, carp, and bullhead). The refuge also provides important habitat for the endangered Higgin's eye mussel.

Trempealeau National Wildlife Refuge

Often overshadowed by the much larger Upper Mississippi River

National Wildlife and Fish Refuge, 6,200-acre Trempealeau is one of the region's hidden gems. A series of dikes built for railroad lines in the 1800s effectively isolated a large swath of Mississippi River backwaters. As a result, it remains an extremely high-quality wetland, its waters protected from siltation, agricultural runoff, and other pollution.

The refuge includes several miles of dikes and service roads that allow you to explore the area on foot or bicycle. The 5-mile interpretive **Wildlife Drive** (pick up a guide booklet at the Refuge Road entrance kiosk) loops through the refuge's range of sand prairie, marsh, and floodplain forest habitats. Though autos are permitted on this gravel route, mountain bikes are even better for seeing and hearing the abundant wildlife. Painted turtles sun on muddy banks, wood ducks nest in tree cavities, great horned owls perch on high limbs, and thousands upon thousands of migratory birds rest and roost in the wetlands. For a water-level view of the wildlife, a boat launch near Kiep's Island provides access for canoes, kayaks, and boats with electric motors only.

Scattered patches of sand prairie are visible throughout the refuge from Wildlife Drive. The prairie originally formed as the prevailing winds blew sand and sediment into large dunes. Grasses later established themselves and stabilized the dunes. Though much of the original prairie was destroyed, remnants remain, including parcels of 6-foot-high big bluestem and Indian grass.

Restoration projects have reestablished 350 acres of prairie, one of the largest in the region.

As part of the restoration efforts, refuge managers must continually fight back invasive species such as black locust trees. Planted here in the 1930s to reduce erosion, black locusts grow quickly in the dry prairie soils, sending shoots up from horizontal roots. Cutting and controlled burns now keep these trees at bay.

Perrot State Park

Fragmented sections of the upper Mississippi bluffs rise up like enormous anthills at this 1,253-acre state park along the river's edge. The Mississippi originally flowed on the west side of these bluffs but was rerouted by glacial silt deposits. State park trails skirt along the backwaters of Trempealeau Bay, zigzag through a 10-acre patch of native hillside prairie, and circle and climb several bluffs.

Three trails scale the highest one, Bradys Bluff, which towers 520 feet above the floodplain. Across from the boat landing on Park Road you can follow the steep 0.5-mile Bradys Bluff West Trail, traveling through 600 million years of geology, ascending layers of sandstone and dolomite, each laid down during a different era.

From the crest of Bradys Bluff, a jigsaw puzzle of islands and channels spill out in front of you. Trempealeau Mountain dominates the view, jutting 385-feet directly out of the water. The tallest island on the Mississippi, it was a well-known landmark for natives and early immigrants alike. ∎

A quiet afternoon on the Kickapoo River

Kickapoo River Valley

■ 12,300 acres ■ Southwestern Wisconsin, 35 miles east of La Crosse ■ Year-round. Best canoeing April-Oct. ■ Camping, hiking, canoeing, fishing, biking, horseback riding, cross-country skiing, snowshoeing, scenic drive ■ Permit required for reserve; adm. fee for state park ■ Contact Kickapoo Valley Reserve, 505 N. Mill St., La Farge, WI 54639, phone 608-625-2960, kvr.state.wi.us; or Wildcat Mountain State Park, P.O. Box 99, Ontario, WI 54651, phone 608-337-4775

THE THICK ICE SHEETS THAT flattened much of the Great Lakes region during the last ice age, more than 10,000 years ago, never advanced across southwestern Wisconsin and the adjacent corners of northwestern Illinois and northeastern Iowa. As a result, the land here is wrinkled into deep furrows and filled with crooked rivers, steep-sided ravines, sandstone outcrops, and limestone escarpments. Because it is free of glacial sediment or drift, this region is known as the driftless area.

The clear, spring-fed Kickapoo River showcases the driftless area perfectly. A crazy corkscrew of a river that twists for 125 miles to cover the 65-mile distance between the communities of Wilton and Wauzeka, the Algonquin Indians named the river Kickapoo—"one who goes there, then here." Less than a mile wide at its broadest, the river valley narrows to just a small gap in many places. Geologists believe the Kickapoo may be among the oldest river systems in the world because the river valley predates the glaciers.

Normally a gentle river perfect for floating in a canoe, the Kickapoo can quickly rise out of its narrow banks after heavy rains. More than a half-dozen major floods occurred between 1907 and 1956, drowning several farming communities and prompting discussion of a flood-control project. After decades of debate, the U.S. Army Corps of Engineers broke ground near La Farge in 1971 on a $24-million dam and reservoir, designed to alleviate flooding and create a lake for recreation.

As environmental groups rallied to stop the project, the corps moved forward, buying up 140 farms, rerouting roads, and building dam towers. Four years later, only partially complete, the dam was mothballed for a host of environmental and economic reasons. (The passage of the Endangered Species Act in 1973 was a contributing factor because one endangered plant and three threatened plants can be found within the project area.)

The 8,569-acre tract sat in limbo until the late 1990s. Now the land has come full circle: A 1,200-acre portion has been returned to the Ho-Chunk Nation and the rest reverted to state public lands as the Kickapoo Valley Reserve for "education, recreation, and low-impact tourism." Together with Wildcat Mountain State Park at its northern boundary, the area offers you ample opportunities to explore its delightfully twisting trails, roads, and riverways.

What to See and Do

Hiking

The well-marked trails at 3,700-acre **Wildcat Mountain State Park** offer a good introduction to the driftless area. The **Old Settlers Trail** begins at the park's prime observation point, high atop a limestone escarpment, then loops 2.8 miles up and down its flank. Pileated woodpecker, ruffed grouse, and wild turkey are common in the woodlands here, a mix of hardwoods and pine plantation. This area is reclaimed farmland and snow-on-the-mountain, a garden plant, now grows wild underfoot. A wide variety of songbirds inhabit the forest edge.

Passing through the Mount Pisgah Hemlock–Hardwoods State Natural Area, the state park's

Hemlock Nature Trail climbs one mile to the 1,220-foot summit of Mount Pisgah. Lacy-needled hemlocks provide a canopy of dappled sunlight well-suited to a range of wildflowers including wild geranium, bluebell, sweet cicely, and cooler-climate species such as wild ginger and bunchberry. The humus-rich rocky ledges support a lush carpet of ferns, lichens, liverworts, and the more unusual puffball and shaggy mane fungi.

Trails within the reserve are less developed, but a little bushwhacking will reward you with old-growth hemlock forests, short-grass prairie remnants, and high sandstone overlooks. To find your way around pick up a map at the reserve office in La Farge. Most

Paddling the Kickapoo River, Wildcat Mountain SP

Eastern wild turkey

Talking Turkey

Eastern wild turkeys once inhabited much of southern Wisconsin, but by the 1880s they had disappeared, the result of overhunting, habitat loss, and diseases transmitted by domestic poultry. In 1976, the Wisconsin Department of Natural Resources began a program to reintroduce the wild turkey. In exchange for ruffed grouse, it obtained a total of 334 birds from Missouri and released them in the southwestern corner of Wisconsin in the heart of the driftless area.

It quickly proved to be one of the most successful reintroduction programs ever. Within just three years, the turkeys had multiplied into the thousands. From this population, about 3,500 turkeys were trapped and relocated to additional counties throughout the state. The current statewide wild turkey count is estimated at 320,000—a remarkable feat of reproduction by any standard.

trailheads begin at lettered campsites, which are marked on maps and in the reserve itself. At Campsite N, follow a horseback/mountain bike route east to a small sign with a hiking icon. This footpath leads north up a spine of mixed hardwood forest to Blackhawk Rock. Follow the trail as it circles the rock for a hawk's-eye view of the serpentine valley below.

Horseback Riding and Mountain Biking

The Kickapoo Valley Reserve has long been regarded among equestrians as one of the most beautiful destinations in the Midwest. The reserve offers approximately 34 miles of riding trails, which follow streams and climb through hollows. One of the prettiest begins at Campsite S north of Rockton and twists north toward Ontario, crossing three creeks before terminating at Campsite U.

Wildcat Mountain State Park also caters to horseback riders (*May–mid-Nov.*), with 15 miles of hilly bridle trails that crest bluffs and wind through woods and fields. The park includes horseback campsites complete with corral, hitching posts, and loading ramp.

From Hay Valley Road in the north, a 10-mile long mountain bike trail runs the length of the reserve to Corps Road in the south. This challenging route includes steep uphill climbs with hairpin turns and passes through hardwood forest, oak savanna, and open meadow. Observe trail etiquette and yield to equines on sections of the path—mostly connector trails—shared with horseback riders.

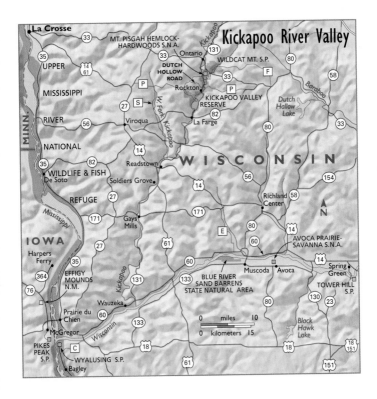

Canoeing and Fishing

Not surprisingly, a canoe is probably the best way to explore the river valley. Though it can become swift and dangerous after storms, the Kickapoo's normally mellow current makes it appropriate even for novice paddlers. (A bigger issue tends to be shallows and logjams that require portaging.) Ontario to La Farge is about a 10-hour paddle; with several put-ins along Wis. 131, you can plan a trip ranging from 2 hours to all day.

As you travel downstream, you'll hug tall sandstone cliffs, which seep moisture and host a variety of lush ferns and mosses. Hemlocks and pines shade much of the river's course. Watch for wildlife: Beavers, muskrat, and otters all glide across its waters, and deer, raccoons, and woodchucks frequent its banks. More than a hundred bird species inhabit the river valley, including the threatened Kentucky warbler and the Louisiana water-thrush. Shorebirds such as tundra swans and sandpipers sometimes make surprise appearances as they migrate through the region.

Many of the Kickapoo's small tributaries, including Billings Creek, offer excellent fishing for brown trout.

Scenic Drive

You can hardly go wrong on any drive in this wrinkled valley, where roads dip through valleys of grazing Holsteins, wind along ridge

Living Fossil Fish

Among the walleye, catfish, and other species inhabiting the upper Mississippi and its tributaries lurk a few remarkable oddities: prehistoric species that have lived in these waters since the days of the dinosaurs. The paddlefish, the gar, and the sturgeon are virtually unchanged from millions of years ago, retaining characteristics long lost by most other modern-day fish.

The largest and most notable of these ancient fishes is the lake sturgeon. Lake sturgeon can reach lengths of eight feet and weigh in at more than 200 pounds. (Other sturgeon species, such as the beluga sturgeon of Russia, can weigh ten times that.) Though sturgeon are considered rare in the U.S., one of the country's largest self-sustaining populations can be found in Wisconsin waterways.

The monstrous sturgeon looks appropriately medieval, clad in an armor of bony, overlapping cartilage plates, each with a sharp pointed spur. Four barbels dangle off the lower side of its short snout, feeling for food as the sturgeon cruises along the lake or river bottom. Sturgeons have no teeth. They suck up snails, small clams, insect larvae, and leeches and then expel the silt, gravel, and other bottom debris through their gills. Opaque eyes and an asymmetric split tail fin (like that of a shark) complete the sturgeon's sinister appearance.

By the early 1900s, the lake sturgeon was nearly harvested to extinction for its roe, or caviar. Its slow reproduction cycle makes for a difficult comeback: Though male sturgeon can live for 50 to 60 years, females can survive over 100 years but don't reach maturity until about age 25. Even then females spawn only every four to nine years.

Loss of habitat also plays a key role. Dams prohibit sturgeon from returning to their spawning grounds, and pollution fouls the lake and river bottoms. It remains to be seen whether this fascinating fish that's a link to the river's past will be part of the river's future.

tops crosshatched with apple trees, skirt Amish farms, and skip back and forth over the Kickapoo.

Begin in Ontario, home to canoe outfitters and other services, for a short 17-mile loop through the Kickapoo Valley Reserve. Follow Wis. 33 southeast as it arcs past Wildcat Mountain State Park high above the valley. At about mile 3, turn west on County Road F, which passes the Mount Pisgah Hemlock–Hardwoods State Natural Area under the shadow of a limestone bluff. Turn south on Wis. 131, which hopscotches from bank to bank across the Kickapoo. You'll pass several trailheads and canoe campsites. After 3 miles on 131, turn right on Dutch Hollow Road. This is one of Wisconsin's Rustic Roads, selected for its scenic characteristics. The road follows high ridgelines and passes some Amish farms, recognizable by the use of horses and hand tools in the fields rather than mechanized equipment. Follow the Rustic Road signs back to Ontario via Sand Hill Road and Lower Ridge Road.

For a longer drive through the Kickapoo Valley, follow the above route, but rather than turning onto Dutch Hollow Road, stay on Wis. 131 to Rockton. From here, follow County Road P as it swings southwest, crossing the Kickapoo and passing the Blackhawk Rock trailhead. Turn south on County Road S which winds alongside the West Fork Kickapoo River down a green agrarian valley. At Reed-stown, the West Fork meets the main Kickapoo; continue south on Wis. 131 to follow the river.

At Gays Mills, the heart of Wisconsin's apple country, turn right on Wis. 171. The gently sloping hillsides provide the orchards with ample sunlight and protection from damaging winter winds. From Gays Mills, Wis. 171 continues another 11 miles to the Mississippi River. ■

Hemlock Trail, Wildcat Mountain SP

Confluence of the Mississippi and Wisconsin Rivers

Lower Wisconsin State Riverway

■ 79,000 acres, encompassing 92 miles of the Wisconsin River ■ Southwest Wisconsin, from Prairie du Sac to the Mississippi River ■ Spring through fall for river activities ■ Camping, hiking, boating (40 hp or less), canoeing, fishing, wildlife viewing, scenic drive ■ Contact Lower Wisconsin State Riverway Board, 202 N. Wisconsin Ave., Muscoda, WI 53573; phone 608-739-3188 or 800-221-3792. lwr.state.wi.us

AS THE WISCONSIN RIVER FLOWS from the state's far north, 26 hydroelectric dams harness its power, earning it the nickname "the hardest working river in the nation." But northwest of Madison, where the river arcs through a broad hairpin turn and swings southwest, its work is done. Below a final dam at Prairie du Sac, the Wisconsin rolls 92 uninterrupted miles to its confluence with the Mississippi—one of the longest stretches of free-flowing river in the eastern United States.

Float down the lower Wisconsin River in a canoe and enjoy scenery remarkably similar to that which Jacques Marquette and Louis Joliet witnessed when they explored this waterway in 1673. The broad river rolls past sand barrens, sedge meadows, wetlands, sandstone bluffs, and tallgrass prairies climbing up hillsides. Designated a state riverway in 1989, a few bridges, power lines, and an oft-hidden highway are all that will mar your 17th-century view. That highway, Wis. 60, parallels the river's north bank all the way to the Mississippi and makes for a fine scenic drive.

At Prairie du Sac, the lower Wisconsin flows through a gorge of sandstone bluffs nearly 4 miles wide. Although part of the state's driftless area (the region not scoured by glaciers), the ice sheets still played a role in the landscape. The meltwater carried tons of sediment through the valley; today the sand riverbed is some 150 feet deep and sandbars frequently appear, disappear, or shift downstream, depending on water levels.

The stretch of river between Prairie du Sac and Spring Green is a favorite recreation area, popular with canoeists, fishermen, and sun-bathers lolling on sandbars. (Be aware that sandbars drop off sharply on the downstream side, and river currents can be deceptively dangerous. Drownings occur almost every summer.) The broad river valley and sinewy hollows inspired architect Frank Lloyd Wright who built Taliesin, his home and architecture school, in Spring Green's Wyoming Valley.

You can find several canoe launches in the Spring Green area. Many paddlers launch at Peck's Landing below the Wis. 23 bridge while others put in at **Tower Hill State Park** (*5805 Cty. Rd. C, Spring Green, WI 53588; 608-588-2116*). The park is named for a shot tower still on the site that was used to manufacture ammuni-tion from the 1830s to the 1850s.

Dawn on the lower Wisconsin

The Lower Wisconsin State Riverway protects one of the larg-est remnants of tallgrass prairie remaining in the eastern United States. The **Avoca Prairie–Savanna State Natural Area,** north of the village of Avoca, in-cludes nearly 1,300 acres of native prairie and sedge meadow. Prairie plants such as little bluestem, but-terfly milkweed, coneflower, spi-derwort, prairie coreopsis, bush clover, and wild rye once covered 9 percent of southern Wisconsin and much of the upper Mississippi River Valley—more than two mil-lion acres in Wisconsin alone. Piece by piece, settlers overgrazed and plowed under the Midwest's vast prairies for cropland. The Avoca tract only hints at what it must have looked like, a sea of delicate blooms and tall grasses bobbing in the summer breeze.

Sand barrens are another rare and vital ecosystem protected along the riverway. Just west of Muscoda, the **Blue River Sand Barrens State Nat-ural Area** harbors dozens of rare plants found few other places in the world. Most recognizable—and to many, most surprising—is the prickly pear cactus, the only cactus native to Wisconsin.

As the river continues on its southwestern path, the valley progres-sively narrows and shifts from predominantly sandstone to limestone. A rural, lightly visited area, paddlers and hikers will likely share this final stretch of river only with the likes of eagles, deer, beavers, and otters. ∎

Wyalusing State Park

■ 2,654 acres ■ Southwestern Wisconsin, south of Prairie du Chien, jct. of Wisconsin and Mississippi Rivers ■ Year-round ■ Camping, hiking, canoeing, fishing, bird-watching, wildlife viewing ■ Adm. fee ■ Contact the park, 13081 State Park Ln., Bagley, WI 53801; phone 608-996-2261

FROM HIGH ATOP A 500-FOOT sandstone bluff on the Sentinel Ridge Trail, a jumble of river channels, sandbars, sloughs, jungle-like backwaters, and forested islands seems to all but obliterate the Mighty Mississippi itself. At Wyalusing State Park you enjoy a true eagle's-eye view of the confluence of the Wisconsin and Mississippi Rivers.

Many park visitors come simply to soak in these views, which are especially brilliant in fall when oaks and sugar maples turn crimson and scarlet. But it's well worth exploring the park, with its web of trails that cling to the bluff faces, wind among the wooded bluffs, pass small caves, and meander along the bottomlands. White-tailed deer are likely to spring across your path, and grouse may startle you as they erupt from the underbrush, flapping away with a loud buzz. Wild turkeys and pheasants are also frequently seen in the park.

The Mississippi River's backwaters lure paddlers with a shallow labyrinth of waterways and waterlogged islands. In late summer, blooms erupt in this lush environment, from rosy pink marsh milkweed and deep purple New York ironweed to the brilliant red cardinal flower and the well-known white water lily. A 6-mile signed **canoe circuit** guides paddlers through the sloughs, away from any boat traffic on the main channel or significant current.

You're likely to spot muskrats gliding quietly through the water with just their noses and rat-like tails breaking the surface. Though mostly herbivorous, they have an appetite for freshwater mussels. Look along the shore for discarded

Marquette and Joliet

The mouth of the Wisconsin River marked the highlight of an epic 2,900-mile journey by Jacques Marquette and Louis Joliet. In 1673, the Frenchmen set out in canoes across the northern shore of Lake Michigan to search for a trade route to the Far East. They had heard from the Indians about a great waterway, Missi Sipi ("big river"), that they thought might flow into the Pacific Ocean.

Marquette and Joliet canoed down Green Bay and then paddled and portaged their way to the Wisconsin River with the help of local Indians guides. It was at this spot near the mouth of the Wisconsin that the two explorers first spotted the fabled Mississippi.

They never discovered an eastern trade route, of course. But their journey and peaceful communications with dozens of Indian tribes added greatly to the white man's knowledge of North American geography.

shells, leftovers from a muskrat meal. You also may spot painted and snapping turtles, which commonly sun on fallen logs and then plop into the water as you approach.

Great egrets and great blue herons stalk through the bottomlands and fish along the water's edge, spearing fish with a quick stab of their beaks. Herons are masters at disguise: They become remarkably still if they feel threatened, freezing in position and stretching their necks to blend in with tall reeds and marsh grasses.

Directly across the Mississippi River, **Pikes Peak State Park** (*15316 Great River Rd., McGregor, IA 52157; 319-873-2341*) offers an almost identical landscape as Wyalusing, with additional hiking, paddling, and camping opportunities. ■

Soaking in the scenery, Wyalusing SP

A field trip to Hopewell Culture NHP

The Mound Builders

Up and down the Mississippi and Ohio River Valleys, many early native cultures built thousands upon thousands of burial and other ceremonial mounds. A handful of these prehistoric treasures remain, protected on federal lands, state parks, or other patchworks of land where someone had the foresight to save them.

The Hopewell Culture (200 B.C.–A.D. 500) built elaborate earthen complexes containing numerous mounds enclosed within earthen walls. Perhaps even more notable than the mounds themselves are the tools and ornaments that have been found within. Unearthed objects have been fashioned out of mica from the Appalachians, obsidian from the Rocky Mountains, seashells and sharks' teeth from the Gulf of Mexico, and copper from the Lake Superior region—evidence that the culture traded far and wide.

The mid-Ohio River Valley contains some of the best-preserved Hopewell sites, including those at Hopewell Culture National Historical Park (6062 State Rte. 104, Chillicothe, OH 45601; 740-774-1125. Adm. fee).

An even more distinct mound-building culture developed in southern Wisconsin and Iowa. Beginning about 500 B.C., the Effigy Mound Culture built mounds in the shape of bears, turtles, falcons, eagles, and other animals. Some are remarkable in size: the Great Bear Mound, north of McGregor, Iowa, is 137 feet long and 70 feet across.

These mound builders were certainly prolific in the upper Mississippi River Valley. More than 10,000 mounds were discovered in northeastern Iowa alone.

Today, the 2,526-acre Effigy Mounds National Monument (151 Cty. Rd. 76, Harpers Ferry, IA 52146; 319-873-3491. Adm. fee) protects 195 known mounds within its borders and helps the public to appreciate this unique culture.

Two Rivers National Wildlife Refuge

■ 8,500 acres ■ 30 miles north of St. Louis, along Mississippi and Illinois Rivers ■ Closed mid-Oct.–mid-Dec.; bald eagles congregate in January; migratory bird-watching best March–May and Sept.–mid-Oct. ■ Walking, kayaking, canoeing, fishing, biking, bird-watching ■ Contact the refuge, HCR 82, Box 107, Brussels, IL 62013; phone 618-883-2524

IF YOU LONG TO WITNESS the majesty of a bald eagle in flight, you will almost certainly get your chance if you plan a January visit to Two Rivers National Wildlife Refuge. Several hundred bald eagles—one of the largest winter populations in the lower 48 states—make their hibernal flight to the 25-mile stretch of the Mississippi River between Lock and Dams 25 and 26. The open waters provide plenty of fish, and the bluffs of the Mississippi and Illinois Rivers provide the updrafts they soar upon.

The topography of the refuge provides ideal habitat for hundreds of bird species. The Illinois River empties into the Mississippi just downstream from here—a typical floodplain habitat of sloughs, marshes, and bottomland forest. Backwaters formed by U.S. Army Corps of Engineers dams, such as 2,400-acre Swan Lake, prove irresistible to large numbers of cormorants, American white pelicans, and waterfowl.

This is the heart of the Mississippi flyway, one of the world's premier avian migration routes. Millions of ducks, raptors, songbirds, and shorebirds travel up and down the river valley each spring and fall. Birders have recorded nearly 250 species in the refuge. Some, such as the eagles, use the refuge as the southern end of their range, wintering here and returning as far north as the Arctic Circle in summer months. For many other species, though, the refuge lies toward the northern end of their migratory route. Songbirds, warblers, and shorebirds such as egrets spend summers here and move south come fall.

A variety of hardwoods grow in the river bottomlands, including willow, elm, river birch, basswood, and cottonwood. A tangle of poison ivy and brushy plants below makes it a difficult place for humans, but provides habitat for coyote, red fox, raccoon, and other small mammals. Bald eagles tend to roost in the highest treetops, especially along the east side of the Illinois River at Gilbert Lake, an old river channel.

Best access to the refuge for hikers is on the Gilbert Lake side, where a 3-mile-long gravel road (autos prohibited) off Ill. 100 parallels the Illinois River. You can also explore the more rugged shoreline of Swan Lake (accessible from visitor center on Deer Plain Rd., 4 miles S of Brussels off Illinois River Rd.). The lake is open to fishing, canoeing, and kayaking. If you walk along the dikes you'll see the downed trees that still remain from the devastating flood of 1993, which left this area under more than 6 feet of water. ■

Following pages: American white pelicans on Swan Lake, Two Rivers NWR

Testing the echo of Hawks' Cave, Ferne Clyffe SP

Illinois Ozarks

■ Approximately 100,000 acres ■ Southern Illinois, west of I-57 to the Mississippi River ■ Best seasons spring-fall ■ Camping, hiking, boating, fishing, scenic drives ■ Contact Shawnee National Forest, 50 State Rte. 145 South, Harrisburg, IL 62946; phone 618-253-7114 or 800-699-6637. ww.fs.fed.us/r9/shawnee

THE PART OF THE SHAWNEE HILLS that extends across the southern tip of Illinois, near the Mississippi River, is often called the Illinois Ozarks because of its similarity to the Missouri Ozarks across the river. Four times during the Pleistone epoch (2 million to 10,000 years ago), lobes of ice hundreds of feet thick crept southward across the Midwest. They covered much of present-day Illinois, bulldozing flat nearly everything in their path.

The boundary line where the ice sheets stopped advancing couldn't be more obvious if someone marked it with flags: From a flat till plain prairie landscape, the topography clearly changes and the land eventually rises into fanciful sandstone bluffs, ledges, and canyons. The Mississippi River also played a role in sculpting the area. Over the centuries it changed its course many times, etching out the valley as it meandered back and forth.

An astounding variety of plant and animal species live in this unique landscape, a diverse blend of forests, wetlands, prairies, and glades. Midwest prairie plants such as big bluestem coexist with southern swamp types like buttonbush, while northern species of ferns and wildflowers find habitat in the cool glens and hollows. The area is a vital breeding ground for dozens of reptiles and amphibians, an important migratory route for birds, and a safe haven for the bobcat, the Indiana bat, and other endangered or threatened species.

What to See and Do

Eons of wind and water eroded the sandstone to create what is now called the **Little Grand Canyon** south of Murphysboro. From the parking lot at the end of Forest Road 251, the 3.5-mile **Little Grand Canyon Trail** follows the rim of this canyon before descending a series of stone steps to a lush bottomland habitat 350 feet below.

Up top, overlooks let you gaze out over the distinctive valleys and floodplains of the Big Muddy River and Turkey Bayou. The Missouri bluffs of the Mississippi River are visible in the hazy distance. Turkey vultures and hawks circle lazily, eyeing the ground for mice and other rodents. Though the large raptors are easiest to spot, the canyon area is also a stopping point for many migratory songbirds in spring and fall.

As the trail descends into the canyon, watch the rock ledges: Timber rattler and copperhead snakes—both venomous—den in the crevices and overhangs. Towering beech and cottonwood trees shade the cooler canyon floor, where many species of ferns hide trickling creeks.

Just east of Ill. 3 and the tiny town of Wolf Lake, scenic 7-mile **Pine Hills Road** (Forest Road 236) runs north along a high ridge in the **Larue-Pine Hills/Otter Pond Research Natural Area.** The bluff is an ancient uplift of limestone, rather than the sandstone that dominates the Little Grand Canyon area. The hills are named for the shortleaf pine (*Pinus echinata*) that grows here. Because the seeds must be in direct contact with soil to propagate, the tree depends on regular fires to clear away duff on the forest floor. The Forest Service conducts prescribed burns to help the trees reproduce.

Dense woods of pin oak and shagbark hickory also flank the twisting road. Pull off at marked observation points such as Crooked Tree (mile 4.8) and Inspiration Point (mile 6.5), where short walks lead you to fine views of the natural area and the Mississippi River and Big Muddy River bottomlands. The 0.75-mile **Inspi-**

ration Point Trail crests a 350-foot bluff with easterly views taking in 4,730-acre Clear Springs Wilderness Area and the adjacent 5,863-acre Bald Knob Wilderness Area.

At the north end of the scenic drive, the road meets up with Forest Road 345 and leads into the LaRue Swamp. An estimated 35 species of snakes hibernate in the crevices of the Pine Hills in winter and in summer hunt and breed in the swamp. To protect the animals during their biannual migration across Forest Road 345—locally known as Snake Road—the road is closed to motor vehicles for two months in spring and fall. Hikers (presumably those without an aversion to creepy crawlies) are welcome to travel the area on foot.

East of the Pine Hills near Makanda, building-sized blocks of sandstone lie scattered through 4,055-acre **Giant City State Park** *(235 Giant City Rd. 618-457-4836)*. Early 1800s pioneers with fanciful imaginations named the area: They said the passageways between the rock formations looked like streets of a giant city.

The 1-mile loop **Giant City Nature Trail** *(trailhead at Shelter #3)* slaloms through these immense sandstone "buildings." Many are cloaked with moss and lichens, which can grow right on the moist, porous rock. The brownish-red lines in the rock were caused by iron that was in the groundwater when the sandstone was formed.

Rappelling off High Bluff, Giant City SP

A large array of wildflowers grows in the park, where the sandstone bluffs offer protection from excessive wind and sun, and small creeks provide ample moisture. In spring, 20 or 30 species may be blooming at one time, including yellow trout lily, yellow celandine poppy, purple larkspur, and white French's shooting star.

Fifty yards beyond the main entrance, the aptly named **Trillium Trail** showcases many of these wildflowers as it wanders along Stonefort Creek. The 2-mile loop then climbs atop a bluff, where the plant community changes drastically. Dry and exposed, it supports a forest of red cedar and post oak. ■

Ohio River Valley

Sunset view over the Ohio from Tower Rock, Shawnee NF

WHAT'S THE OHIO RIVER VALLEY doing in a guidebook
about the Great Lakes, you ask? It does seem to be a geographical and emotional stretch. The paddle wheelers and
magnolia trees of the Ohio River seem to have a lot more
in common with the Deep South than the sea kayaks and
pine forests of the North Woods.

In fact, the Ohio River Valley is a natural boundary
between the Great Lakes region and the Ozarks, Appalachians, and America's South. While the waters of the

Great Lakes lap at the northern shores of Illinois and Ohio, travel south through these large states and maples soon give way to sycamores, catfish and bass replace cool-water trout, and brilliant azaleas grace plantation-style homes. In a few spots, such as the Cache River basin in the southern tip of Illinois, the Gulf Coastal Plain even licks north into the region, with bald cypress and black tupelo swamps. North, meet South.

The Ohio River proper begins in western Pennsylvania, where the Allegheny and Monongahela Rivers merge at Pittsburgh. It courses southwestward for 981 miles, forming the scribbled southern boundary of three Great Lakes states—Ohio, Indiana, and Illinois—before flowing into the Mississippi River at Cairo, Illinois.

Glaciers in four ice ages—from 1.3 million years ago to just 10,000 years ago—played a role in the formation of the Ohio River Valley just as they did over much of the rest of the Great Lakes region. Massive lobes of ice ground their way across the landscape, scouring much of it into flat, fertile plains and leaving behind a trail of debris and meltwater that

created lakes and carved river valleys. Some of the ice sheets blocked existing rivers; several of these waterways that once drained into the ancestral Mississippi were rerouted south, widening and deepening the river that would become the Ohio.

In what is today southeastern Ohio, the foothills of the Appalachian Mountains stopped the advancing glaciers. In present-day southern Indiana, tall knobs of limestone—layers of sediment laid down by ancient tropical seas, then subsequently uplifted—had the same barrier effect. As a result, the banks of the Ohio River are lined with steep hills and sinewy valleys.

The eastern reaches of the Ohio River Valley are characterized by the region's steepest hills and thinnest soil. Under rugged highlands and deep valleys lie some of the nation's richest deposits of coal, oil, natural gas, and salt. Such mineral riches have made Ohio one of the nation's leading industrial centers. Moving downstream, the rumpled southern hills of Indiana lie atop a patch of earth riddled with holes like Swiss cheese. This is the heart of Indiana's karst area, where eons of dripping and flowing acidic waters have worn through the region's limestone, diverting the water into subterranean routes and carving out caves, sinkholes, and sinking springs. Indiana's karst area is one of the most significant cave regions in the United States, and part of the same geological phenomenon that formed Mammoth Cave in Kentucky, the world's largest known cave system. In southern Illinois, the sedimentary rock—largely sandstone—was uplifted; subsequent wind and water erosion created the dramatic bluffs and rock formations of the Shawnee Hills.

Up until the 19th century, hardwood forests—vast stands of beech, hickory, oak, poplar, cottonwood, and sycamore—covered much of the Ohio River Valley. The woods harbored mammals large and small, but the bears, cougars, and wolves disappeared along with the forests, which were largely leveled in the 1800s for farmland. Today, the white-tailed deer is the only large mammal that remains in any significant numbers, keeping company with a host of smaller species such as squirrel, chipmunk, muskrat, raccoon, red fox, and woodchuck.

Thankfully, birds of all kinds remain prevalent, from small song-birds to peregrine falcons and other powerful birds of prey. Ducks, geese, and other waterfowl migrate through the region by the millions, resting and feeding at the many preserves and refuges established along the riverway. It is not unusual to spot dozens of species congregating at any one time along the Ohio's stretches, from American white pelicans to black-crowned night herons to sandpipers.

The Ohio River has not only shaped the land, it has shaped our culture. Indians lived along the shores of the Ohio for thousands of years, and more recent tribes like the Shawnee and Miami used the river as a convenient source of transportation. So did European explorers and traders, and adventurers like Meriwether Lewis and William Clark, who began their famed exploration of the American West near present-day Louisville, Kentucky.

Although steamboats and later, barges, turned the Ohio River into a main commercial artery for the young United States, the advent of railroads eventually shifted much of the region's industrial centers farther north. Over recent generations, the Ohio River Valley has regained—or rather retained—the somnolent air of the Old South, as thick and rich as syrup. As a result, the valley is a lovely place to hike, bird-watch, or simply explore, easing along at the pace of the river.

Beginning just east of the Ohio's confluence with the Mississippi, this chapter travels upstream through the Ohio River Valley. We first visit the curious cypress swamps of the Cache River basin, then explore fantastic sandstone formations in the Garden of the Gods in Shawnee National Forest, then the cave country of southern Indiana. The jour-ney concludes in the deeply folded landscapes of the Hocking Hills and Wayne National Forest, where the rolling hills and vales give way to the Appalachian Mountains. ∎

Big Wyandotte Cave, Wyandotte Caves State Recreation Area

Cache River State Natural Area

■ 11,971 acres ■ Southern Illinois, southwest of Vienna off US 45 ■ Best seasons spring and fall ■ Hiking, kayaking, canoeing, wildlife viewing ■ Contact the natural area, 930 Sunflower Ln., Belknap, IL 62908; phone 618-634-9678. www.dnr.state.il.us/lands/landmgt/parks/cachervr.htm

YOU COULD EASILY MISTAKE the Cache River State Natural Area for a Deep South bayou: Coffee-colored water bleeds through a dark canopy of bald cypress and tupelo gum trees. Tree frogs and a chorus of insects sing from the high branches. Herons and egrets stalk the shadows, while catfish and gar hide under floating carpets of brilliant emerald duckweed.

So what's it doing in Illinois? Though seemingly out of place, Cache River is a true southern swamp at the northernmost edge of its range. UNESCO lists the largely undisturbed Cache River basin as one of 15 "Wetlands of International Importance," along with select company like the Florida Everglades. Several cypress trees here are more than a thousand years old and, at last count, the area contained 56 state-threatened or endangered plant and animal species. Bobcats, river otters, and rare yellow-crowned night-herons are among the area's more elusive inhabitants.

View of cypress-tupelo swamp, Heron Pond Trail, Cache River SNA

What to See and Do

Hiking into the wetlands is surprisingly good from all directions; stop at the visitor center for a map that shows designated access points. If you have time for only one trail, make it the 1.5-mile **Heron Pond Trail** in the lush northeastern corner. A floating boardwalk leads into the heart of the swamp, where cypress trees, fortified by broad buttresses that widen as the trees age, rise up from the water. Continue on the 2.4-mile **Linkage Trail** to see the 100-foot-tall state champion cherrybark oak (circumference: 22.5 ft.) and to reach the 5.5-mile **Little Black Slough Trail.** This difficult trail fords the Cache

and wanders through a variety of habitats, from tupelo swamps to sandstone bluffs. Watch your step: Though reclusive, cottonmouths, copperheads, and timber rattlesnakes all call the basin home.

Perhaps the best way to experience this wonderfully saturated world is by canoe or kayak. In the **Buttonland Swamp** area, yellow arrows or blazes mark 3- and 6-mile routes for the **Lower Cache River Canoe Trail,** which twists through thickets of buttonbush before emerging in an open pool dominated by a commanding bald cypress. Measuring more than 40 feet around, it's the state's largest. ∎

Garden of the Gods, Shawnee National Forest

Shawnee Hills

■ Approx. 175,000 acres ■ Southern Illinois, roughly I-24 to Ohio River
■ Year-round ■ Camping, hiking, backpacking, boating, swimming, fishing, horse-back riding, bird-watching, wildlife viewing, scenic drives ■ Contact Shawnee National Forest, 50 State Rte. 145 South, Harrisburg, IL 62946; phone 618-253-7114 or 800-699-6637. www.fs.fed.us/r9/shawnee

ILLINOIS CALLS ITSELF "THE PRAIRIE STATE," a motto that seems apt enough as you drive the length of this leggy state. Acres after acres of field corn and soybeans roll in waves to the horizon like an endless golden sea. Until you hit Illinois's southernmost tip, that is—that triangle of land down beyond the 38th parallel, where the Ohio River squiggles southwest toward the Mississippi. The glaciers that flattened the prairie stopped here, leaving untouched the Shawnee Hills, a region defined by deeply etched sandstone hills, remarkable rock outcroppings, pine barrens, and river bottomlands. It is undeniably the most scenic and, from a natural resources standpoint, the most significant corner of the state.

Together with a handful of state parks and other preserves, Shawnee National Forest encompasses most of the Shawnee Hills. The vast 278,000-acre national forest spans the entire width of the state, stretching from the Mississippi River to the Ohio. Perhaps because of their proximity to Missouri, the western Shawnee Hills are often referred to as the Illinois Ozarks (see pp. 242-45). Most of the sites in the eastern Shawnee Hills are found within a region roughly bordered by Ill. 13 to the north, Ill. 145 to the west, Ill. 146 to the south, and the Ohio River to the east. Although you'll need a car to access various points of interest, once there, hiking trails and wilderness areas abound, affording you ample opportunities to get out among nature.

What to See and Do

Begin your visit at Forest Service Headquarters in Harrisburg for maps and other information. Then head east toward the Ohio River and south on Ill. 1. At Karber's Ridge Road, turn east to dip and climb through black, white, and scarlet oaks along one of the prettiest routes in the forest.

Your first stop is the **Pounds Hollow Recreation Area,** where in 1939, the Civilian Conservation Corps built a dam to create a 25-acre lake. This popular spot for fishing, boating, swimming *(fee)*, and camping lies tucked into a sylvan hollow typical of the Shawnee Hills. From the beach house, follow the half-mile **Beaver Trail** to the **Rim Rock Trail.** This short loop trail passes a sandstone barrens— where plant growth is stunted by shallow, infertile soils and a hot, dry southwestern exposure—and

traces the edge of the Rim Rock escarpment. Descending into a valley, the trail squeezes between two-story-high sandstone blocks before reaching **Ox Lot Cave,** a recess where pioneers once corralled livestock. A natural spring trickles through the ferny valley.

Garden of the Gods

Continue about 10 miles farther along Karber's Ridge Road to the national forest's showpiece: the Garden of the Gods. Eons of wind and water have eroded the sandstone bluffs into fantastically shaped overhangs, crevices, balanced rocks, and towers, contorted like dissolving sandcastles.

More than 300 million years ago, a warm inland sea covered this region; it laid down layer upon layer of sediments, which eventually compacted into sandstone. In

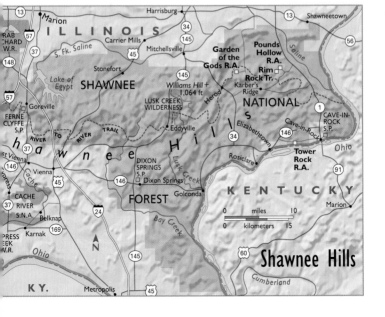

the Garden of the Gods area, these layers were more than 4 miles thick. After they uplifted into the Shawnee Hills, the erosive forces of nature took over.

The quarter-mile **Garden of the Gods Observation Trail** (*access via Glen-O-Jones Rd., 1.5 miles N of Karber's Ridge Rd.*) winds among the garden's most dramatic formations, protruding high above the thick oak forest. The trail sidles right up against the formations, so you can see features like the dark liesegang bands—strata created when iron-rich water seeped into the still-underwater sandstone. They stick out like bas-relief sculpture because they resist erosion better than sandstone.

Lusk Creek Wilderness Vicinity

Return to Karber's Ridge Road and follow it west to Herod, where nearby Williams Hill—the second-highest point in Illinois—climbs to 1,064 feet. Just beyond Herod, the **River to River Trail** crosses Ill. 34. This hiking and horseback riding trail winds across public lands for 176 miles and links the Ohio and Mississippi Rivers. It crosses five of the forest's seven wilderness areas; the popular 18-mile stretch from the Garden of the Gods west to the Lusk Creek Wilderness is deemed one of its finest sections.

The 4,500-acre **Lusk Creek Wilderness** protects broad, flat ridge tops and terraces overlooking narrow ravines and deep sandstone gulches. Lusk Creek itself flows through small tracts of virgin timber and spring wildflowers, including wild columbine and French's shooting star. You can hike, camp, ride horseback, and

fish for bass and bluegill throughout this secluded area.

Dixon Springs and Cave-in-Rock State Parks

South of Lusk Creek near Ill. 145, Dixon Springs State Park (*618-949-3394*) was once the site of a 19th-century health spa; guests flocked to the "healing waters" of its seven mineral springs. Today those waters flow as brooks and streams, tunneling through 100-year-old hemlocks and cascading over hills and crags. Boulders overgrown with lichen and moss lay scattered among the hillsides, and blooming catalpa and dogwood trees brighten the forest in spring.

From Dixon Springs head east on Ill. 146 and stop at **Tower Rock.** Hike the nature trail that climbs 160 feet up a bluff for an eagle's-eye view of the Ohio and its broad expanse of floodplains.

About five miles farther east, Cave-in-Rock State Park (*618-289-4325*) overlooks the Ohio from a mile-long stretch of 60-foot-high hills and bluffs. The marquee attraction is the gaping cryptlike cave at water's edge. More than 160 feet deep, it made a perfect hideout in the late 1700s and early 1800s for bandits and pirates, who lured unwary river travelers into it to rob and murder them. After this grisly period, the cave became a well-known shelter for pioneers; its location is marked on some of the nation's earliest maps. The park is a popular picnicking spot, and boat launches offer good access to fishing and other water sports on the river. Follow Ill. 1 north to return to your starting point at Karber's Ridge Road. ■

Fanciful erosion in the Garden of the Gods, Shawnee National Forest

Hemlock Cliffs Trail, Hoosier NF

Hoosier National Forest

■ 198,000 acres ■ South-central Indiana, 80 miles south of Indianapolis ■ Best seasons spring and fall ■ Camping, hiking, fishing, mountain biking, horseback riding, caving ■ Contact the national forest, 811 Constitution Ave., Bedford, IN 47421; phone 812-275-5987. www.fs.fed.us/r9/hoosier

IN A STATE AS HEAVILY FARMED AS INDIANA, Hoosier National Forest strives to preserve—or in many cases, restore—a swath of the state's native ecosystems. Overlain by open prairie and rolling hills forested in hardwoods, subterranean oddities—such as caves, sinkholes, springs, rise pools, and underground rivers—riddle the national forest's karst terrain. (In compliance with the Federal Cave Resources Protection Act, the national forest does not publicize the locations of its caves; however, local

The Old Buffalo Trace

For centuries, southern Indiana served as a main thoroughfare for massive herds of migrating American bison, commonly known as buffalo. By the thousands, they migrated from salt licks in northern Kentucky and converged near present-day Louisville, where they crossed the Ohio River at its shallowest point and headed west to summer pasture in the grass prairies of the Great Plains.

In a cloud of dust that could be seen for miles, millions of hooves beat a well-worn path across the state. The annual migration cut a 20-foot-wide swath through forests and, in places, wore a 12-foot-deep rut into solid rock. The scars still remain visible in places.

Indians, early settlers, westward pioneers, stagecoach lines, and even stretches of modern highway have all followed the "Old Buffalo Trace." Though the name has disappeared from maps and the bison from the landscape, the Buffalo Trace has left an indelible mark in more ways than one.

cave clubs explore these areas using low-impact caving techniques. The Forest Service can provide contact information for visiting cavers.)

The **Wesley Chapel Gulf** *(2 miles E of Orangeville, off Cty. Rd. 350 West)*, provides a rare glimpse of a river on its subterranean path. More than 1,000 feet long with walls as high as 95 feet, this exceptionally large gulf began as a sinkhole, which collapsed and obstructed the free passage of the underground **Lost River.** The artesian waters of the Lost River bubble up from a rise pool at the southern end of the gulf—surfacing calmly through placid azure waters or frothing forth violently depending on the river's volume—only to disappear again through a labyrinth of swallow holes and channels, back to their secret river route.

For aboveground exploring, hike the 0.8-mile linear path *(access via Ind. 37, 1.5 miles S of Paoli)* within **Pioneer Mother's Memorial Forest.** This 88-acre parcel filled with centuries-old walnuts and oaks represents the largest tract of old-growth forest left in Indiana. Three miles north of the junction of I-64 and Ind. 37 (follow signs), **Hemlock Cliffs** features sandstone cliffs, seasonal waterfalls, and lush ravines where cool-weather species like wintergreen, mountain laurel, and yes, hemlocks, thrive. The 1.2-mile-long **Hemlock Cliffs Trail** leads you down into a shady canyon.

In the southern tip of Hoosier National Forest, near Derby, the **German Ridge Trail** winds past sandstone rock outcrops and hilly terrain with views of the Ohio River. Its many loops total 25 miles and nearly all are open to hikers, mountain bikers, and horseback riders *(access via Gerald and German Ridge Rds. off Ind. 70).*

Hoosier also protects Indiana's only designated wilderness area. The 13,000-acre **Charles Deam Wilderness,** 15 miles southeast of Bloomington, offers a 36-mile-long interconnected trail system that wanders through hollows and sycamore forest *(access via Blackwell Horsecamp, Grubb Ridge, and Hickory Ridge Firetower trailheads on Tower Rd., off Ind. 446).* ∎

Wyandotte Caves State Recreation Area

■ 2,100 acres ■ South-central Indiana, 32 miles west of Louisville, Ky.
■ Year-round ■ Hiking, cave tours ■ Adm. fee to caves. Cave access by tour only ■ Wear sturdy shoes and a jacket ■ Contact the recreation area, 7315 S. Wyandotte Cave Rd., Leavenworth, IN 47137; phone 812-738-2782. www.in.gov/dnr/forestry/property/wyandtcv.htm

LYING IN THE HEART of Indiana's karst area—where dripping and flowing acidic waters have worn through the limestone and left behind a Swiss-cheese patchwork of caves, sinkholes, and underground rivers—this recreation area's two caves offer an informative introduction to a dark, damp netherworld. Big and Little Wyandotte Caves feature more than 10 miles of passageways filled with delicate, flowing formations.

Big Wyandotte features an impressive underground "mountain"—185 feet of fallen rock covered with stalagmites—in a soaring cavern room, along with well-preserved and rare, twisted formations called helictites. It also contains one of the largest known stalagmites, the **Pillar of the Constitution,** which stands 35 feet high and 75 feet in circumference. Seeing the pillar, however, requires a half-day spelunking journey that involves a climb into the **Animal Pit,** and a squeeze through **The Straits.** This tour is only open to those with a 46-inch or less chest size.

Fortunately, Wyandotte also offers a menu of less-intense cave tours that give you a good look at fantastical speleothems along lighted pas-

Pillared Palace area, Big Wyandotte Cave, Wyandotte Caves SRA

sageways. A knowledgeable guided narration helps make sense of it all. The two-hour **Monument Mountain Tour** features Big Wyandotte's underground mountain, helictites, and prehistoric flint quarries. In winter months, you can often spot the endangered Indiana bat; some 30,000, one-tenth of the entire estimated population, hibernate here. True cave enthusiasts can opt for the **All-Day Tour** that showcases some splendid columns and even the occasional waterfall, but also requires lots of climbing and crawling—not a good choice for anyone even remotely claustrophobic. The **Little Wyandotte Tour,** the only one offered in the smaller cave, provides a quick and easy 45-minute glimpse of some flowstone and dripstone calcium-carbonate mineral deposits.

Cave Crazy?
Several private enterprises in the area also offer cave tours. For quality caves, consider the exceptionally beautiful national landmark **Marengo Cave** *(812-365-2705)* in Marengo, with dramatic flowstone deposits, mazes of stalagmites, and huge corridors. You'll see multilevel underground waterfalls and cavern pools hosting albino crayfish in **Squire Boone Caverns** *(812-732-4382)* near Corydon.

   The caves lie beneath Wyandotte Caves State Recreation Area, which encompasses a steep-sided escarpment overlooking the meandering, spring-fed Blue River, a tributary of the Ohio River. More than 15 miles of trails wind through oaks and other hardwoods within the 2,100-acre recreation area. You can also access the 30-mile **Adventure Trail,** which continues on into the surrounding 39,000-acre **Harrison/Crawford State Forest** *(812-738-8232)*. ■

Spring Mill State Park

■ 1,322 acres ■ South-central Indiana, 30 miles south of Bloomington ■ Year-round. Cave boat tours only Mem. Day–Labor Day ■ Camping, hiking, fishing, cave tours, pioneer village ■ Contact the park, Box 376, Mitchell, IN 47446; phone 812-849-4129. www.state.in.us/dnr/parklake/parks/springmill.html

YOU'LL FIND A SAMPLER PLATTER of the state's most notable natural and cultural resources within the relatively modest borders of Spring Mill State Park. The park serves up a national-landmark virgin hardwood forest, five caves, and a well-preserved 1814 gristmill and pioneer village. Nine miles of hiking trails link it all together. The park even contains an inn (Spring Mill Inn 812-849-4081), so you can explore to your heart's content and have a spot to relax come nightfall.

   In the heart of the park, just north of the visitor center, a long flight of steps leads down a wooded ravine to the moss-covered limestone portal of **Donaldson Cave.** Visitors can poke around the entrance to the cave a bit—bring a flashlight—or delve a little deeper with a park naturalist on

Restored gristmill, Spring Mill SP

occasional interpretive tours. (Inquire at the park office.) The unusual northern blind cave fish—an endangered species first discovered here—lives in a stream that rises up within the cave. The naturalists, taking advantage of an underground stream, also lead seasonal boat trips *(fee)* 500 feet into **Twin Caves.**

The waters flowing from the Spring Mill cave system feed **Spring Mill Lake,** an impoundment created by the Civilian Conservation Corps (CCC) in the 1930s. The water has receded in recent years, but the lake remains a popular fishing spot for bass, bluegill, and even trout, which survive thanks to the ongoing replenishment of cool cave waters. The mile-long **Trail 5** loops pleasantly around the lake.

Donaldson Woods Nature Preserve protects a stand of 300-year-old native trees in the park's southeast corner. This airy, open forest lets you experience untouched Indiana, where sturdy oak, hickory, and maple rise high overhead, mixed with a more delicate understory of beech, ash, and tulip poplar. The 2.5-mile **Trail 3** loop bisects the preserve and continues on past Twin, Bronson, and Donaldson Caves. Don't venture off the trail: The landscape is pockmarked with sinkholes, just waiting for erosion to create another cave entrance.

Like Donaldson Cave, the woods commemorate George Donaldson, a Scottish immigrant who purchased this land in 1865. Donaldson stalwartly refused to allow any hunting or logging on his property in an era when harvesting natural resources was de rigueur.

Even before Donaldson's day, by the early 1800s the land just to the west was a thriving community of more than 300 families. Spring Mill's economy was tied to its limestone gristmill, powered by waters flowing from nearby Hamer Cave. After the railroad passed Spring Mill by in the mid 19th-century, the town slowly began deteriorating; however, the CCC commenced restoration efforts in the 1930s. Today, the gristmill once again operates and interpreters bring Spring Mill back to life in historically accurate shops and houses (*April-Oct.*). ■

Falls of the Ohio State Park

■ 68 acres ■ South central Indiana, across Ohio River from Louisville, Ky. ■ Year-round; biggest variety of fossils usually visible in autumn ■ Hiking, boating, canoeing, bird-watching, fossil viewing ■ Contact the park, P.O. Box 1327, Jeffersonville, IN 47131; phone 812-280-9970. www.fallsoftheohio.org

ENVISION A CLEAR TROPICAL SEA, teeming with fish, corals, snails, scallops, and a host of smaller creatures. Now imagine what it would be like if you could part the waters and see the seafloor, complete with all its life-forms. That's essentially what you'll experience at Falls of the Ohio State Park, where fluctuating water levels reveal 170 acres of a fossilized ancient seafloor along the banks of the Ohio River. This fossil bed—laid down between 425 million and 300 million years ago—is one of the largest exposed beds in the world. The same formation lies in western New York and southern Ontario, but here you can walk right across the bed and, with virtually every step, examine a panoply of organisms embedded in the limestone.

The fossil bed is 50 feet thick and made up of several layers, each preserving a different time period. The oldest layer, containing Silurian coral from 425 million years ago, is found in the lowest part of the fossil bed, located in the center of the river. It remains under water much of the year, exposed only when water levels are extremely low (most reliably in September and October).

The upper fossil layers are almost always exposed. They represent the Lower and Middle Devonian periods—approximately 300 to 390 million years ago—and contain the greatest quantity and variety of fossils. You're likely to spot horn coral; a fan-shaped shell called a brachiopod; a crinoid, which looks like a threaded bolt, but is an arm of a cup-shaped animal; and giant snails 3 or 4 inches in diameter. In all, this remarkable fossil bed preserves an estimated 600 species of prehistoric animals.

Although you may walk around the 170-acre fossil bed on your own (*June-Aug.; weekends Sept.-Oct.*), consider joining one of the free ranger-led hikes. The park naturalists point out interesting specimens and help you make sense of it all. At the very least, be sure to visit the excellent interpretive center (*fee*) at the park's entrance for a good geological and historical overview of the falls area.

The falls themselves are practically indiscernible. The Ohio River drops 26 feet in 2.5 miles—hardly dramatic. Nonetheless, the long, shallow course of limestone ledges once caused this length to be one of the few unnavigable stretches of the Ohio. Dams and canals were constructed in the mid-1800s to rectify this situation; however, they also flooded what would otherwise be 300 more acres of exposed fossil bed. Silt and scrub trees have covered an additional 50 acres in recent decades.

The waters attract a variety of birds, from sandpipers skittering along the river's edge to majestic ospreys wheeling overhead. An impressive 265 species have been recorded, including the peregrine falcon, great blue heron, black-crowned night-heron, and ring-billed gull. They no doubt inspired John James Audubon (see sidebar at right), who sketched more than 200 of his famous illustrations while living in Louisville. ∎

Fossil viewers, Falls of the Ohio SP

Portrait of J. J. Audubon, late 1840s

Birdman of Ohio

Though born in Haiti and raised in France, John James Audubon (1785-1851) is best known for his studies and paintings of North American birds, a legacy he began building along the Ohio River.

In 1803, the teenager began studying birds in earnest at his father's estate in Philadelphia. He was soon banding waterfowl to learn more about their migratory patterns; others he shot, stuffed, and wired in lifelike positions so he could draw them accurately. He is considered to be one of the first to study and paint North American birds in their natural surroundings.

In 1807, Audubon moved to northern Kentucky, near a deep horseshoe bend in the Ohio River. Apparently enthralled with the wealth of birdlife in the valley, his general store and other business ventures went bankrupt while he wandered the countryside, observing and drawing birds. He was even jailed briefly for debt.

Still, Audubon remained dedicated to his drawing. In 1820, he decided to pursue his dream of painting every American bird species, traveling the Great Lakes and up and down the Ohio and Mississippi Rivers to learn everything he could about Canada geese, wild turkeys, great white herons, and other species.

By 1824, Audubon had assembled a large body of work. Unable to find an American publisher, he went to England and Scotland in 1826. A British engraver agreed to reproduce the collection, which depicted birds both life-size and in their natural environments. *Birds of America* created a sensation, selling at an extraordinary $1,000 per set.

Subsequent volumes of ornithological writings and watercolors secured Audubon's reputation as the premier natural history artist of the 19th century. By the end of his life, he had completed more than 400 paintings, was a member of the Royal Society of Victorian England, and established a name that, for generations to come, would be inextricably linked to the birds that so fascinated him.

Clifton Gorge, Clifton Gorge State Nature Preserve

Little Miami River Valley

■ 105 miles long ■ Southern Ohio, 15 miles east of Dayton ■ Year-round
■ Camping, hiking, canoeing, fishing, biking, bird-watching ■ Contact Ohio Division of Natural Areas and Preserves, 1889 Fountain Square Ct., Columbus, OH 43224; phone 614-265-6453

BEGINNING AS A NEEDLE-THIN CREEK, the Little Miami River soon threads through a slender, 100-foot deep gorge before eventually widening into floodplains more than a mile wide. Ohio's first state and nationally designated scenic river, the Little Miami's upper reaches showcase the effects of the glaciers that scrubbed and scoured the landscape.

When the Wisconsinan glacier retreated from the area, a glacial meltwater river flowed over the tough Silurian dolomite and cut into the softer limestone and shale below, carving deeper and deeper over time. The river also widened; it undercut the dolomite in places, creating slump blocks (huge rock slabs fallen away from the rock face) and recesses. Today the Little Miami follows the path of this glacial river.

What to See and Do

The cool, shaded recesses of **Clifton Gorge State Nature Preserve** protect the Little Miami's headwaters and provide habitat for several plants uncommon in Ohio, including Canada yew, redberry elder, wall rue fern, and the state-threatened red baneberry. Wildflowers erupt in spring and early summer, a brilliant show of snow trillium, hepatica, Virginia bluebell, wild ginger, Dutchman's-breeches, and more than 300 others.

The half-mile-long **Narrows Trail** (off Ohio 343 W of Clifton) and the connecting **Gorge Trail** offer the best views of the gorge, where the Little Miami bolts over small waterfalls and swirls through potholes. The 269-acre preserve permits hiking on the north side of the river only; the south side is restricted for scientific study. You can also access the preserve from the adjacent **John Bryan State Park** (937-767-1274), which has several miles of pleasant wooded trails along the river.

Nearby, Antioch University in Yellow Springs protects 1,000 acres of woods and riverway in the **Glen Helen Nature Preserve.** You're welcome to hike around; the iron-rich springs that gave the town its name still bubble forth in oddly colorful hues. The preserve also includes a **raptor center** (937-767-9292; by appt.), where injured hawks and other birds of prey are nursed back to health.

Farther south, in 463-acre **Caesar Creek Gorge State Nature Preserve**—a lightly traveled blend of oak and hickory woodlands and rippling streams—Caesar Creek flows through its own glacier-formed gorge before joining the Little Miami. This deep gorge exposes some of the oldest rock in the Midwest: 500-million-year-old Ordovician shale and limestone embedded with brachiopods, trilobites, and other fossils. To find it, enter from the west side on Corwin Road, three miles north of Oregonia.

The terrific **Little Miami Scenic Trail** roughly parallels the river for nearly 70 miles, from Springfield to Milford. The path is paved for cyclists, in-line skaters, and those in wheelchairs, while a softer adjacent surface is maintained for walkers, runners, and horseback riders. Several communities along the route, such as Xenia and Yellow Springs, provide easy access. ■

The Ohio Buckeye

Aesculus glabra—the Buckeye State's namesake tree—reaches heights of 70 feet and grows wild along rich moist river bottomlands. It produces lovely yellowish-cream flower spikes in spring, and later bears a 1- to 2-inch-diameter chestnut-shaped fruit. Native Americans called the fruit *hetuck,* or "eye of the buck," in reference to the light beige spot on the dark nut. They ground the nut into powder and sprinkled it in pools of water to stun fish and make them easy to harvest. Today, the buckeye is grown mostly as a smaller ornamental variety, found in gardens throughout the central U.S. and parts of Europe.

Hocking Hills State Park

■ 2,000 acres ■ South-central Ohio, 50 miles southeast of Columbus ■ Year-round ■ Camping, hiking, fishing ■ Contact the park, 20160 State Rte. 664, Logan, OH 43138; phone 740-385-6841. www.hockinghillspark.com

ASK OHIOANS TO NAME THE PRETTIEST SPOT in the state and many will undoubtedly point you to the Hocking Hills. Surrounded by the gentle agrarian landscape of south-central Ohio, the earth suddenly folds into deep creases and high ridges, hiding cool gorges, gaping sandstone amphitheaters, moss-coated cliffs, waterfalls, and an array of other surprises.

The signature of the Hocking Hills is its dramatic formations of blackhand sandstone—named after similar rock 50 miles to the north, where Indians used soot to inscribe the outline of a human hand into a cliff face. The area's bedrock—mostly sandstone and some shale—was created more than 300 million years ago, when a shallow sea covered the region. As water rushed down from the young Appalachian Mountains rising to the southeast, a delta formed here, depositing layer after layer of sand and other sediment. Over millions of years, it compacted and cemented together with silica or iron oxide. Within the Hocking Hills, the sandstone lies 150 feet thick in places.

Wind and water took over next, scouring the rock to create recess caves, cliffs, overhangs, and gorges. Later, retreating glaciers, which stopped just 6 miles short of these hills, left large chunks of ice that plugged waterways and formed a bottle-shaped gorge north of Lancaster. In the 1700s, Wyandot Indians called the river running through it *hock-hocking,* or "bottle river," and gave the Hocking Hills their name.

The shady, moist environment found deep in the hills' gorges mimics a much cooler climate. As a result, Canada yew, yellow birch, stately old-growth stands of hemlock, and other species normally found much farther north thrive here. This collision of climatic zones also makes for an interesting cross section of animals. Copperhead and ring-necked snakes sun on high rock ledges, while red-backed salamanders and box turtles hide on the ferny forest floor. Common mammals include the white-tailed deer, red fox, and gray squirrel.

What to See and Do

The park, along with Hocking Hills State Forest, encompasses within an area south of Logan—roughly outlined by Ohio 664, 56, 374, and 33—most of the Hocking Hills region. The park's six units are each named for its most notable attractions: Old Man's Cave, Cedar Falls, Ash Cave, Conkles Hollow, Rock House, and Cantwell Cliffs. All are within a ten-minute drive of one another.

For better or for worse, good road access makes it easy to reach the most remarkable rock formations in the Hocking Hills. To get

Ash Cave, Hocking Hills State Park

your bearings, pick up a map and trail guide from the park office, across from Old Man's Cave on Ohio 664.

The trails within each unit tend to be rather short—not more than a mile or two long— but **Hocking Hills State Forest** (*740-385-4402*) surrounds and weaves among the state park units, offering even more hiking and camping opportunities. Forest headquarters are on Ohio 374 near Conkles Hollow.

Ash Cave and Cedar Falls

The most dramatic unit may be Ash Cave (*parking area is W of intersection of Ohio 374 and 56*). The trail to Ash Cave begins as a pleasant stroll along a stream shaded by pines and hemlocks and surrounded by the blooms of trillium, jack-in-the-pulpit, and other wildflowers. As you walk northward on the quarter-mile trail, the walls of the gorge narrow, then suddenly converge at a magnificent amphitheater of sandstone, where a narrow waterfall plunges into a pool below.

Follow the trail right up to the concave wall, where it arcs above you and gives you a dizzying sense of its scale. **Ash Cave** stretches 700 feet wide, 90 feet high, and about 100 feet deep, like a band shell. Like other recess caves in the park, Ash Cave was formed when the softer middle layer of blackhand sandstone eroded more quickly than the more resistant top and bottom layers. The cave is named after a huge mound of ashes—several thousand bushels worth, believed to have been the remains of

Indian bonfires built over the course of hundreds of years— discovered here by early settlers.

Stairs to the right of the cave climb up to its rim. From here, you can follow the **Rim Trail** back to the parking area, or pick up the **Grandma Gatewood Trail,** which heads north 3 miles to the next park unit, Cedar Falls. (Some maps and signs list the Grandma Gatewood Trail as the Buckeye Trail, a statewide route.)

Though you can also reach Cedar Falls by car, it seems far more appropriate to arrive by foot since this lovely grotto is among the most secluded in the park. **Queer Creek** carves chasms and basins into the sandstone before gushing over a final ledge, the most voluminous falls within the Hocking Hills. Don't bother looking for the area's namesake cedars, though—settlers named the spot after misidentifying the tall hemlocks.

Old Man's Cave

From Cedar Falls, the Grandma Gatewood Trail continues another 3 miles to Old Man's Cave, the park's most popular unit. Named for a hermit who lived here in the early 1800s, this area offers a little bit of everything—upper and lower waterfalls, a narrow gorge, potholes and other formations carved out by the flowing water, and the 200-foot-long cave. Most notable is the gorge, which cuts through the entire thickness of the blackhand sandstone. You'll follow a 300-million-year-old time line by walking the half-mile trail through the gorge from the upper to lower waterfalls!

Hiking the rim trail, Conkles Hollow, Hocking Hills SP

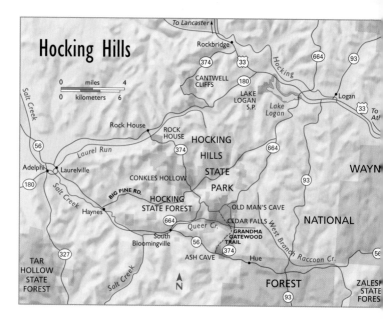

Hocking Hills

Conkles Hollow

The Conkles Hollow area offers some of the best options for hikers *(on Ohio 374, a few miles NW of Old Man's Cave)*. The 2.5-mile **rim trail** traces the edge of Conkles Hollow and allows you to peer 250 feet down into what is believed to be the deepest gorge in the state. Vistas at almost every turn take in the lush valley floor or look off across the forested hills.

A small parking area on Big Pine Road, about a mile east of Conkles Hollow, serves as the trailhead for a couple of state forest trails. As you tramp along you'll encounter **Big Spring Hollow**, a horseshoe-shaped recessed cave near a 100-foot waterfall, a scenic rock outcropping called Airplane Rock, and a double-level cave.

Cantwell Cliffs

From Conkles Hollow, Ohio 374 twists and turns for 13 miles to

Old Man's Cave, Hocking Hills SP

Of Mules and Men

With the Ohio River leading the way, Ohio's web of rivers served as the region's transportation network long before the advent of railroads and roadways. Its efficiency prompted industrious Ohioans to add to their good fortune: Link man-made waterways with natural ones, they reasoned, and money would soon be flowing through the state right along with merchandise.

They took note of the new Erie Canal linking New York City to the Great Lakes. Thousands of boats were suddenly moving between Albany and Buffalo, creating boomtowns and dramatically shifting economies. Delighted to be on the receiving end of the Erie Canal trade, Ohioans immediately started to survey possible north-south canal routes that would connect Lake Erie with the Ohio River. An ambitious era of canal building began in 1825.

The Ohio and Erie Canal, stretching 308 miles from Portsmouth north to Cleveland, was rushed through to completion by 1832. The 249-mile Miami and Erie Canal between Cincinnati and Toledo opened in 1849. Several branches followed until "ditch diggers" had carved a labyrinth of 40-foot-wide pathways across the state.

Transportation was slow and methodical. Towing loaded barges, mules or horses, coaxed along by a canal driver on foot, trudged along a pathway adjacent to the canal. Their speeds rarely exceeded 1.5 miles per hour.

Alas, the canal era was short-lived. By the 1860s, railroads crisscrossed the state, largely superseding the need for canals. Only in recent years have these historic canal corridors found a new role: Hundreds of miles of towpaths now serve as multiuse trails enjoyed by hikers and bikers.

Cantwell Cliffs, the park's hidden jewel. The cliffs—yet another dramatic example of eroded blackhand sandstone—plunge 150 feet straight down, as if the rock was sliced away with a knife. The gorge below is a broad horseshoe-shaped glen, a peaceful world of ferns, mossy limestone walls, and trickling creeks.

The 2.5-mile **trail** leading down into the gorge is the highlight of the place. From the parking area on Ohio 374, head left at the fork in the trail and you'll soon be descending through a tight maze of slump blocks, large chunks of sandstone that have broken away from the cliff. The passage named Fat Woman's Squeeze gives you an idea of trail width here. The trail next passes a concave rock shelter, then crosses the floor of the gorge before climbing up the other side and looping back to the parking area.

Rock House

A half-mile **trail** off Ohio 374 leads to a recess cave that, according to local folklore, once harbored bootleggers and horse thieves. Weathering sculpted the unusual formation by widening cracks found in the softer middle layer of sandstone. ■

Sugar maples in fall, Wayne National Forest

Wayne National Forest

■ 229,600 acres ■ Southeast Ohio, two units near Marietta and one near Ironton ■ Year-round ■ Camping, hiking, canoeing, fishing, mountain biking, horseback riding, scenic drive ■ Contact the national forest, Route 1, Box 132, Marietta, OH 45750; phone 740-373-9055. www.fs.fed.us/r9/wayne

THE OHIO RIVER MAY BE ITS MOST MAJESTIC where it forms the border between southeast Ohio and West Virginia. Arcing in broad sinewy curves, it flows wide and stately through the folds of the Appalachian foothills—a dark ribbon among the pale shoots and blossoms of spring, a mirror of fiery bronze come autumn.

Two of Wayne National Forest's three units hug the river valley here, a mix of thickly wooded hillsides, twisting tributaries, quiet back roads, grand river views, and reclaimed farmland. Much of the national forest comprises farmland abandoned during the Great Depression and later sold by the state to the Forest Service to recoup delinquent taxes. Farming has never been an easy life here, where soil is thin and floods periodically destroy the sweet corn, tomatoes, and other local crops.

While these lands harbor the occasional special treat—wild orchids sprouting under brambles, shy deer hiding among the pines—the national forest is best suited for recreation. Whether on foot, mountain bike, or horseback, this neck of the woods is a fine spot to get out and enjoy a sparsely populated and particularly lovely stretch of the Ohio River Valley.

Begin at the Forest Service office in either Marietta or Ironton. If you plan on doing any extended hiking or riding, purchase the appropriate topographic maps—the free Forest Service maps can be difficult to read.

What to See and Do

The simply named **Scenic River Trail** provides an appropriate introduction to the area. Park at the **Leith Run Recreation Area** (*about 18 miles NE of Marietta, near the small town of Wade*) along Ohio 7; observation decks here overlook the Ohio River and its backwaters, where a variety of ducks, herons, and the occasional osprey gather.

The 3.4-mile trail climbs through a bottomland of blackberry thickets and walnut trees, then switchbacks up a steep hillside. As you stop and catch your breath, you'll be treated to classic Huck Finn river views and probably a passing tugboat pushing a barge or two. The trail continues along a ridgeline through stands of poplars frequented by woodpeckers and songbirds. At about mile 3, a secondary trail forks to the left and loops back to Ohio 7. Otherwise, the trail terminates at another small parking area on County Road 9.

Due north of the County Road 9 trailhead lies the **Archers Fork Trail.** One of the most unique trails in the forest, this 9-mile loop winds along rock shelters and outcrops and over a natural rock bridge. Erosion weathered a hole in the sandstone rock, leaving behind an arch 51 feet long and 39 feet high. The trail also links with a 3-mile segment of the North Country National Scenic Trail.

North of New Matamoras (*off Ohio 7*), the **Ohio View Trail** parallels the Ohio for seven miles; it offers river vistas and terrain similar to the shorter Scenic River Trail, and links up with the North Country National Scenic Trail.

In the Ironton District, 25 miles of trails scribble through the **Vesuvius Recreation Area,** including the 18-mile **Backpack Trail.** The 8-mile **Lakeshore Trail** outlines man-made Lake Vesuvius, passing through a variety of habitats, from river bottomlands to high rock outcrops. Although the lake was recently drained and its channels cleared, you might spy a beaver. This is also a good area to spot wild turkeys, which favor forest edges.

Nearby, explore the stone chimney and other remnants of the **Vesuvius Furnace.** Built in 1833, it was one of 46 charcoal furnaces in southern Ohio that produced iron for everything from wagon wheels to Civil War cannons.

Near Gallipolis, the 6-mile **Symmes Creek Trail** showcases large rock outcrops and natural wetlands. Though access to Symmes Creek is unimproved, in spring and fall, the creek offers pretty paddling through classic pastoral scenery.

Several bridle paths (many double as mountain bike trails) stitch through the region. The 16-mile **Kinderhook Horse Trail** (*trailhead off Cty. Rd. 244*) traverses some of the forest's steepest hills and passes through a tangle of brushland and mature forest.

Mountain bikes are permitted on all marked trails within the national forest but require a permit (*fee; available at any forest service office*).

Cover Story

Today we view covered bridges as quaint and romantic, but they were simple utilitarian structures in their day. Though each carpenter had his own specific design, bridges in the 1800s were engineered with wooden trusses, a triangular pattern that allowed bridge builders to span distances 200 feet or more. Exposed to rain, snow, and hot summer sun, those trusses would rot in just a couple of decades. When walls and roofs were added to protect the trusses from the elements, the bridges could last for more than a century—as Ohio's 19th-century covered bridges so endearingly demonstrate.

Scenic Drive

For a classic cruise through Ohio River Valley country consider a 65-mile loop along the Ohio and Little Muskingum Rivers. This quintessential river route runs alongside the broad Ohio for 33 miles and twists between wooded hillsides of buckeye, hickory, and oak. You'll pass trailheads for the Scenic River and Ohio View Trails along the way.

Begin in the pretty redbrick town of Marietta, founded in 1788 as the first capital of the Northwest Territories. Follow Ohio 7 northeast toward New Matamoras. At New Matamoras, turn west on Ohio 260. Just after it crosses the Little Muskingum River, turn south on Ohio 26. As the road corkscrews through this pretty farmland, you'll notice several small oil and gas wells, testament to the pockets of crude oil and natural gas that lie under roughly half the state.

Watch along the east side of the road for the 1879 **Hune Bridge**, one of several covered bridges along this road. More than 12,000 covered bridges once dotted the U.S. countryside, more than a fourth of them spanning the numerous rivers and streams of Ohio. Fewer than 1,000 remain today, 136 of them in Ohio.

At the Hune Bridge, you'll find a trailhead for the **Covered Bridge Trail.** This trail wanders for five miles along streams and bottomlands and erupts in wildflowers in spring. The trail also connects with a segment of the North Country National Scenic Trail, which traces a 41-mile north-south route through the national forest.

The Hune Bridge trailhead also features a canoe launch. Though river levels drop in summer, the **Little Muskingum** ranks as one of the state's most appealing canoe rivers, slicing through bluffs and rural farmland, and under the shade of pearly sycamore trees. Fishing can be excellent along the river, especially for smallmouth bass, catfish, and panfish. The river also harbors the endangered stream muskellunge and Ohio brook lamprey.

Continuing south on Ohio 26, you'll pass another covered bridge, which dates to 1875, and barns painted with "Mail Pouch Tobacco" signs, now American cultural icons. Continue south on Ohio 26 to return to Marietta. ■

Hune Bridge, Ohio 26, Wayne National Forest

Other Sites

The following is a select list of additional Great Lakes sites.

Lake Superior and the Canadian Shield

Brule River State Forest

Known as "the river of presidents," the fruitful Brule has attracted five—including Teddy Roosevelt and Dwight Eisenhower—to fish its famous trout waters. Brule River State Forest straddles the river for more than 30 miles, all the way to its mouth on Lake Superior east of Superior, Wisconsin. Old-growth red and white pines rise from its banks, and the elusive timber wolf finds solitude in its deep woods. White-water paddlers favor the lower stretch, where the Brule squeezes through a narrow valley and drops an average 17 feet per mile. Camping, hiking, and cross-country skiing are also popular in the 41,000-acre forest. Contact the forest, 6250 South Ranger Rd., Brule, WI 54820; phone 715-372-5678.

Pattison State Park

Thirteen miles south of Superior, this park preserves Big Manitou Falls—Wisconsin's highest waterfall—where the Black River plummets 165 feet. Hike below the falls on a short trail that skirts the gorge, giving you views of the dark, dramatic basalt cliffs that gave the river its name. Contact the park, 6294 S. State Rd. 35, Superior, WI 54880; phone 715-399-3111.

Northern Highlands

Flambeau River State Forest

The Flambeau is a picture-perfect example of a North Woods river, flowing free through boreal forest of red and white pine, white spruce, and balsam fir in north-central Wisconsin. The 90,000-acre forest protects 60 miles of river; most pristine is the Upper North Fork, with virgin stands of cedar and virtually no development. Bald eagles and ospreys nest above its banks, and the rare lake sturgeon still thrives in its waters. Contact the forest, West 1613 Cty. Rd. W, Winter, WI 54896; phone 715-332-5271.

Great Lakes Shipwreck Museum

Located in Whitefish Point, this fine, compact museum, with dim lighting and appropriately ominous music, traces the history of Great Lakes commerce and the disasters that sometimes attended it. Several shipwrecks are chronicled here, each with a scale model, photos or drawings, artifacts from the wreck, and a description of how and why it went down. Don't miss the *Edmund Fitzgerald* exhibit. Open May-Oct.; adm. fee. Contact the museum, 111 Ashmun St., Sault Ste. Marie, MI 49783; phone 877-744-7973. www.shipwreck museum.com

Michigan Riding and Hiking Trail

Also known as the Shore-to-Shore Trail, this 210-mile trail for trekkers and equestrians stretches across the Lower Peninsula from Lake Michigan to Lake Huron. Oscoda and Empire are the main east-west trailheads; Stoney Creek and Cadillac are the trailheads for the north and south spurs. A substantial portion of the trail follows the Au Sable River as it courses through Huron National Forest. Contact the Michigan Trail Riders Association, 3010 North Mich. 52, Stockbridge, MI 49285; 989-851-7554. www.mtra.org

Spread Eagle Barrens State Natural Area

An anomaly created by glaciers, Spread Eagle Barrens is a naturally formed open area of sandy hills, bracken grasslands, low shrubs, and solitary pines and scrub oaks. Located in northeastern Wisconsin, the 8,850-acre barrens area stands in stark contrast to the thick forests that surround it. In addition, its ecological communities are as distinctly different as its looks. It is a biologically rich landscape, notable for its birds and butterflies. Easiest access is from the town of Florence. Contact the Wisconsin Department of Natural Resources, Florence Office, HC 1, Box 81, Florence, WI 54121; phone 715-528-4400.

Great Lakes Plains

Cuyahoga Valley National Park

Established only in 2000, this national park was originally a national recreation area; it preserves some 33,000 acres along 22 miles of the Cuyahoga River in northwestern Ohio, near Lake Erie. The park has both hiking and horseback riding trails; it also offers opportunities for biking and canoeing (Ohio license required for latter). Contact the national park, 15610 Vaughn Road, Brecksville, OH 44141; phone 216-524-1497. www.nps.gov/cuva

Goose Lake Prairie State Natural Area

Before immigrant farmers began tilling the land, a continuous sea of grass stretched from Indiana to the Rockies. You can experience this lost landscape 50 miles southwest of Chicago at 2,838-acre Goose Lake Prairie, the largest prairie remnant in Illinois. About 60 percent of the preserve is tallgrass prairie, comprising Indian grass, big bluestem, switch grass, and 10-foot-high prairie cordgrass. Seven miles of trails wind through the grasslands and along ponds and marshes. Contact the natural area, 5010 N. Jugtown Rd., Morris, IL 60450; phone 815-942-2899. http://dnr.state.il .us/lands/landmgt/parks/i%2 6/east/goose/home.htm

H. H. Bennett Studio and History Center

In 1875, fledgling photographer Henry Hamilton Bennett began photographing the grand sandstone escarpments of the Wisconsin Dells. His glass-plate negative prints, created just a few decades after the earliest recorded photographs were made, played an integral role in promoting the Wisconsin Dells. They also helped launch America's tourism industry. Bennett's original studio (the nation's oldest to be owned and operated by one family) is now a state historic site. Restored and transformed into an interactive museum, it celebrates both Bennett's work and the cultural evolution of the Wisconsin Dells. Contact the history center, 215 Broadway, Wisconsin Dells, WI 53965; phone 608-253-3523. www.shsw.wisc.edu/sites/bennett

Loda Lake Wildflower Sanctuary

Glaciers formed the mix of marsh, dunes, forest, and lake in this 800-acre tract of Manistee National Forest, a diverse ecosystem that supports an equally diverse array of wildflowers. A 1.5-mile trail meanders through the property, and numbered posts identify hundreds of native species, including ferns, sedges, wild roses, lilies, orchids, and more. Contact Baldwin/White Cloud Ranger District, Manistee National Forest, 650 N. Michigan Ave., Baldwin, MI 49304; phone 231-745-4631.

Upper Mississippi River Valley

Mississippi Headwaters River Trail

During the first 400 miles of its 2,350-mile journey to the Gulf of Mexico, the mighty Mississippi curls gently through marshes, lakes, and piney woods across north-central Minnesota. It's an idyllic waterway for paddling, hence the designation of this trail. The Chippewa National Forest, as well as county and state parks, offers numerous access points along the way. Contact the Mississippi Headwaters Board, Cass County Courthouse, P.O. Box 3000, Walker, MN 56484; phone 218-547-7263. www.mississippiheadwaters.org

Mississippi Palisades State Park

Named for the steep, lofty limestone cliffs that rise up from the Mississippi, this park in northwestern Illinois was untouched by the glaciers that flattened much of the state. Thirteen miles of trails stitch through the park, many of them along the 250-foot-high river bluffs, which are riddled with caves and sinkholes. The park is an excellent vantage point for observing the spring and fall bird migration up and down the river, which includes hundreds of raptors, shorebirds, songbirds, and waterfowl. Contact the park, 16327A Illinois Rte. 84, Savanna, IL 61074; phone 815-273-2731. http://dnr.state.il.us/lands/landmgt/parks/palisade.htm

Ohio River Valley

Shawnee State Park

This state park—and the surrounding 60,000-acre state forest—in southeast Ohio marks the northern edge of Appalachia, where the Appalachian Plateau descends to the lowlands of the broad Ohio River Valley. Sometimes called the "Little Smokies," the densely forested hill country supports thick stands of oak and hickory. In spring, the forest erupts with flowering dogwood and redbud trees, and a showy display of Dutchman's-breeches, wild blue phlox, wild geraniums, and other woodland wildflowers. More than 60 miles of hiking trails wind over ridges and into deep valleys carved by numerous streams and rivers. Contact the park, 4404 State Rte. 125, Portsmouth, OH 45663; phone 740-858-6652. www.dnr.state.oh.us/parks/parks/shawnee.htm

The Buckeye Trail

The Buckeye Trail—an ambitious, 1,200-mile-long hiking and horseback trail—forms a continuous loop through Ohio, traversing nearly half the counties in the state. The trail leads from the shores of Lake Erie to the Amish country of the Tuscarawas Valley to the rugged and remotely populated Hocking Hills; from there it threads the fruit belt of Medina County and follows the old Miami and Erie Canal towpath. This impressive accomplishment gives hikers and horseback riders a unique opportunity to explore the corners of this diverse state. The Buckeye Trail is marked with blue blazes; sectional trail maps are available. Contact Buckeye Trail Association, Box 254, Worthington, OH 43085. www.buckeyetrail.org

Resources

The following is a select list of resources. Contact state and local associations for additional outfitter and lodging options. For chain hotels in the Great Lakes states, see p. 283.

Current information about road conditions is available for Illinois at 800-452-4368 or www.dot.state.il.us; for Indiana at 800-261-7623 or www.ai.org/dot; for Michigan at 800-411-4823 or www.mdot.state.mi.us; for Minnesota at 800-542-0220 or www.dot.state.mn.us; and for Wisconsin at 800-762-3947 or www.dot.state.wi.us.

The U.S.D.A. Forest Service operates campgrounds throughout the national forests found in the Great Lake states. Call specific national forests for details or contact the National Recreation Reservation Service (877-444-6777. www.reserveusa.com). Information on some campgrounds can be found at the Great Outdoors Recreation Page (www.gorp.com).

Many state forests and parks provide camping facilities;

contact the specific forest or park for more information. State tourism bureaus can provide information on both private and state-owned campgrounds.

ILLINOIS

Federal and State Agencies

Illinois Bureau of Tourism
620 E. Adams St.
Springfield, IL 62701
800-226-6632
www.enjoyillinois.com
Information on state attractions, activities, events, lodging, camping, and more.

Illinois Dept. of Natural Resources
524 S. Second St.
Springfield, IL 62701
217-782-7454
www.dnr.state.il.us
Information on state parks and forests, fishing, and other recreation.

Outfitters and Activities

Cache Core Canoe Rental
RR #1 Box 71AA
Ullin, IL 62992
618-845-3817
Canoe rentals near Cache River State Natural Area.

Lodging

Giant City Lodge
336 S. Church Rd.
Makanda, IL 62958
618-457-4921
Rustic sandstone lodge and cabins located in Giant City SP in heart of Shawnee Hills.

INDIANA

Federal and State Agencies

Indiana Dept. of Natural Resources
402 W. Washington St., Rm. W160
Indianapolis, IN 46204
317-232-4200
www.state.in.us/dnr
Information on state parks and forests, fishing, and other recreation.

Indiana Tourism Division
1 North Capitol, Ste. 700
Indianapolis, IN 46204
888-ENJOY-IN
www.enjoyindiana.com
Information on state attractions, activities, events, lodging, camping, and more.

Outfitters and Activities

Indiana Outfitters
www.indianaoutfitters .com
Web directory of outfitters for hiking, paddling, caving, climbing, fishing, and more. Also provides maps and weather information.

Lodging

The Leavenworth Inn
State Route 2
Leavenworth, IN 47137
812-739-2021
www.leavenworthinn.com
Near Wyandotte Caves, this turn-of-the-19th-century inn consists of two houses on six acres of Ohio River shore.

Spring Mill Inn
P.O. Box 68
Mitchell, IN 47446
812-849-4081
www.state.in.us/dnr/park lake/inns/springmill/index. html
A CCC project of the 1930s, the inn offers 74 rooms, 2 pools, and a public dining room.

MICHIGAN

Federal and State Agencies

Isle Royale National Park
800 East Lakeshore Dr.
Houghton, MI 49931
906-482-0984
www.nps.gov/isro
General information on Isle Royale National Park, and ferry service to the park from Houghton.

Michigan Dept. of Natural Resources
P.O. Box 30028
Lansing, MI 48909
800-275-3474
www.dnr.state.mi.us

Fishing and other wildlife information.

North Country National Scenic Trail
700 Rayovac Dr., Ste. 100
Madison, WI 53711
608-441-5610
www.nps.gov/noco
Information on cultural, historic, natural, scenic, and recreational activities along 7-state hiking trail.

Parks and Recreation Division, Michigan Dept. of Natural Resources
P.O. Box 30257
Lansing, MI 48909
800-44-PARKS
www.dnr.state.mi.us
Information on camping, state parks, trails, and other recreation areas.

Travel Michigan
P.O. Box 30226
Lansing, MI 48909
888-78-GREAT
http://travel.michigan.org
Information on state attractions, activities, events, lodging, camping, and more.

Upper Peninsula Travel and Recreation Association
P.O. Box 400
Iron Mountain, MI 49801
800-562-7134
www.uptravel.com
Information on Upper Peninsula attractions, activities, snow reports, events, campgrounds, and more.

Outfitters and Activities

The Buck Sporting Lodge and Triple Creek Kennels
P.O. Box 156
Rapid River, MI 49878
800-DOGSLED (outside Michigan)
906-446-3360 (Michigan)
www.updogsledding.com
Dogsled trips and wilderness lodging in the Upper Peninsula.

Great Northern Adventures
P.O. Box 361
Marquette, MI 49855
906-225-TOUR
www.greatnorthernadven tures.com
Kayak, mountain bike, cross-country ski, snow-

shoe, and sled-dog adventure tours in the Upper Peninsula.

The Isle Royale Line
Box 24
Copper Harbor, MI 49918
906-289-4437
www.up.net/~isroyale
Ferry service to Isle
Royale National Park
from Copper Harbor.

Isle Royale Seaplane Service
P.O. Box 366
Houghton, MI 49931
906-482-8850 (mid-May
–Sept.) or
715-526-5103 (Oct.–
mid-May)
Seaplane service to Isle
Royale National Park
from Houghton.

Northern Waters Adventures
1200 Commercial St.
Munising, MI 49862
906-387-2323
www.northernwaters
.com
Kayak rentals and guided
trips to Pictured Rocks
NL and Grand Island
NRA.

Pictured Rocks Cruises
P.O. Box 355
Munising, MI 49862
906-387-2379
Offers 2.5-hour trips
along Pictured Rocks
National Lakeshore. Late
May–mid-Oct.

Sylvania Outfitters
23423 Hwy. 2 West
Watersmeet, MI 49969
906-358-4766
www.sylvaniaoutfitters
.com
Canoe, camping, and fishing outfitters for Sylvania
Wilderness and Ottawa
National Forest.

**Outdoor Education
and Resources**

North Country Trail
Association
229 East Main St.
Lowell, MI 4933
888-454-6282
www.northcountrytrail
.org.
Trail descriptions and
contacts for the North
Country NST. Trail condi-

tions, maps, books, and
more.

Michigan Underwater
Preserve Council
11 S. State St.
St. Ignace, MI 49781
906-643-8717
Information on locations
of protected shipwreck
sites and dive charters
that serve them.

Lodging

Grand Hotel
Grand Ave.
Mackinac Island, MI 49757
906-847-3331 or
800-33-GRAND
1887 stately hotel overlooking the Straits of
Mackinac.

Rock Harbor Lodge
P.O. Box 605
Houghton, MI 49931
906-337-4993 (summer)
270-773-2191 (winter)
Rooms and cottages on
Isle Royale.

MINNESOTA

Federal and
State Agencies

Minnesota Dept. of Natural
Resources Information
Center
500 Lafayette Rd.
St. Paul, MN 55155
888-MINNDNR
www.dnr.state.mn.us
Information on state
parks and forests, fishing,
and other recreation.

Minnesota Office of
Tourism
100 Metro Square Bldg.
121 7th Place E.
St. Paul, MN 55101
800-657-3700
www.exploreminnesota
.com
Information on state
attractions, activities,
events, lodging, camping,
and more.

Outfitters and Activities

Cascade Kayaks
20 E. First St.
P.O. Box 215
Grand Marais, MN 55604
218-387-2360 or

800-720-2809
www.cascadekayaks.com
Kayak rentals, courses,
and guided trips throughout the North Shore
region.

Grand Portage Isle Royale
Transportation Line, Inc.
1507 N. First St.
Superior, WI 54880
715-392-2100 or
888-746-2305
www.grand-isle-
royale.com
Ferry service to Isle
Royale National Park
from Grand Portage.

Hungry Jack Outfitters
318 S. Hungry Jack Rd.
Grand Marais, MN 55604
218-388-2275 or
800-648-2922
www.hjo.com
Cabins and canoe
rentals/outfitting for
the Boundary Waters.

Sawbill Canoe Outfitters
4620 Sawbill Trail
Tofte, MN 55615
218-663-7150
www.sawbill.com
Canoe rentals and outfitting for the Boundary
Waters.

Wintergreen Dogsled
Lodge
1101 Ring Rock Rd.
Ely, MN 55731
218-365-6022 or
800-585-9425
www.dogsledding.com
Lodge-to-lodge dogsledding adventures in the
Boundary Waters, with
one of the nation's oldest
dogsledding operations,
owned by renowned arctic explorer Paul Schurke.

**Outdoor Education
and Resources**

International Wolf Center
1396 Hwy. 169
Ely, MN 55731
218-365-4695 or
800-ELY-WOLF
www.wolf.org
Exhibits, programs, and
a resident wolf pack to
educate the public about
wolves.

Superior Hiking Trail Assn.
731 7th Ave.

Two Harbors, MN 55616
218-834-2700
www.shta.org
Information on 200-mile
hiking trail that parallels
the North Shore of Lake
Superior.

Lodging

Clearwater Canoe Outfit-
ters and Lodge
774 Clearwater Rd.
Grand Marais, MN 55604
218-388-2254 or
800-527-0554
www.canoebwca.com
This historic log lodge on
Clearwater Lake by the
Gunflint Trail offers canoe
and kayak excursions in
the Boundary Waters.

Kettle Falls Hotel
10502 Gamma Rd.
Lake Kabetogama, MN
56669
218-374-4404 or
888-534-6835
www.kettlefallshotel.com
A renovated 1910 hotel in
Voyageurs NP; accessible
by boat or floatplane only.

OHIO

Federal and
State Agencies

Division of Parks and
Recreation, Ohio Dept. of
Natural Resources
1952 Belcher Dr., Bldg. C
Columbus, OH 43224
614-265-6561
www.dnr.state.oh.us
Information on state
parks and forests, fishing,
and other recreation.

Division of Travel and
Tourism, Ohio Dept. of
Development
P.O. Box 1001
Columbus, OH 43266
800-BUCKEYE
www.ohiotourism.com
Information on state
attractions, activities,
events, lodging, camping,
and more.

Outfitters and Activities

Northcoast Sea-Kayaking
Adventures
2014 W. 16th St.
Ashtabula, OH 44004

440-964-2932 or
888-636-8625
Day and overnight trips
in northeastern Ohio.

Lodging

Hocking Hills Lodging Co.
16099 Pike St.
Laurelville, OH 43135
740-332-0212
www.hockinghills.com/
hhlc/
Information, recommen-
dations, and reservations
for area lodgings.

Lafayette Hotel
101 Front St.
Marietta, OH 45750
740-373-5522 or
800-331-9336
www.lafayettehotel.com
Historic, riverboat-era
hotel on the banks of the
Ohio, with 78 rooms and
modern amenities.

WISCONSIN

Federal and
State Agencies

Wisconsin Dept. of Natural
Resources
P.O. Box 7921
Madison, WI 53707
608-266-2621
www.dnr.state.wi.us
Information on state
parks and forests, fishing,
and other recreation.

Wisconsin Dept. of Tourism
P.O. Box 7976
Madison, WI 53707
800-432-TRIP
www.travelwisconsin.com
Information on state
attractions, activities,
events, lodging, camping,
and more.

Outfitters and Activities

Original Wisconsin Ducks
1890 Wisconsin Dells
Pkwy.
Wisconsin Dells, WI
53965
608-254-8751
World War II amphibious
vehicle tours of the Wis-
consin Dells. April-Oct.

Trek & Trail
P.O. Box 906
Bayfield, WI 54814

800-354-8735
www.trek-trail.com
Kayak rentals, lessons,
and tours in the Apostle
Islands and Pictured
Rocks National
Lakeshores and beyond;
dogsledding tours.

Wild River Outfitters
15177 State Rd. 70
Grantsburg, WI 54840
715-463-2254
www.wildriverpaddling
.com
Canoe and kayak rentals,
and shuttle service for St.
Croix and Namekagon
Rivers.

Outdoor Education
and Resources

Ice Age Park & Trail
Foundation, Inc.
207 E. Buffalo St., Ste. 515
Milwaukee, WI 53202
800-227-0046
www.iceagetrail.org
Information on statewide
hiking trail that traces the
farthest advance of the
glaciers.

Lodging

Bear Paw Outdoor Adven-
ture Resort
N3494 Hwy. 55
White Lake, WI 54491
715-882-3502
www.bearpawinn.com
Inn, cabins, and camp-
ground on 80 acres adja-
cent to the Wolf River.
Gear and courses for
white-water and quiet-
water paddling, fly-fishing,
and mountain biking.

Wisconsin Bed and Break-
fast Association
108 S. Cleveland St.
Merrill, WI 54452
715-539-9222
www.wbba.org
Accommodations include
historic properties, log
homes, and farmhouses
in Door County and
throughout the state.

ONTARIO, CANADA

Federal and Provincial
Agencies

Arts in the Wild

Queen's Park
Toronto, ON M7A 2R9
416-314-0944 or
800-ONTARIO
www.artsinthewild.com
Painting, Photography, pottery, performing arts in the outdoor. Offers more than sixty outfitters and learning vacations. Arts experiences and outdoor adventure.

Ontario Parks
300 Water St.
P.O. Box 7000
Peterborough, ON
K9J 8M5
416-314-0944 or
800-ONTARIO
www.ontarioparks.com
Information on Ontario's more than 270 natural areas. For campsite reservations call 888-668-7275.

Ontario Tourism
Queen's Park
Toronto, ON M7A 2R9
www.ontariotravel.net
Complete lodging, camping, transportation, and park information.

Parks Canada
111 Water St. E.
Cornwall, ON K6H 6S3
800-839-8221 or
613-938-5879
www.parkscanada.pch
.gc.ca

Information on Ontario's national parks (descriptions, fees, etc.).

Outfitters and Activities

Canoe Canada Outfitters
300 O'Brien Street,
P.O. Box 1810
Atikokan, ON P0T 1C0
807-597-6418
www.canoecanada.com
Fully supported fishing and canoeing in Quetico Park.

Paddling Ontario
Queen's Park
Toronto, ON M7A 2R9
416-314-0944 or
800-ONTARIO
www.paddlingOntario
.com
Information on flat-water, white-water, sea kayaking, and canoeing.

Lodging and Camping

Ontario Private Campground Association
R.R. 5
Owen Sound, ON
N4K 5N7
519-371-3393
www.campgrounds.org
400 privately owned campgrounds, representing 70,000 campsites; accommodating needs from tent camping to RVs.

Hotel and Motel Chains

Accommodations are available in all states unless otherwise noted.

Best Western International
800-528-1234
Comfort Inns
800-228-5150
Courtyard by Marriott
800-321-2211
Days Inn
800-325-2525
Econo Lodge
800-446-6900
Embassy Suites
800-362-2776
Fairfield Inns by Marriott
800-228-2800
Hampton Inn
800-HAMPTON
Holiday Inns
800-HOLIDAY
Independent Motels of America
800-841-0255
Marriott Hotels
800-228-9290
Motel 6
800-466-8356
Ramada Inns
800-2RAMADA
Red Roof Inns
800-843-7663
Super 8
800-255-3050

About the Author/Photographer

A native of the Great Lakes states, **Tina Lassen** has worked as a freelance writer since 1988. She writes about travel and outdoor sports for a number of national magazines, including *National Geographic Adventure*. She divides her time between Madison, Wisconsin and Hood River, Oregon.

Photographer **Mark R. Godfrey** has shot two previous books—*Mighty Aztecs* and *Frontiers of Science*—for National Geographic. He began his career as a photographer by covering the Vietnam War for *Life* magazine. After serving as Photography Director of *U.S. News & World Report* for nine years, he returned to his first love—taking pictures.

Illustrations Credits

All images by Mark R. Godfrey except for the following:

p. 26, The Granger Collection, New York; p. 27, Culver Pictures; p. 35, Brown Brothers, Sterling PA; p. 104, ©Minnesota Historical Society/CORBIS; p. 105, ©CORBIS; p. 131, ©Ralph White/CORBIS; p. 137, ©Doris Sampson 1990, Duluth, MN; p. 176, ©Layne Kennedy/CORBIS; p. 230, Raymond Gehman/NGS Image Collection; p. 265, Transparency #1822 (photo by Logan), courtesy the Library, American Museum of Natural History

Index

National Geographic Guide to America's Outdoors: Great Lakes
by Tina Lassen
Photographed by Mark R. Godfrey

Published by the National Geographic Society
John M. Fahey, Jr., *President and Chief Executive Officer*
Gilbert M. Grosvenor, *Chairman of the Board*
Nina D. Hoffman, *Executive Vice President,*
  President, Books and School Publishing

Guides to America's Outdoors
Elizabeth L. Newhouse, *Director of Travel Publishing*
Allan Fallow, *Senior Editor and Series Director*
Cinda Rose, *Art Director*
Barbara Noe, *Senior Editor*
Caroline Hickey, *Senior Researcher*
Carl Mehler, *Director of Maps*

Staff for this Book
Jane Sunderland, *Book Manager*
Robin Currie, Sean M. Groom, Kim Kostyal, *Editors*
Kay A. Hankins, *Designer*
Sadie Quarrier, *Illustrations Editor*
Sean M. Groom, Victoria Garrett Jones, Keith R. Moore, *Researchers*
Michele T. Callaghan, *Copy Editor*
Nicholas P. Rosenbach, *Map Manager*
Matt Chwastyk, Jerome N. Cookson, Sven M. Dolling,
  Thomas L. Gray, Joseph F. Ochlak, Gregory Ugiansky,
  National Geographic Maps, The M Factory, Mapping
  Specialists, *Map Edit, Research, and Production*
Tibor Tóth, *Map Relief*
R. Gary Colbert, *Production Director*
Cynthia Combs, *Illustrations Assistant*
Elisabeth MacRae-Bobynskyj, *Indexer*
Larry Porges, *Program Assistant*
Deb Antonini, *Contributor*

Manufacturing and Quality Control
George V. White, *Director*; John T. Dunn, *Associate Director*;
Vincent P. Ryan, *Manager;* Phillip L. Schlosser, *Financial Analyst*

Library of Congress Cataloging-in-Publication Data
Lassen, Tina.
    Great Lakes / by Tina Lassen ; photography by Mark Godfrey.
      p.   cm. —(Guide to America's Outdoors)
      Includes index.
      ISBN 0-7922-7754-6
      1. Great Lakes Region—Guidebooks. 2. National parks and reserves—Great Lakes
    Region—Guidebooks. 3. Outdoor recreation—Great Lakes Region—Guidebooks. I.
    Godfrey, Mark. II. Title. III. Series.

    F551.L37 2001
    917.704'34—dc21   2001042809
                                                                       CIP

The information in this book has been carefully checked and is accurate as of press date.
However, details are subject to change, and the National Geographic Society cannot be
responsible for such changes, or for errors or omissions. Assessments of sites are based on
the authors' subjective opinions, which do not necessarily reflect the publisher's opinion.
The publisher cannot be responsible for any consequences arising from the use of this book.